Dear Hugh J.
Hope you enjoy the Book,

all the Best,

John OB

Festival Legends: Songs & Stories

John O'Brien, Jr.

Bloomington, IN Milton Keynes, UK
authorHOUSE

AuthorHouse™
1663 Liberty Drive, Suite 200
Bloomington, IN 47403
www.authorhouse.com
Phone: 1-800-839-8640

AuthorHouse™ UK Ltd.
500 Avebury Boulevard
Central Milton Keynes, MK9 2BE
www.authorhouse.co.uk
Phone: 08001974150

First published by AuthorHouse 4/13/2006

ISBN: 1-4259-1738-0 (sc)

Printed in the United States of America
Bloomington, Indiana

This book is printed on acid-free paper.

This goes out to Derek, you should be in here too.
Bless you for all the joy you brought.
God has an exclusive now.

Preface:

Raised on Songs and Stories,
Heroes of Renown.
Of the passing tales and glories...

The happiest times in my life are those spent around festivals, especially the afters parties. Whether with the festival that I am involved with in Cleveland, or at others in places like Pittsburgh, Milwaukee, Dublin, Ohio, Indy or the myriad of others throughout the United States that I have been fortunate enough to be able to attend, I have always had a fantastic time; learning, laughing, dancing ... and being inspired.

It is these afters parties held at the end of each day at the festival, after hours, that really stick out in my memory. It is there that I enjoyed more than a passing hello, with time to actually talk to those I term "Legends" for more than a minute and share a story, or a song or two. I have gotten the opportunity to get to know these men and women as people, not as performers.

This has been seed of inspiration for writing this book, seeing these amazing and genuine people, up close and off camera. When I tried to find out more information about them, where they came from, in the sense of what made them who they are, beyond just the town they were born in, there was so little information available. That was the kindling. I decided to change that.

Derek McCormack's sudden passing lit the fire, reemphasized the need for me to get these wonderful histories, filled with humor, jaw-dropping accomplishments and stories, and deep love for the Irish heritage, from those who know it best, the performers themselves. I have strived to eliminate any inaccuracies, myths, false stories and general lack of hard information about each of these legends and present it in their own words.

I wouldn't give up the time spent with Tommy, Danny, Liam, Joanie, Sean, John, Alec, Johnny, Tom, Brendan, Batt, Dennis, Rory, Shane, Conor, Mickey and Liam and so many others, both in this book and not. Not for anything. The respect and admiration I have for these folks, dedicated, above and beyond, to preserving and spreading the Irish music, stories and history of an incredibly rich and broad culture, cannot be articulated.

There are others that should be included. Folks like; Paddy Reilly, Dermot Henry, Foster & Allen, Mick Moloney, The Fureys, Kilfenora Ceili Band, The Irish Rovers, Liz Carroll, Joe Burke ... and the list goes on, and on, and on. Room and access have limited it to this dozen, for now. The second book in this series, *Festival Legends, Trads & Ceili's,* and the third, *Festival Legends, The Balladeers,* will hopefully address that. See www.songsandstories.net, for updates, release dates and more.

While researching this book over an almost two year period, I have been able to have prolonged discussions with these men and women that I call legends, in multiple settings; festivals, restaurants and over the phone. It has been one of the most joyful, fun and interesting experiences of my life. I hope you will find this book a great experience for you as well.

A Tommy Makem fan, when asked if she knew what music is, responded: "It is the soul of the world expressed in sound." To me, Tommy Makem, and the other Festival Legends featured here in this book, express the soul of the whole world, Irish or not, in each and every performance they give, in Dolby surround sound.

Acknowledgements:

There are so many to thank, for all their help and guidance. First and foremost, would be those featured in this book. They were incredibly open, honest and very patient with my constant follow ups and additional questions. They also provided insight and stories on some of the other Legends as well. I am forever grateful.

Quite a few people in the business, not featured in Festival Legends (yet!) or are part of a larger group, helped in the writing of this book. They generously provided quotes, backgrounds, contact information and much more. Robbie O'Connell, Heidi Talbot, Eileen Ivers, Jerry O'Sullivan, Rosin Dillon, Mick Moloney, Jimmy Sweeney, Liam Tiernan, Mary Coogan, Philippa Shine, Mirella Murray & Aiofe Clancy - Thank You.

Outside of performers, Ed Ward must also be thanked. Not only for his contributions to this book, but for his help in driving the quality and breathe of festivals. His contributions are seen, not just in Milwaukee, where he founded Milwaukee Irish Fest, the largest Irish festival in the world, but also in helping other festivals; with ideas, grants and most importantly, ready advice, just a phone call away. A class act through and through.

Nick Kelly, who runs www.theballadeers.com, was a fantastic source for accurate information on performer discographies and very helpful in sorting through all the conflicting release and compilation information. This is the best site out there for this kind of information and Nick does a fantastic job.

Rich Croft, of Vertical Lift Web Design (www.vertlift.com), for the fantastic website he designed for me (www.songsandstories.net), his unbelievable creativity and wide ranging expertise in many design areas, graphics and more. His input is invaluable and saved me a lot of work, time and money.

Last, but in no way least, are my family. My father, who provided the immersion, and genuine respect, for the rich Irish culture growing up, and my mother and sister, Tricia, who never stopped supporting and praying for me, through all the hard stuff, over all the years. Thank You Lord for you.

"The music business is a cruel and shallow money trench -- A long plastic hallway where thieves and pimps run free and good men die like dogs. There's also a negative side...."
-Hunter S. Thompson

Contents

Tommy Makem

"I was born in Keady, the hub of the universe." - Tommy Maken

The Godfather of Irish Music, The modern Bard of Armagh. Of course, Tommy is, was, and always will be - first.

There is no one who has done more for Irish music; in the United States, Ireland, and around the world. He is revered, not only because of the chart-topping and award winning songs, more than four hundred of them, that he has written and recorded, but even more so because of the vision, action, dedication and deep love for all things that honor the traditions of the Irish culture that Tommy lives out each and every day. Although musically gifted himself, his greatest gift to others is in providing inspiration and guidance, illimination to countless musicians, singers, bands, festivals, schools, programs and the list goes on and on, not only by his music, but his deep passion for the Irish culture and willingness to speak up and, most importantly, to take action to preserve it.

"Ahh, fantastic source of songs. He holds the audience in the palm of his hand, for as long as he wants. Tommy's a gentleman, a real Ambassador."- Sean McGuinness, Dublin City Ramblers.

"Tommy is simply 'the Boss.' I love his passion and envy him his treasure-house of knowledge. I'm studying hard to catch up but I never will. He has too much of a start on me. He is the reincarnation of some ancient Bard or other, constantly channeling, it seems, a deep mother lode of song and story." - Danny Doyle

Many have given so much to Irish music in writing, recording and performing songs. Tommy has done this and then gone on to do so much more, by his actions, when he is not on stage. That active involvement is his legacy. Tommy has infused an unbreakable pride in Irish culture and in being Irish by broadening parameters previously undefined. He has made it cool to be Irish and then instilled in others a thirst to find out what that means. Not surprisingly, he even wrote a song about it.

Singers

by Tommy Makem

I am of the stock
Of those who raised their harps
And sang the story
Of all our people;
The Parthalonians, the Nemedians,
The Fomorians, the Firbolg,
The Tuatha de Danaan and the Milesians.
Those seer-singers
Who filled our souls,
Our minds, our hearts,
With gilded pride
In and of
The glorious legacy
They passed to our keeping.

I charge you now
To nourish that legacy,
To revel in it,
To bask in its magnificence.
Accept no diminishing,
Nor revision,
Of that culture,
But pass it on enhanced
To the generations
Who follow us,
And the generations
Yet unborn,
Charging them,
As I charge you now,
To complete the circle.

Tommy Makem was born November 4th in the Year of Our Lord to remain unnamed. He has a middle name, "but I never use it and will never tell what it is." His brogue is soft, especially for one from the North of Ireland - Keady, in South Armagh, Northern Ireland - the hub of the universe. He is often joking and you have to pay careful attention to know just when he is pulling your leg. "Some people came around to my house collecting for an orphanage, so I gave them four orphans."

The humor reflecting in his keen and animated blue eyes pervades his music, his performances and his life. His shows are filled with poetry and fantastic ballads; ballads that tell a story, all with humorous, educational or timely introductions, and all delivered with a serious face that almost hides the makings of a smile that is constantly tugging at the corners of his mouth. He is known to throw in a joke or three.

Tommy often tells of the Irish boy who wanted a bicycle "but his mother said, 'where would I get the money for a bicycle?' So he decided to pray to Jesus, saying, 'Dear Lord, if you get me a bike, I'll...', but the boy desisted because he knew it wouldn't work. Better write to him, he thought. So he started a letter: 'Dear Lord, please let me have a bike...' and then he stopped because he recalled writing to Santa Claus for things these three years and he'd got nothing at all. Looking around the room, his eye fell on a statue of the Virgin, and he was inspired. He got down on his knees and prayed: 'Dear Jesus, if you ever want to see your mother again...'"

But don't let all the laughter, great fun and subliminal education you are getting during a Tommy Makem performance fool you. Tommy Makem is deadly serious when it comes to spreading his message on the preservation of the things he cares so deeply about; the song tradition, the Irish culture, and the history of those who came before.

The story of Tommy Makem begins with the story of the international renowned source singer and song collector, Sarah Makem (1900 - 1982) - Tommy's mother.

"My mother was a source singer; she had all of these songs, hundreds of them, hundreds and hundreds and hundreds of songs in her head. These collectors came over and they'd be looking for big ballads. James Francis Childs came out and collected in the Appalachians and he got a lot of pure ballads from Scotland and Ireland and England. They hadn't been changed at all. Now, if they heard one of those somewhere, and maybe a version of it, all of them would prick their ears up.

"So they got to my mother, and all the other local source singers, like Mrs. Cronin in Cork, Elizabeth Cronin, and Paddy Tunney. They found that these people had different versions of those same songs. For instance, my mother had a version of *Barbara Allen*, which is internationally known. But she had a version that none of them had ever heard before. It was a different melody, most of the Barbara Allens you hear, most of them were set in the spring time of the year. But my mother's version was set at Michealsmas (Fall season, September 29th), which was more in tune with the somber, dead, dramatic atmosphere of the song.

'Michealmas day, being a day in the year,
When the brown leaves they were falling,
Young Jemmy Grove on his death bed lay
For the love of Barbara Allen.'

"She had a verse that no one else sang;
*'Look at my bed foot, he said
And there you'll see the legacy
Bloody feet and bloody shirt
I sweat them for you Allen.'*

"But that's what a source singer would be. They might have versions of major songs, and they might have other songs that people had never heard before, that collectors would give their eyes for.

"They are the source of these songs. My mother was the source of many of the songs, like *When I Roved Out* would have been one. She was the source singer for *The Little Beggerman,* which has now passed into the American main stream folk music, as an American song. They were the source of these songs [that had long been forgotten].

"She learned a lot of songs working in the mill, as did my grandmother and anyone who worked in the mills. They used to sing all the time. My mother told me if anyone ever brought a new song into the mills, it was like a great gift for everyone. And everyone in the mill learned the new song."

"I immigrated to America. I came to Dover, New Hampshire, to relatives. My mother's entire family emigrated here. She had two sisters and four brothers. My Auntie Annie came out first, in 1911, she saved whatever she could to help pay her brother Johnny's fare out [and so on]. The last one came out around 1918 or so. My father was the only one in his family to marry, the only man. My mother's entire family came out here; they were all weavers and spinners."   Many of those in the linen mills of South Armagh left for the textile jobs of Dover, and the broader opportunities work in the States offered. Eventually Tommy left his family in Keady to join his family in Dover, New Hampshire.

"As a matter of fact, people, mostly from around Keady, which was a small market town and one of the centers for the linen industry in Ireland, were brought out [to the U.S.] to work in the cotton mills, around the 1830's or so, because of this experience that they had. They also built a church in town, the church that I go to in Dover here, called St. Mary's. It was the first Catholic Church in the diocese of Manchester. It was built by people, most of them, from around Keady. They worked twelve hours a day in the mills and then they went out in the evenings and worked to build this church and got nickels and pennies together and eventually [built this church].

"On September the 25th, [2005] they celebrated their 175th Anniversary and I figured I owed the old people something, only for them, I wouldn't be in Dover, New Hampshire. So I wrote a mass for the 175th Anniversary. Six or seven pieces, maybe. This was arranged for the four; soprano, alto, tenor and base. And it was performed at the mass on the 25th of September. I advised them to invite the Archbishop of Armagh over for it and they did and he accepted! So we had a big blowout."

"My father worked in the flax industry, which was the original material for making linen. He worked in the flax mill, my mother's entire family worked in the weaving and spinning. My mother never stopped singing, she always sang, she wouldn't have known a folk song if she tripped over it. She just knew hundreds and hundreds and hundreds of songs and she would know all the verses to any song she was asked. But it could be a 16th century ballad or it could be a song she heard on the radio two weeks ago. She had the great capacity for remembering lyrics and tunes and keeping them in her head. So she had, if not thousands, certainly hundreds of songs and she sang all the time.

"Then back in 1953 or '54, A man called Peter Kennedy came from England to Ireland and he was collecting folk songs in Ireland, England, Scotland and Wales, and a man called Sean O'Boyle from the city of Armagh, which is seven miles from Keady, knew of my mother and he brought Peter Kennedy to our house.

"Sean O'Boyle would have been a Gaelic scholar; certainly a fluent Gaelic speaker and he would have been a musician of high repute. And he had served his time with Carl Hardaback, who was a noted folk song collector. But O'Boyle brought Peter Kennedy to our house and he sort of hit a gold mine when he arrived there. They were there, for I would say the guts of two weeks. Every evening, they came and set up the big real-to-reel tape recorders and my mother sang piles and piles of songs for them, as did neighbors, who came in.

"He took all of his tapes that he had collected back with him and eventually, he got on to the BBC and the BBC decided to do, what I would consider, a very early folk music program [it started in 1950], called *As I Roved Out,* on BBC World Services network. My mother only had two verses of As I Roved Out, but she recorded it for Peter Kennedy and that's the title they chose for the program. My mother's recording was also the signature tune for the program. So they opened the program and they closed the program with my mother's singing of As I Roved Out. And that went out to the world every Sunday morning at ten o'clock.

As I Roved Out

Traditional, as collected by Peter Kennedy from Sarah Makem

As I roved out on a May morning
On a May morning right early
I met my love upon the way
Oh, Lord but she was early

Chorus:
And she sang lilt-a-doodle, lilt-a-doodle, lilt-a-doodle-dee,-
And she hi-di-lan-di-dee, and she hi-di-lan-di-dee and she lan- day
Her boots were black and her stockings white
her buckles shone like silver
She had a dark and a rolling eye
And her ear-rings tipped her shoulder

Chorus

Years later, Tommy Makem collected verses from the dozens of different versions floating about and put some of them into one song (the original melody was called *The Trooper and the Maid*). In Tommy's version, it started as above and then continued:

What age are you my bonny wee lass
What age are you my honey?
Right modestly she answered me
I'll be seventeen on Sunday

Chorus

Where do you live my bonny wee lass
Where do you live my honey?
In a wee house up on the top of the hill
And I live there with my mammy

Chorus

If I went to the house on the top of the hill
When the moon was shining clearly
Would you arise and let me in
And your mammy not to hear you?

Chorus

I went to the house on the top of the hill
When the moon was shining clearly
She arose to let me in
But her mammy chanced to hear her

Chorus

She caught her by the hair of the head
And down to the room she brought her
And with the butt of a hazel twig
She was the well-beat daughter

Chorus

Will you marry me now my soldier lad
Will you marry me now or never?
Will you marry me now my soldier lad
For you see I'm done forever

Chorus

I can't marry you my bonny wee lass
I can't marry you my honey
For I have got a wife at home
And how could I disown her?

Chorus

A pint at night is my delight
And a gallon in the morning
The old women are my heart break
But the young ones is my darling

Chorus

"Other collectors came to my mother, people like Jean Ritchie, who would be, I suppose the queen of American folk collectors. People came from Germany and France and various other places. Pete Seeger was over and collected some stuff from her."

Tommy saw first-hand his mother being visited by many of these now legendary song collectors mentioned above, as well as such luminaries as Jean Ritchie, who recorded Sarah over the winter of 1952-53, Diane Hamilton (Guggenheim), who first arrived in 1955, and scores of singers and musicians, all in search of new material, no matter how old it was. The impact that his mother, and her songs, were having persisted most of Tommy's life.

Tommy illustrates: "I remember arriving home one day on vacation from the States. I came to the house, I had a hired car and got my bag and my banjo out and I couldn't get into the kitchen because there was a class on, some university way down in the southwest, of this country [the U.S.] and their professors. They were all sitting on our kitchen floor and scullery floor and living room floor, all the students taking notes of what my mother was saying. And my father laughing his head off as these people were taking down what my mother was saying. And he was trying to ignore it all his life.

"But I couldn't get into the kitchen so I went up the stairs, left my bag and banjo and left until they got all their notes taken and whatever she sang for them. But I thought it was quite funny."

Sarah was also a member of the *Singing Greenes of Keady*. She was recorded on multiple compilation records and had at least three recordings of her own; *Sarah Makem, Ulster Ballad Singer* and *May Morning Dew*, all under the name of Mrs. Sarah Makem.

Visits from these song collectors inspired young Tommy to continue to collect songs from the surrounding areas, long after the collectors had gone back to whatever country they called home.

Although it appears that Tommy was born to be a fantastic singer, given the family passion and history, first the mandatory education, formal and life, had to be "got out of the way."

"I went to St. Clare's convent for infants class [pre-school] and wait until you hear this one, 'Senior Infants' [kindergarten] and then went down to the brothers, we had the De la Salle Brothers. And I went through grade one thru seven, and it was called Cross Mor Monastery Public Elementary School, in Keady. It was a very fancy name for it.

"I went to the Irish Christian Brothers, Armagh City [for post-elementary education] but, I only went for, maybe six months, and then I figured my education was all done and I got a job, in Keady. I was a clerk in Nugent's Garage and Taxi Service. I did the bookwork. It was all wonderful, great stories all through. I learned a lot from working there. I was fifteen, maybe.

"I worked there for a number of years and the garage changed hands a couple of times. So, then I left the garage and got a job as a barman in Mone's Bar. James Mone was the name of the father. They had a shop, a grocery store, and they sold meal to farmers and all that kind of thing and then they had a bar as well.

"So I was the barman. No experience, they just liked the way I could talk to people. And they showed me how to pour. Well there was no mixing of drinks in it. If somebody wanted a glass of whiskey, you could get that for them or a gin and tonic maybe but it was mostly beer and the stout of course, bottles of stout. We did not have pumps for the pints.

"And generally that, keeping it tidy and polishing the counter and washing the floors and scrubbing the back room out, cleaning the mirrors and the glasses. Ahh, I enjoyed it. Actually, when I was there, I became a correspondent for the *Armagh Observer*, the newspaper, at a penny a line. But I was working in the bar at the same time.

"But there was a lot going on around Keady, a lot of very good cultural things. We didn't realize it at the time, it just part of what happened. But it was very, very, very powerful, the culture was. Keady would be sort of the gateway to South Armagh. William Butler Yeats and AE [pen name for famous Irish poet George Russell, from Lurgan] rated Slieve Gullion [*shleeve gull yun*], South Armagh, the most mystical mountain in Ireland. And every major figure in Irish Mythology is associated with Slieve Gullion. At the foot of Slieve Gullion, in the 19th century, there was a school of poets, and they were regarded as the greatest poets in their own language in Western Europe and they all lived within an eight mile radius of each other.

"And of course, I was involved in all kinds of things in the community. I was in the church choir, had been since I was six years old, and then my voice changed when I was fourteen, soon as it changed back again [stopped fluctuating], I was put back into the choir because I could nearly sight read, I was taught. We had a wonderful priest there, Canon Pentony, and he had a phenomenal choir, a men and boy's choir. He had, I'll say, maybe twenty men and maybe forty boys. He bought us books, we could all read playing chants, like the monks used to sing, the Gregorian chants. And he taught us Motets [called Shaped Notes Music here - the inflections and voice strengths, rather than the times of the notes], and harmonies singing and he taught us about the voice, if you paid attention, and he was very picky that you paid attention.

"I couldn't write a piano chart, I couldn't put down a piano line of music but if he gave me a piece of a song, and the music there, I could pick out the melody. We had choir practice two evenings a week. Then I was in the dramatic society, amateur dramatics. The group I belonged to, called the *Keady Dramatic Society,* had been going on for one hundred and twenty years, non-stop. For a small country town, that was a great achievement.

"We got through a number of amateur theatrical contests. As a matter of fact, we made it to the All-Ireland Finals in Athlone. I got some sort of a prize, I don't remember what it was, for production of a Sean O'Casey play.

"Meanwhile, I was in a dance band. I was the singer in a dance band, a show band of some kind [called *The Clippertones & Tommy Makem*], then I also played in a couple of ceili bands [Tommy started his first ceili band at fifteen years old], where I played the whistle or a piccolo, a pipe kind of thing, sometimes there were drums. So all of that, I played football [Gaelic] and hurling and I was in the marching pipe band in Keady, as was my father, the base drummer, and Jack [Tommy's brother] would have been one of the leading pipers in the pipe band.

"I didn't read a lot. When I was a kid I remember going over and buying a copy of a play. And they were all concerned that I was spending my one and six pence on a play 'This is a theatrical play, you know, it is not a story.' I said, 'I know that is why I'm buyin' it," Tommy relates, recreating the exasperation he felt as a young man."

The Makem musical legacy didn't start with Sarah and end with Tommy. "All of us in the family knew the hundreds of songs that my mother, incessantly, all the time, sang. So sort of by osmosis, you got to know all these songs you'd hear her singing around the house, and later on, in years whenever I got involved in singing over here, I could go back and remember all these songs that my mother sang. I didn't have to sit down to learn them, they were there, always had been."

The Makem family legacy spreads far and wide. Tommy's three sons; Shane, Conor and Rory, formed the *Makem Brothers* in 1989, holding strong to the Song Tradition, they perform ballads and original tunes all across the country and in Ireland. They joined with Liam and Mickey Spain, themselves from a musical family, in 2003, and now perform as *The Makem & Spain Brothers*. If your eyes are closed, Rory's renditions of his father's songs can yield a feeling of displacement. Is that Tommy singing there?

Tommy also has a daughter, Katie, the oldest of Tommy and Mary's four children, and a grandchild, Molly. Tommy met his wife, Mary Catherine Shanahan, in her hometown of Chicago in 1961.

"The Clancy Brothers and myself were playing at the *Gate of Horn*, in Chicago, on State Street. I had played in it when it was on Chicago Avenue, the old Gate of Horn, and it burned down. They built a new one on State Street and the Clancys and myself were playing then and people like Lenny Bruce and Josh White.

"We were in for three weeks, I suppose. It was a folk and jazz club. My wife's mother and father were both from County Kerry and a cousin from Kerry had gotten a couple of tickets to come see these boys play. She had a cousin who was a waitress in the Gate of Horn and they thought we were hilarious – almost with straw growing out of our ears - but not quite.

"Her cousin had two tickets and he couldn't find anyone to go with him. So she was sort of dragged to it, she didn't really want to go because her mother and father used to have on this Irish 'diddly –dee' bits on the radio on a Saturday. She wasn't too impressed with what they were playing. But she came to the show and she thoroughly enjoyed the show and she came back, herself and a girl friend. I saw her sitting and she was drinking something, I don't know what the hell it was, I asked her if it was shampoo. That's where we met.

"We got married in 1963, in Chicago, at Our Lady O' Sorrows Basilica. "It was a great choice, she was a fantastic woman [Mary passed away in 2001 of cancer at the age of fifty-eight]. I just lucked out that she turned out to be a great woman."

The Makem legacy is not just a straight line, from Sarah, through Tommy, to his sons. Peter Makem, Tommy's father, was a fiddler and Peter's brother, Jack, was a bagpipe player and even created bagpipes himself. Tommy's own brother, Jack, was a musician as well.

"Jack was a phenomenal character, played the fiddle, the uileann pipes, the war pipes. He was a great whistle player. He's the one who taught me how to play the whistle. I'm the youngest. I had Jack and then I had three sisters, Peggy, Mona and Nancy, and Nancy died [in June, 2005]. So I'm the last one left standing.

"When I was maybe seven, the man who taught everyone around Keady to play the fiddle, his name was John Conway. He taught my sister Mona. He came to teach me the fiddle as well and he gave me a scale and told me to practice it and he'd be back the following week. When he came back, I was trying to play a tune on it, I had forgotten about the scales he had written down. He got disgusted at that and he threw it up in the air and he never came back to me. So that is how I did *not* become a fiddle player.

"Later on in life, he would have claimed me as one of his pupils," Tommy laughingly recounts. "He was a great one, he taught a lot of people to play the fiddle. He kept it alive and going when it was not the great thing to do. It wasn't as popular as it is now. He had a ceili band, John Conway did, and my sister Mona played in the ceili band with him. And he would also do house parties, just himself and the fiddle. He'd play for dancing at a house party or weddings and things like that, in the house. He was one of the men that kept the flame burning.

"But there was always music around the house, my sister Mona was a great fiddle player. Mona would be Tom and Jimmy Sweeney's mother, both of Barley Bree. So she was a great fiddle player, but the day she got married she left it down and I don't think she ever lifted it after that."

"He was there at the beginning when it all started," said Tom Sweeney. "That break was quite phenomenal, but he was prepared for it, he knew all the stuff as did the brothers [the Clancys], they were steeped in it, and I couldn't think of a better thing to say about Tommy. He was a man in the right place at the right time and he has been an absolute beacon for Irish singers ever since, and he continues to be a great inspiration for so many young aspiring singers today." - Tom Sweeney, another Festival Legend, successful solo performer, former member of Barley Bree - and Tommy's nephew.

Tommy Makem continues on about the Makem family's continued involvement in and dedication to, the Irish arts, "I have a nephew, Peter, Jack's oldest son. Peter would be an excellent, a very, very good poet. He has two or three books out that he has written. He also writes for an American newspaper, called the *Irish Edition*, out of Philadelphia. His brothers; Eddie, who also performs, and Tom Makem, who plays the banjo and sings, and Gerry Makem is an uileann piper."

Jack has three daughters as well; Kathleen, Mary and Monica. All of Jack's sons; Peter, Eddie, Tom, Gerry and John Makem are all not only involved in Irish music but passionate about the preservation of the Irish culture in all that they do. Tommy provides an example of their deep love for the Irish heritage and the efforts to preserve and honor the stories of those that came before, "On the foundations of an old house that had been on their land, land that had once belonged to a woman named Makem and her husband, named Connolly, the brothers built a new cultural center.

"In the bad old days, the landlord came around and threw them out of the house and burned it to the ground because they didn't have the rent. So they went down to my father's place, to the Makems, oh maybe a couple of miles down the valley,. He didn't have any room to put them up but built them a house out of sod. This couple lived in it for a while, until they got themselves on their feet and got another place to live."

The cultural center, where music sessions, lectures, singing and presentations on many aspects of the Irish heritage and culture are held, is called *Toffee's Hotel*, after a Neil Doran song that mentions Toffee's Hotel. Neil is from the area and he composed hundreds of songs over the years. So the Makem brothers decided this would be a great name for the cottage. "It is a privately raised cultural center. They do it for love of it," Tommy said.

The cultural center sits next to the site of the old Makem/Connolly house. The hard times caused the massive emigration of millions from Ireland. These emigrants are paid tribute by the elder Makem brothers, who raised a five ton standing stone on the former Makem/Connolly homestead. They called it *the Emigration Stone*, to salute anyone who had ever emigrated from Ireland to anywhere in the world.

The teaching and preservation continues, as Tommy explains, "John teaches in the high school in Keady. They have a few acres, off what they call the mountain, it is a big hill called Mullyard [*mull lee yard*]. They don't grow flax anymore, so John, about ten years ago, put in a quarter acre of flax so his students could see what it was like and the work that was involved in pulling the flax and drowning it in a Flax Hole, as they called it, or a Lint Hole. That's where Linseed comes from. Linseed oil would be flax seed oil.

"John put in this ¼ of acre, it was covered by Ulster television and newspapers, showing how it was grown and the terrible slavery it was to pull the flax and drown it and wait for it to dry and bring it to be scutched. John got a man to come in and hand-scutch it, for there were no scutch mills anymore, which is what my father used to work at.

"In the scutch mill [in the old days], there were a row of eight scutchers and each of them had a little area, sort of like a box, to themselves almost. There was a big shaft in behind that and on the shaft there were blades, like airplane propellers. Except the blades were made from ash (wood), so after the flax was drowned, it was spread out on the ground. The smell of it was horrendous; aw you could smell it for miles and miles. It was spread out on the fields in rows, to dry, just lying on the field. Whenever it got dried, they tied it up in sheaves again, bundles, and tightened it with a rush band, made from rushes. But the dried flax was taken to the mill and it was cut through.

"The first process was like rollers, long steel rolls with teeth on that broke the flax up a bit. The linen or flax thread was up, sort of almost like a straw but not quite as big as a straw, and the rollers broke up the outer casing of it. Then it was brought in, in 'streaks,' handfuls, and it was twisted and left with the scutcher, who took it and fed it very carefully onto this propeller that was flying around the 'handles,' as they called them. The scutcher was a tough job and most of them got hit at one point or another, hit on their knuckles or their thumb or index fingers, by the handles. They all got broken fingers.

"The handles beat the reed like stuff out of it and left it just mostly, like hair, like thread. You were left with this dried, sort of golden hair colored flax, threadlike. It was the raw material of the flax and that was the basis of the threads for linen."

Tommy again returned to talking about the Makem family's talent and involvement in the Irish performing arts. "Eddie Makem's daughter, Stephanie, is one of the finest singers I've heard in years and years and years. I didn't hear her singing until maybe two or three years ago. When I heard her sing, it struck me, she sang very like my mother, who would be her great grandmother. But she was a little more decorative [demonstrative]. Northern singing is very straightforward. A bit of decoration, but not too much.

"Stephanie had a little bit more decoration than my mother had. And Stephanie is married to a young fella, a teacher, from Monaghan. His name is Tiarnan *[Tear nan]* Dinkins, and Tiarnan would be one of the better uileann pipers in Ireland, among the young people. He is a scholar with the music and the general culture.

"Stephanie plays the fiddle as well. And then she has a sister Judith, who plays the flute and another sister, Emma, who plays the keyboard. They used to play together and sing a bit in harmony but I was surprised when I heard Stephanie sing, the fourth generation. And there's some of the rest of them at it as well. My other sister's people, well most of the Sweeney's sing, I think, the whole Sweeney family, there were eight of them.

"As a matter of fact, I brought a small nylon string guitar home and gave it to Jimmy [Sweeney] when he was a kid and he learned to play it, and I also got some records and things, not only of what the Clancys and myself were doing but I brought the family some American folk songs recordings, like the Weavers and people like that. And their father, Frank Sweeney, he would have been into classical music quite a bit and he played the cornet in a silver and reed band, so he got very interested in the music and he had the boys singing.

"One time, Jimmy and Tom were singing together, they were nine or ten years old and Frank got a tape recorder from somewhere and he taped the boys singing and singing in harmony and singing these songs that they heard, not only their Uncle Tommy doing, but the Clancys and their Uncle Tommy and some songs the Weavers would have done and various other people, the Irish Ramblers, for instance.

"The father sent me a tape of the two boys singing, he wanted to let me hear what they were about and what they were doing. Jimmy had learned the guitar. And the tape sat here for years and years in the cupboard here. About two or three years ago, Rory was poking through a cupboard and he found this tape and put it on a CD. Their father, Frank, he would introduce the songs on it and talk to me on it and he got his wife, my sister Mona, to say hello and so forth.

"Rory made up a number of CDs and they were given to the Sweeney family as a Christmas present. Of the two boys, when they were lads, singing and their mother and their father talking on there. Apparently there was weeping and gnashing of teeth when they got it!"

The Makem family, in all its breadth and talent, keeps the legacy, the ancient tradition, alive and new.

"The great Dublin singer Frank Harte [who passed away in July, 2005] observed that while America and Britain had their folksong revivals, "we in this country have been spared the sacredness of a revival due to the fact that the tradition of singing of songs has never died."[1] Tommy continues to make sure that the wonderful traditions of the Irish never die, in the U.S., Ireland, or anywhere else Irish and folk music lovers gather.

The Makem family continues to inspire and influence Irish music fans the world over. But one of the previously mentioned song collector's, Diane Hamilton [Guggenheim], would go on to have significant influence on Tommy himself, opening doors and creating opportunities leading from his dreams of acting in the U.S., to a fateful meeting with Liam Clancy, to stardom never before seen in the Irish music world.

Diane Hamilton's search for the folk songs of Ireland had led her to Sarah Makem. Tommy explains, "Diane Hamilton put out an album on Traditions Records, called *The Lark in the Morning*, and those were of some of the tapes she collected around Ireland and wonderful ones they were that she had. She had Paddy Tunney on it, a phenomenal singer. My mother, of course was on it and Mrs. Clancy and Liam, and I was on it doing something.

"She also had Mrs. Cronin from Cork, who was a great singer and she went around and collected Padraic O'Keefe, down in Kerry and Liam Clancy, that's where he and I met. She had a big tape recorder, and it would take maybe a horse, maybe two donkeys to carry it. Nowadays, you can put your tape recorder in your breast pocket. But at that time it was a big reel-to-reel thing, so Liam got the job of carrying this around.

"Diane had gone to Carrick-on Suir to visit Mrs. Clancy because she knew Paddy and Tom Clancy in New York. Then Liam and Diane Hamilton came up to collect songs from my mother and Liam and I found out each of us was going to head to the States and that each of us were interested in the theatre, in being actors. So I emigrated December 1st, of '55 and Liam emigrated early the next year [January, 1956]."

"I knew I would never be going back, why was I leaving in the first place? There was no place for you to go [in Ireland].You could've found a job, but the job you'd of been at, if it was not what you wanted to do, you were stuck. Out here you could see more opportunity to work and find something that you would like. But I had it [locked] in my head that I wanted to be an actor and I thought there were more opportunities out here.

"At the All-Ireland Amateur Theatrical [competition], there was an adjudicator over from England, a judge, and his name was Hugh Hunt, Sir Hugh Hunt, and he was a director of the old Vic, in England, which does classical theatre. And he offered me a job in England, at the old Vic. But I began to think that there was a lot of very good Irish and English actors, and Scottish as well, and I began to think that America is a much bigger country and much more opportunity there, so I didn't go to the old Vic. I came to America instead, to become an actor."

Liam Clancy recounts his early Tommy Makem memories: "The recording sessions at the Makem's house were memorable. Peter, the man of the house, with his pipe and fiddle…and Jack, his son…Tommy, the youngest son, in the corner nearly as shy as myself…. And they all buzzed around the queen bee herself, Sarah Makem, as she sat placid in the eye of the hurricane.

"It was so much like the Clancy household it was uncanny, in our case Mammy Clancy being the queen bee. All that was different was the accents.

"The young Tommy Makem and I struck up an instant friendship. Out interests were so similar; girls, theatre and singing, in that order. He was heading to America soon, he told me, to try his luck at acting. We agreed to keep in touch. One night we went to a dance in Newry. The band knew Tommy and invited him up on the stage to sing a song. The hall was mobbed and I thought, 'My God, this crowd will never listen.' He got onstage and asked for a chair. Putting his right foot up on his left knee, he started to make a motion of mending his shoe. He began, 'Oh me name is Dick Darby, I'm a cobbler.' Those in front started shushing those behind, and before he'd finished the first verse, there was total silence. I was impressed." - Liam Clancy [2]

Liam and Tommy hit it off, and about a year after they met, headed for America (separately) to try their luck at acting – both on stage and on television. But the legendary *Clancy Brothers & Tommy Makem* seeds had been planted in a small village in South Armagh, and would blossom and multiply beyond anyone's dreams.

Tommy's ambition to become an actor had taken him to New York. He sang professionally while acting, including playing the Gate of Horn and opening for Josh White (in 1958). After a brief but rewarding career in live television, summer stock and Off Broadway plays, he teamed up with Liam, Tom, and Paddy Clancy, after numerous sessiuns and sing-alongs at the White Horse Tavern in Greenwich Village.

"The only thing for Irish songs at that time, early on, John McCormack and people like Bing Crosby. Here we came, and maybe we had one mike for the four of us to sing on. So you roared as loudly as you could so you could be heard," recalled Tommy Makem, to Ronan Nolan in a 2002 interview.[3]

"Someone [Kenny Goldstein] had gotten on to Paddy Clancy to do an album of Irish Rebels songs," Tommy says, "and Diane Hamilton said 'Well why don't you do them for yourself, start a record company?' So Diane Hamilton and Paddy and Tom and I think Liam were involved, I wasn't involved in it, started *Tradition Records.*"

Paddy Clancy credits Tommy Makem for the idea to start the group performing professionally, when Tommy came into Tradition Records one day and wanted to make a record. That gave Paddy the idea for taking the boys from where they were just gathering around, singing for a few bucks and for fun, to singing professionally, as a band.

The Clancy Brothers & Tommy Makem's first professional appearance was at *Circle in the Square Theatre* in Greenwich Village. Then John Hammond of Columbia Records signed them to a recording contract in 1961 (Columbia bought the Clancy/Guggenheim Traditions Records the same year).

After a brief trip home, in 1958, Tommy returned to New York and completed a Camera Three Special for St. Patrick's Day, called *The Rising of the Moon, Irish Songs of Rebellion.*

"Almost immediately after Tommy arrived, we started work on another album,' Liam Clancy recounts, "This time a collection of drinking songs. We rehearsed by day at Tradition's office on Christopher Street and belted out the songs by night at the White Horse Tavern."[2]

Tommy recalls *The Rising of the Moon* - "... they had asked me to do this recording with them. We went up to Kenny Goldstein's apartment; he lived off of Fordham Road I think, in the Bronx. He had a tape recorder. We went up to his apartment and recorded, unaccompanied.

"They had a young baby at the time, and his wife Rochelle had us stay there and put our hand over the baby's mouth, if it was going to cry while we were doing the recording. The album cover was done by an artist called Louis Le Brocquy [*pron* Leh Brockey], who would be one of the major artists in Ireland at the time. And he designed the cover for *The Rising of the Moon*, which was green with a little bit of linen cut out in the shape of the moon, a quarter moon. And a shirt, of the same sort of linen, cut into the shape of a shirt, with a bit of red over where the heart would be. That's called the Rising of the Moon and the album cover won a number of awards, art awards.

"He also designed the cover for Diane Hamilton's *The Lark in the Morning*. He used the carvings on the entrance stones to Newgrange, just the grain of the stone on these carvings. It won a number of awards as well."

During this same time period, at the beginning of the 1960's, Tommy also appeared at the Newport Folk Festival, where he and Joan Baez were chosen the two most promising newcomers on the American folk scene.

"It was just a couple of great days up in Newport, Rhode Island. Got a lift up, maybe Charlie Rothschild had a little Volkswagen, and he gave me a lift up. I think I had been there the year before. But it was later on that the New York Times published that [list of Award winners]. Ahh, it was nice of them, but I didn't think too much more of it at the time.

"But I remember being up at Tradition Records one day and Paddy Clancy was sitting behind the desk and he has some papers and sitting on the papers was some little gramophone or a phonograph, with the loudspeaker on it.

"And I said 'Paddy, where'd ya get the wee gramophone?'

"'Sure I don't know, somebody sent it to me.'

"And it was years later that I realized, and I don't know if he ever realized, it was a nomination for a Grammy. I don't know what happened to it. I don't know if we won one or not, but certainly were nominated for one. But he didn't know what it was. I [certainly] didn't. He was using it as a paperweight."

"All of us were acting and the Rising of the Moon was out and about and doing fairly well, people were getting to know about it and we had *Come Fill Your Glass with Us* and they were both out and about and people were looking for us to perform. I remember that offers started to come in for singing but we were doing whatever plays we could get, find to do, on and off-Broadway. Acting jobs and bits of television and things like that. We had a mass meeting, all four of us, to see of we were going to carry on with our proper in the theatre or if we were going to take this singing nonsense, 'cause we kept getting offers to go sing. We were getting more offers to sing than plays we could find. So we came to a unanimous decision, the four of us together. 'We'll give this singing lag six months and see if we can survive for six months on it.' And then of course six months turned into whatever number of years. [It has been almost fifty years since Rising of the Moon was released].

"It was the Gate of Horn in Chicago where we got our name. There was a fella called Alan Ribback, who was one of the owners of Gate of Horn. They had heard this Rising of the Moon album and this album of drinking songs called Come Fill Your Glass With Us. The folk music boom was just getting started. So they got in touch with Tradition Records to see if we would perform at the Gate of Horn and why not, we were all looking for jobs acting. Tom was an actor on Broadway, Paddy was running Tradition Records by this time, Liam and I were doing off-Broadway things. The Gate of Horn got in touch with us to see if we'd go out and do some time there.

"And we did, but we spent a few days trying to, we must have filled five or six or seven or eight foolscap pages [large yellow lined pads of paper] with names, looking for names for the group. Like The Moonshiners, and we had The Chieftains, I know and the Blacksmiths, The Druids, and all of us had to agree to it. And someone would have an objection to this and someone would object to that. And eventually, we didn't have a name when we were going out to the Gate of Horn and when we arrived out they had our names up at the Gate of Horn, *The Clancy Brothers and Tommy Makem* and that's where we got our title. They decided it for us."

Most Irish music fans know that when The *Clancy Brothers & Tommy Makem* appeared on *The Ed Sullivan Show,* Irish music came into its own. The appearances weren't just pivotal, they were ground breaking. That these four young guys could take songs, songs that everyone in Ireland had known, maybe for generations, and perform them in a way that all audiences, not just the Irish ones, could appreciate and enjoy, started an elemental change in the Irish psyche. The days of being belittled, just for being Irish, the *No Irish Need Apply* times, were over, and a new pride, a new recognition, that if our music is accepted and celebrated, then we must be acceptable and celebrated. It really was an event, a progression, that literally started to transform the Irish people.

The Ed Sullivan Show was one of the highest rated shows on television, drawing over eighty million viewers for each Sunday night show. But it was not their first appearance on the Ed Sullivan Show that shook the foundations of Irish music in America, as most believe. The Clancy Brothers & Tommy Makem appeared on the Ed Sullivan Show four times. Although each show had progressively more impact, saving the best for last, the final appearance is the episode that changed history and altered the path, and the adoption, of Irish music, the world over.

The first appearance was on March 12, 1961, when The Clancy Brothers & Tommy Makem sang *Brennan on the Moor.* Other entertainers included actress Tammy Grimes, Actor Pat O'Brien and Irish singers Brendan O'Dowda and Mary O'Hara. Backstage, Liam Clancy was a bit nervous and had gotten a nose bleed. He was leaning forward, bent over the guitar strapped to his chest, to insure the blood didn't get on his white Aran sweater. A producer came up and made sure they were ready. When he told them how many people would be watching, Liam's nose bleed immediately dried up.

Their second appearance was on December 16th, 1962 and included Liberace, Abbe Lane, Xavier Cugat and Barbra Streisand, who would go on to open for The Clancy Brothers & Tommy Makem, on their own tour, soon after. They performed *Whistling Gypsy* and *South Australia*.

March 14th, 1965, the Clancy Brothers & Tommy Makem made their third appearance, where they sang *Wild Colonial Boy*. Other guests on that show included Petula Clark, Nancy Walker and Burt Lahr.

But it was the fourth appearance, on March 13th, 1966, that altered the future, the prestige, and the acceptance, of Irish music in America, and in Ireland too. It also did well for The Clancy Brothers & Tommy Makem! Other guests included Wayne & Shuster, the McNiff Dancers and Mary O'Hara. Pearl Bailey was scheduled to be the headliner, but did not show.

Liam Clancy recalls the producer coming to them, the next act, in a panic.

"'We've got a problem. Could you guys improvise three extra songs?'

"[Liam thought to himself...] That would leave us with about fifteen minutes out of a one hour show. ...

"'Be good gentlemen. Remember – there's eighty million people watching you!'"[2]

The group had rehearsed two songs, but now five were required. For sixteen minutes, an Ed Sullivan Show record, they held the stage – and most of the television tuned world, in the palm of their hands. It was more time than anyone had ever done on the Ed Sullivan Show, including the Beatles, and Elvis.

"The times we did the Ed Sullivan show, we had no idea of the enormous impact it would have. No idea at all," Tommy recalls. The young performers didn't waste the opportunity. Their performance sent the Clancy Brothers & Tommy Makem on an unprecedented path to stardom.

Tommy plays the banjo, tin whistle, war pipes (bagpipes, also called Irish Union Pipes), drums, piccolo, guitar and bodhran. He also played the drums in ceili bands when he was younger but these were snare and base drums with little wooden box for rhythms. His aversion to the big drum kits of today is well known.

"Ahh Lord, anytime when I see a major set of drums. When I see a major set of drums, with the side drums and the cymbals and the whole bit, I shudder. I now come to call those I.M.D.'s. That's *Instruments of Mass Destruction* - and unlike the weapons of mass destruction, there available everywhere! There is a difference between a percussionist and a drummer. Rock drummers just pound everything as heavily and as hard and as far into the dirt as they can. They obliterate any idea of graciousness in a melody. They blank out whatever meaning the words, the lyrics would have. Songs that started out with melodies have now been reduced to three notes. It covers a lot of sins and creates a lot of them as well."

"Tommy Makem was a gentleman. By his own definition, a gentleman is a fellow who can play the bagpipes, but won't," says Liam Clancy. "Tommy was a piper. The first time we played the *hungry i* in San Francisco, Tommy had not yet learned to become a gentleman. He insisted on playing his bloody warpipes. I have nothing against bagpipes as long as they play their hellish instruments on a mountaintop… But the Highland pipes played indoors at close range are an abomination and a health hazard."[2]

Tommy reluctantly gave up performing the bagpipes as part of the Clancy Brothers & Tommy Makem, when the group came to realize that because of the loud sound of the warpipes, playing them indoors at a show knocked the band members out of tune for the following songs. But not too long after that, for very different reasons, Tommy had to give up the bagpipes for good.

"I can play a tune or two on the uileann pipes, but when I came to this country first, I had my hand crushed, my left hand, the fingers won't, they'd be all right for a minute or two but then would begin to slip and they would slide off the holes because they [the holes] were wider apart [on the uileann pipes] than on the tin whistle.

"I was working here in New Hampshire in a foundry [1956] trying to earn a few dollars so I wouldn't starve to death when I went to New York to become an actor. The side of a printing press slipped as it was unchained. I was turning it over onto two horses (wooden horses). I put my hand to it to balance it so it wouldn't [fall over] but it slipped and came down and bounced on a cement floor, my left hand under it. So I tore the tendons out of three fingers [severed the tendons connecting the fingers to the palm].

"And that night, there were three or four doctors there looking at it. A couple of them thought they should probably cut the fingers off. I was only over from Ireland a couple of months. There was one young doctor who was just out of medical school, and his forte was tendons.

"The young fella said, 'That's rather drastic, why don't you let me see if I can save the fingers.' So the other doctors said, 'Sure, if you think you can do anything.'

"He took me, and I had seven or eight surgeries on my hand. He took tendons out of my wrist and out of my feet, and he transplanted them into my fingers. That's why I still have fingers on my left hand.

"[At the time], it wasn't sore because the weight of this hanging form, bouncing on the floor, it sort of numbed my hand and so I didn't feel any pain. Matter of fact, they wanted to send me up to the hospital but I went home and I took a bath. It was filthy dirty working in the foundry. I took a bath and then went to the hospital.

"So the pain wasn't great. But the young doctor who did it, his father had come over from Greece and was a cobbler in the town of Dover, here. This young man had worked his way through college and through medical school. His name is Dr. Demopolous and he now lives down at the end of this street I live on. So I see him all the time, he's retired.

"I remember coming out of the anesthesia one time [after one of the surgeries] and I was making this great anti-English speech, roarin' and shoutin' and waving my good arm and he thought this was great because Greece and Turkey and Britain were having rows about Cyprus at the time. So he thought this was wonderful.

"He was only out of medical school at that time and there was a man in Boston, who was considered the expert on tendons in the United

States, and he had written a number of books about working with tendons and so forth. I was sent to him by the insurance company for him to look at my hand

"He said 'Who did this work?'

"'Dr. Demopolous in Dover, New Hampshire,' I said.

"'He's to be congratulated, I couldn't have done a job as good as that.'"

"And I came home and told that to Dr. Demopolous. You'd have thought I had given him a million dollars, because of this man's reputation."

Another brilliant performer who had life-changing impact on Tommy was Pete Seeger. "Seein' him, that first time when I came to New York, when I got the $30 for singing a couple of songs [on St. Patrick's Day, 1956, the first time that making money for singing would register with Tommy as a viable source of income while the acting dreams were being pursued]. I had my hand in a cast, as a matter of fact. It was a midnight concert at a theatre called the Circle in the Square, down in Greenwich Village. After the concert, two men came in to see me, dressed in lovely wool overcoats and scarves and hats, the caps, and talked to me about the songs and about my singing.

"I had no idea who they were but when they left, Diane Hamilton explained that it was Pete Seeger and Alan Lomax. I said 'Who's Pete Seeger? Who's Alan Lomax?' So they told me. Pete sang with a group called *The Weavers*. I went out and I bought a couple of records of The Weavers and brought them back to New Hampshire from New York and sat down to listen to them when I got back and I thought 'Oh my God, they're singing all my mother's songs - but they have the wrong tunes to them!' They were doing different versions of a lot of the songs that I would have heard my mother sing.

"I was very impressed with the Weavers, especially Pete. Then I got to do a couple of concerts with them, on my own. Those I enjoyed thoroughly.

"Alan Lomax was the premier American folk song collector, he and his father, John, before him as well. Alan Lomax collected songs from all over the world. He has a book out, a huge book about American folk music and it has a lot of songs in it. But Alan Lomax would have been the collectors name if you talked about folk song collectors, he would be the major name in American folk song. He did a lot of work for Congress [Library of Congress] and he put out lots of recordings and they have reissued a lot of his stuff from the Library of Congress. He brought to prominence great performers like Lead Belly [Hudie Ledbetter].

"Sisco Houston, a great pal of Woodie Guthrie's [was also a big influence on Tommy]. Sisco Houston used to sing a song called '*The Cat Came Back*.' And I heard him singing it in *Gertie's Folk City* [originally called *Gertie's Fifth Peg*, located on 4th Street, near Broadway in Manhattan] one night. I thought, 'God, there's another man singing one of my mother's songs.' My mother used to sing this song. I don't know where she got it. I do believe it was an American song but I don't know where she got it. [Starts to sing, 'The cat came back the very next day, the cat came back, 'cause she couldn't stay away']."

Gertie's Fifth Peg is one of the early platforms for Tommy and Liam Clancy; where they first got their start. Tom and Paddy Clancy would stop by an odd night and they'd all get up and belt out a few songs. They were in a play together at the time and were offered money to go and sing. Eventually Gertie's moved to around 6th Avenue.

"But Pete, and the Weavers, would have had a very big impact [on me]. And then I got to see him perform and the electricity, just oozing out of this man across the audience, you know, and himself on the banjo. And I thought the banjo was a great instrument for accompanying the songs of that time, folk songs. So I got interested in the banjo.

"I bought a banjo in a shop on Fordham Road one time. I think it cost me $30.00. So [it was] like a piece of tin. Wasn't a very good banjo and it was in a cardboard case. I was up at Tradition Records, in the office one day, and I'd gotten Pete Seeger's book, *How to Play the 5-String Banjo*. I was putting my fingers on the cords, the fingers that were working, and on the strings, and trying to strum and who came into the office of Tradition Records, but Diane Hamilton. She looked and she said, 'Ohhhh, Are you learning to play the banjo?' and I said 'Yeah, it's tough.' [Be]cause I had no one to teach me, I was learning out of the book.

"The next day that I was over there, Diane Hamilton arrived over. She had gone to the Folklore Center on MacDougal Street (down in the Village, A.B. Young used to run the Folklore Center), and she had bought me a banjo, a beautiful banjo, with a hand carved neck. This was a small short-neck banjo, not the long-neck one like I play now. I still have that. It was a much more expensive banjo than the one I had bought for thirty bucks!

"I learned to play the banjo after I had the hand fixed. My index finger on my left hand doesn't bend very well. That's why I have to use a capo all the time. I can't chord, I can't put the finger out straight to go into a different key. It is a physical thing."

Together with the Clancy Brothers, Tommy has appeared on *the Ed Sullivan Show, the Tonight Show, Arthur Godfrey's Talent Scouts, the Morning Show, PM East* and *PM West*, and on every major television network show in the United States.

He has many favorite performances but a few stick out in his mind: "Performing at the dinner for JFK [January 31, 1963] when he was President, and getting to meet him. Oh it was phenomenal. There was a dinner put on, called *Dinner with the President* and there was a television show done of it. Robert Preston, the actor, was Master of Ceremonies for the program. There were all sorts of singers on it, folk singers, like our friend Josh White, and I think maybe Judy Collins was on it, but I'm not certain of that.

"We were representing the Irish of John Fitzgerald Kennedy. But the whole program, and the dinner, was produced by B'nai Brath, to honor President Kennedy. I had rewritten an old song, called *We Want No Irish Here,* one of the songs we played, and I had written new words to it, and they got a great shot of JFK and behind him, the insignia of the President of the United States, [with] JFK laughing his head off at this song - great, great shot. And then he came up afterwards to meet all of the people who were [performing]. He came up onto the stage and shook hands with all of us. It was wonderful.

We Want No Irish Here

words by Tommy Makem, air: Traditional, Are You There Moriarity?

Our ship it docked in New York town
And we took our bags ashore
This was the land of the free they said
We'd see hard times no more
But when we looked for work next day
Wherever we'd appear
The boss so proud, would shout out loud
"We want no Irish here"

Chorus:
We have loyal hearts and willing hands
Of work we have no fear
But when we'd ask for a job they'd say
"We want no Irish here"

We traveled 'round from town to town
We traveled south and north
We tried our best to get a job
So we could prove our worth
But everywhere, it was the same
We searched both far and near
We'd get in line, then see the sign
"We want no Irish here"

Chorus

But prejudice soon fades away
When you find a heart that's true
And all we needed was the chance
To prove what we could do
We fought in wars and drove street cars
Built railroads far and near

Were cops, wrote news, paid our union dues
Now the Irish are welcome here.

We have loyal hearts and willing hands
Of work we have no fear
If you're out for fun or a job well done
You'll find the Irish here

"We did parties, parties for the United Nations people, the American crowd who would be at the United Nations - there were all sorts of big name politicians, who enjoyed all of the craic.

"Certainly the first time we played in Dublin, the Clancys and myself, was very special. We had no idea that these songs were so well known or that they were so popular.

"In Dublin, there was a fella called Ciaran MacMathuna, [*Keer an Mac Mahuna*], who worked for RTE in Dublin and had a radio program, *Job of Journeywork*, who came over here around 1962. He'd find men and women who had emigrated from Ireland, thirty years previously, who played the fiddle, or the flute, or squeezebox, or whatever and he would go around and record programs with them. And at one point, in every apartment that he went into in New York or Chicago or wherever he happened to be recording that week, he saw these pictures of these boys in Aran sweaters on LP's sitting beside the record player. He got interested and took a handful of them home, of whatever we had out at the time, and he started to play them on Radio Eireann and then the regular disk jockeys got on to it and they started playing the songs and they just exploded, because Ciaran was bringing it all back home.

"But we had no idea when we arrived in Ireland. Ciaran MacMathuna was involved in promoting that first tour that we did, because of the popularity on the radio. So when we went to the theatre to do this show. We had no idea what the reception would be like. They could have booed us off the place or they could have ignored us or whatever. But we found to our surprise, the theatre was jam packed, there were actually people sitting in the aisle.

"There was a crowd of people sitting outside that couldn't get in and it was a very wet evening. We were looking out through a dressing room window and these people were out in the street, standing in the rain. When we looked out, we were waving down to them and they shouted out 'Sing us a song.' So we sang two or three songs out the window to the crowd outside. And they all stood in the rain and sang the songs with us. Then we went down onto the stage to do the concert and the place was jammed. I thought it was fantastic. We had been used to good audiences in the States. We were playing colleges and universities and concert halls. But going home and having this happen was absolutely sensational. You'd start to sing a song and you almost wouldn't have to bother finishing it, they would finish it for you. You would get enthusiastic too when they were singing. [Feeding off the crowd]...You'd have to; it's what comes back to you. And there is no high like it, getting feedback, the electricity from an audience. They knew every song we sang and every word of every song. So it just skyrocketed from there on."

"People keep asking me all the time what's my favorite song and I have to tell them, whenever I wake up in the morning, whatever's in my head, that's my favorite song for the day."

"I got a tune one time, I was down in Kerry and I went out one morning about eight o'clock. There was a blackbird in the hedge and it was staking its claim to this hedge and I whistled back and imitated the tune that the blackbird was singing. It followed me, for, maybe a mile or a mile and a half up the road, telling me that this was its territory. I always carry a little notebook with me and I wrote down the notes that the blackbird was singing - it was a whole eight bars. So I put another eight bars to it and I had a whole new tune. I called it *The Listowel Blackbird*."

In 1969 Tommy left the Clancy Brothers to pursue a solo career and immediately sold out *The Felt Forum in Madison Square Garden* in New York. His popularity soared, and he went on to three sold out concert tours of Australia, including Sydney's *Opera House*, three in the United States and several in Canada, Ireland, England, Scotland and Wales, all within a two year period of time. Tommy found time between concert tours to do two TV series for Scottish Television, one series for the BBC and one for Ulster Television. He then went on to do a network series for the CBC in Canada and a four year syndicated series for CHCH-

TV out of Hamilton, Ontario. There were no thirteen week seasons in those days. The show ran for all fifty-two weeks each year.

"I wrote the commercial that was shown during the moon landing in 1969. We did a commercial, for, Gulf Oil Company, I think. They had a big tanker, the biggest tanker in the world, in and out of Bantry Bay. I wrote words to it, called *Bringing Home the Oil,* to the tune of *Gallant Forty Twa.'* I wrote two or three songs and that was the one they picked. It was played all during the moon landing, in network."

Tommy continued his concert career on a solo basis until July of 1975, when he was booked for a folk festival in Cleveland, Ohio. Liam Clancy was booked as a solo act for the same festival. In a hallway, Tommy and Liam chatted and decided to do one set together.

"We were both booked separately. There was a stage outside and one inside at Pickle Bills, down in the Flats. And he was doing a show outside and I was doing one inside and then I would go out and do one outside and he would come in and do one inside. And we met in the hallway and had a bit of a yarn and we decided 'We'll do a few of the old songs,' we didn't have to rehearse them or anything, that we had done for years and years and years with the Clancy Brothers & Tommy Makem.

"So we both went outside and got up on the stage and got like a five minute standing ovation, before we sang a note. So we did a few of the old pot boilers. It was great, there was great reception.

"Then my wife Mary, Lord have mercy on her, was doing the bookings here and we decided, "We should do a few of these shows together, and Mary booked us into a lovely little folk club, which was like a theatre, it was called the *Raven Gallery,* in Detroit. And we went in there and played for a week and we worked out a whole lot of the new material that we were doing, or wanted to do. That's where we worked it out.

"And then I had been doing the television show up in Canada, CHCH TV, and we invited Liam to do it. He went out to live in Calgary at one point and he had a local show out in Calgary and invited me out there to do his show. And then the following year, we did a little show in Calgary, the two of us. Then we did the one in New Hampshire here."

Tommy Makem was a guest on Liam's show in 1975. That episode won *The Best Canadian Variety Show of the Year* award   Tommy won an Emmy with Liam Clancy for a thirteen part series called *Makem & Clancy*.

"Then we started to get bookings. Mary was booking us in various places, booking us in places like Point Barrow, Alaska, in February, where it was sixty below. I think she did that to torture us.

"It was a little village - no grass, no trees, no bushes, no flowers – tundra, five hundred miles from the North Pole. We were playing there in February and we were the only ones who got off the plane who had suitcases. Everybody else was carrying gear, people who were working on the pipeline.

"We came out of the motel to go to the concert and I had my bodhran in a bodhran case. Liam had a bodhran hanging in a shoulder case he had. And the minute he walked out the door, it was sixty degrees below zero, the bodhran burst, with a great bang! You had to wear a scarf over your mouth because at that temperature, there would have been the possibility of your lungs freezing.

"We were trying to figure out what we were going to sing for these people and we decided maybe we should sing some whaling songs and some sea songs. I went out front, and it was in a beautiful new high school. A very beautiful Inupiat woman, very well dressed, came over to me and she said "Would you do a request for me?

"I said 'I will if I can.'

"She said, 'Would you sing *Four Green Fields*?'

"So I figured that one will have to go in [Tommy recounts with a bit of laughter and a small dose of pride]. The place was full, of the entire village of Point Barrow, they were all Inupiat, except for one guy who was from Mayo! He was working on the pipeline and made his way to see us when he heard this Irish stuff was going on."

The coincidental booking of both performers at the folk festival in Cleveland, Ohio, in 1975, and the success of the television show the same year led to the duo deciding to reunite, as *Makem & Clancy*, with the television show becoming *The Liam Clancy - Tommy Makem Show*. Makem &Clancy recorded nearly a dozen albums, including; *We've Come A Long Way, Two For The Early Dew, Live at The National*

Concert Hall, In Person at Carnegie Hall, Sing Of The Sea, Tommy and Liam, which went Gold, and the Platinum selling *Tommy and Liam in Concert*. They also won international recognition for their recordings of Michael Peter Smith's *The Dutchman* and Eric Bogle's *"The Band Played Waltzing Matilda,* [recorded live for the album *The Makem and Clancy Concert*, on July 25-30, 1977, at the Gaiety Theatre, Dublin].

Tommy also had a four year syndicated series for CHCH TV in Hamilton, Ontario called *Tommy Makem and Ryan's Fancy* [a well known group of performers from Newfoundland]. Scottish TV (STV) was also the host for *Makem Country* a two- series program. "They thought I was going to do country music but I was doing my own country's music," Tommy recounts with a laugh.

Around the same time, Tommy also did a series for the BBC, Northern Ireland, in Belfast, called *Makem Sings.*

The magical combination of *Makem & Clancy* was to last until March of 1988 and garnered them an Emmy nomination for the TV series done with New Hampshire Public Television, as well as several platinum and gold records. After thirteen years of almost constant touring, television, recording and major concerts, both Tommy and Liam were suffering from burnout and decided a break was in order. They each returned to their homes for a while, but did not stop performing, still doing sold out solo shows, television specials, recordings and much more, over the next several years.

In 1994 Tommy completed a life long dream when, together with WMHT public Television, Schenectady, N.Y., he taped *Tommy Makem's Ireland,* a two part guided video tour of Ireland, each part approximately sixty minutes. The two 'Parts', were renamed *Part I* and *Part II*. Combined, this two-hour television special ran four times in the following years. On its last showing it was picked up by 320 stations nationwide. In February of 2000, Tommy took a crew back to Ireland to begin filming for *Parts III* and *IV*. The original Tommy Makem's Ireland was re-released as two one hour shows, with Parts III and IV then becoming *The Road Taken.*

"I did all the research for that and I wanted to see places that don't normally get mentioned and I think they are of extreme importance; the Dolmens and Burial Mounds, Cairns. All the ancient sites, that were before five thousand years old, and I think Newgrange is actually a phenomenon.

"So I actually started out my first [tour] at Newgrange, because it is the oldest man made building in the world, built some five thousand years ago [3150 BC]. It outdates the pyramids in Egypt, it would outdate Stonehenge, in England by at least a thousand years, if not fifteen hundred [years]. As far as I'm concerned, it is much more important than Stonehenge ... because this is where a lot of us came from, not necessarily [us directly from] Newgrange but the people before us.* And then I went around the country from there.

"A lot of mythological places, some bits of history and of course the fantastic scenery. But there was all this bits of information about every place we went. Not singing, interviews, filmed inside the sites. We went to Knowth, what went on there, what it was all about. And then I went from there."

"The first time I went into Newgrange, I had a hard time finding it, because there were no signs for it, no signs for Tara, anything. As I was walking up to the entrance to the mound, the hair started to rise on the back of my neck and I figured, 'I have been here before,' although I had never been there before. I went off, walked, and the hair kept up, standing on the back of my neck. I walked up into the passageway, up through the carved stone, dropping to the very center, and there was a young girl doing a lecture on the carved stones and the different carvings on the lozenges and talking about the corbel group** and the spirals that were carved and the big stone basins that were there and why they were there." The triple spiral decoration has now become the symbol of Newgrange.

"When she finished her lecture, she says 'Anybody have any questions?'

---

* Newgrange has been open to the public since 1699, when a farmer accidentally discovered it when he fell into an open hole in the structure while gathering material for constructing a road. It was officially excavated from 1962 until 1975 by University College, Cork (now the National University of Ireland, Cork) Professor Michael J. O'Kelly and his wife Claire, both archeologists.

** Layered rock ceiling, which allowed the water to drain off, leaving the interior of the chamber dry.

"I said, 'Yeah, is there a feather here somewhere?'

And she said, 'Oh no, I nearly forgot, and she stepped away from in front where she had been standing. 'It's not a feather, it's a fern.'

"And there was a fern carved on it. Now, I had never seen it, never been in there, but I knew it was there."

"Mary arranged to get me into Newgrange for the winter solstice (shortest day of the year, December 21ˢᵗ), on the morning of the winter solstice in 1994. It was the most phenomenal feeling and something to witness that I ever had in my life. The sun obliged us that morning and it was very bright when we came in. I saw it straining up the passage and illuminating the whole back wall [on this day, the sun through the passage illuminates the chamber for nineteen minutes].

So I was one of the lucky ones. It is very difficult to get in. Those people, five thousand years ago, knew where the sun was, they had lined up the entrance to the sun arriving on the horizon on the 21ˢᵗ of December!

"There are two other mounds in the Newgrange Complex. One is called Knowth, which has been excavated [Knowth dates back 3000 to 2500 B.C.]. The other is called Dowth, which has not. Each of them are about a mile and a half on either side of Newgrange. Knowth has two passageways that are tuned to the vernal, the spring equinox. Dowth has an opening that is exposed to the setting sun on December 21ˢᵗ. Can you imagine what these people knew that we don't know? They knew where all the planets were and how they operated. Newgrange spoke to me and I knew I had been there before.

"We also went to Grianan off Aileach (pron. *gree ahn an* off *Il e yack*) on the Innishone Peninsula in Donegal, a big circular building, like the coliseum in Rome. It was built 1700 B.C., with walls fifteen and sixteen feet thick. It is a temple. Later on in history, the great O'Neills, who are descendants of Niall of the Nine Hostages, they used Grianan off Aileach as their center, where their kings ruled. The view is sensational. It is on an eight hundred foot hill and on your right, the city of Derry is only ten miles away. Also on your right Loch Foyle and the River Foyle both run into Loch Foyle in Derry. On your left, is Loch Swilley, where the *Flight of the Earls* took place, where the O'Neills and the O'Donnells left when they were leaving Ireland, going to Europe.

38

"We also went to Galway, to Yeats grave at Coole, near Gorte, where Lady Gregory lived (of Yeats poem, *White Swans at Coole*). We saw her estate and the big tree there where all the people came and carved their initials on this huge Copper Beech tree, like George Bernard Shaw and Yeats and such."

"I took all those notes that I had, and I put them into a book and St. Martin's Press published the book. It was called *Tommy Makem's Secret Ireland*. [No longer available]. And then I did the second television thing, another two hour job, (as mentioned above) *The Road Taken* and I went to different places. The Road Taken was just shown, for the fourth or fifth time in March there, PBS took it and they updated it for digital. So it went out over the network and any station that wanted it could pick it up, digitally improved and apparently it was spectacular. I saw a little bit of it, I was up in Albany, I was connecting in New York, doing a pitch for *Tommy Makem's Ireland*.

"It was just to be... the pictures in it were absolutely sensational. Those are available on DVD at Makem.com."

Tommy has worked with WMHT to produce seven other one hour musical specials, in which Ireland's well known and hidden treasures are explored during a video tour, including song, music and poetry.

"If your bones they are weary and your mind is uneasy, the troubles of life, they are taking their toll, come with me to a green land of laughter and legend, there's rest for the body and peace for the soul." - Tommy Makem, "In That Land"

In September of 1999, Tommy fulfilled another lifelong dream, combining it with his love of Irish mythology: "Something I wanted to do all my life, to put together a one-man show on Irish mythology, and I did that. I performed it in New York City at the Irish Repertory Theatre, for three weeks. We had sold out for all three weeks. It was called *Irish Invasions & Legacies* and it was based on the five prehistoric invasions of the Irish. That was the Invasions part and then the Legacies, the second half of the show, I came out and did some songs, bits of poetry and 'this is why we have these songs and this is why I'm singing them this way and this poetry that exists is because of what went on in those invasions.' [The people who invaded], they all left something of themselves in the soil."

Tommy's love for Irish mythology was born of the deep and rich history that thrived around his own hometown, where he could, and did, visit and see for himself the ancient sites and place the ancient stories. "I prefer Irish mythology but have read others, Greek and such. I read *The Odyssey*. The Irish stuff had a much more immediacy for me because I could go to these places. I found out where they were and went to them. I started going to Newgrange … I didn't know about it when I was growing up. I didn't even know about Emhain Macha, [*Owen Maher*] which is in [County] Armagh, which is one of the most important archeological sights in Western Europe.

"Known as the *Navan Fort* in Armagh, Emhain Macha was the sight of the Kings of Ulster for about a thousand years and it is also where King Conor McNeff and the Red Branch Knights and Cuchulain [*Coo hullin*] roamed. South east of Keady, between Keady and Newtownhamilton, there is a gateway to the Ring of Gullion and also to the Mourne Mountains. It is called Carrick-Atuck [*Carrick a tooke*]. In mythology it was called Sliebh Fuadh [*Sleeve Foo idd*]. Slieve means mountain. It is one of the most important sights in Irish mythology. Reputedly that is where King Lir's [from the story of the *Children of Lir*], palace was, on top of Slieve Fuahd.

"Also, Conor McNeff, who was the King of Ulster, throughout The Great Ulster Cycle of Tales, which is Ireland's greatest contribution to Medieval Literature, lived there.

"These are all the things that I was pushing when I started the song festival.* And especially for South Armagh, which has been battered and hammered for the last thirty-five years, so you'd think there was nothing there and only people killing each other, and rottenness and badness. [The presence of the British, their forts and constant helicopters overhead is a daily part of life. But people haven't gone into their shell there].

---

* The first *Tommy Makem International Festival of Song* was held in South Armagh in June, 2000. Because of Tommy's busy touring schedule, it is now carried on by his nephew, Peter Makem.

"One area in Ireland has a continuous line going back to ancient Ireland. Sliebh Gullion and South Armagh has a continual line of people having lived there for over six thousand years. South Armagh, along with Barcelona and Rome, were the three cultural centers of the world in medieval times. And no one knew this and I thought it should really be brought out. It is really a cultural gem, all of South Armagh."

Two great stories somehow stand out from all the other amazing tales shown and presented in *Tommy Makem's Ireland*. Tommy is called the *modern Bard of Armagh*. In the video, Tommy tells the story of the original Bard of Armagh, Archbishop Donnelly, who was one of the parish priests there. During Penal Times, priests were forbidden to say mass. Often they were killed or tortured if caught, whether saying mass or not. So the way Archbishop Donnelly gathered the congregation was by going around disguised as a bard, with a harp on his shoulder, playing music and singing. When enough of a crowd of people gathered around him, he would then say mass. Naturally, the town of Armagh is deeply involved in the Bard of Armagh, because he was a priest there. A song written about him, called the *Bard of Armagh*, influenced one of the great American folk songs, a cowboy song called *The Streets of Laredo*. It was originally the tune called *The Bard of Armagh*, according to Tommy.

The second story Tommy tells deals with Blarney Castle and the tradition of kissing the Blarney Stone. The word Blarney to describe someone not always telling the truth stems from this area. Blarney, or the gift of gab, originated in the 17th century. One Cormac McCarthy, the Lord of Muskerry, who lived in Blarney Castle, used his great eloquence to avoid accepting the authority of Queen Elizabeth I of England. The queen became angry at his evasiveness and declared in exasperation that everything the Lord of Muskerry said was blarney, what he said he never meant. And so the term, *Blarney*, came into the popular lexicon.

Tommy's singing has led to extensive television work, where he has become a prolific contributor of over seventy educational and entertaining programs. These include a number of series for the BBC, Ulster and Scottish TV and a 1992 ninety minute special, called *Tommy*

Makem and Friends, for a New York TV station. A network series for CBC, Canada, out of Vancouver, that was a summer replacement show, is also on Tommy's television resume.

In addition, Tommy was asked to do a special song for Channel 2 in Boston, WGDH Public TV, for a St. Patrick's Day Special. The station provided Tommy with a list of famous Irish names and asked him to include as many as he could in a song. The result, *No Irish Need Apply,* about Irish success in America, has been recorded and sung throughout the world.

No Irish Need Apply

by Tommy Makem

Just think of all the presidents who came from Irish folk
There was Wilson and Buchanan, there was Jackson, Grant and Polk
There was Cleveland and McKinley and the brave Jack Kennedy
And many more whose names have joined that goodly company

Chorus:
And they told us no Irish need apply!
Yes, they told us no Irish need apply!

You've heard about James Curley, that man of great renown
And Honey Fitz, who proved his worth as Mayor of Boston town
And Rose and Ted and Bob and Jack and all the Kennedy clan
And the noble John McCormack, who is honored through the land

Chorus

Did you know John Hancock's family came from the County Down?
And composer Victor Herbert, he was born in Dublin town
And the blood in Davy Crockett's veins
was Irish through and through
And Connie Mack, the baseball great, well he was Irish too

Chorus

The father of the navy, John Barry was his name
He was a gallant Irishman, from Wexford town he came
To the many Irish giants in the literary field
You can add F. Scott Fitzgerald and the great Eugene O'Neill

Chorus

Whenever people talk about great service to mankind
No doubt, the name of Boston's Cardinal Cushing comes to mind
And Doctor Thomas Dooley should be leader of the van
His entire life was spent in helping out his fellow man

Chorus

In the noble art of self-defense, as you'll already know
We had men like John L. Sullivan, who never feared a foe
And gentleman Jim Corbett was among the very best
Likewise the bold Gene Tunney and Jack Dempsey and the rest

Chorus

We're the men who built the railroads,
we're the men who fought the wars
We're the men who manned the police force,
we're the men who drove street cars
We're the men who formed your unions,
we're the men who sang your songs
We're the men who filled your history and
tried to right your wrongs

Chorus

Asked if he had any plans to retire, Tommy replied "Yes, of course, I retire every night and in the morning when I awake I realize just how lucky and privileged I am to be able to continue doing the things I love to do."[4]

For fifty-five years, Tommy has shared himself and the music and culture of his home country with the world. We are privileged to know him. It's nice to be able to give *The Godfather* a little thanks, as Milwaukee Irish Fest did, with the help of Founder and President of the Board of Milwaukee Irish Fest, Ed Ward:

"The best memories of Tommy would be of course the shows he and Liam did together. Anyone who never saw Liam and Tommy as a duo can't even imagine what they missed. However, a few years ago, when Tommy was celebrating his 50th anniversary in the music business, we booked Tommy, and Rory came with him. Unbeknownst to Tommy, we decided to fly Conor, Shane, Tommy's daughter Katie, and his granddaughter Molly in, as well as agent Kevin O'Shea, to make a surprise appearance with cake and candles and all, at his Saturday night show.

"Shane, Conor and Kevin had to stay holed up in a hotel all day Saturday because we aware afraid someone would recognize them and mention it to Tommy. They didn't leave their hotel until Tommy's show had already started. It couldn't have gone any better. About 3/4 of the way thru the show, Rory has Eugene Byrne come out on stage. Eugene has great flair and he builds up the surprise and has Kevin come out, then Shane and Conor, and then - to Tommy's amazement - Katie and Molly. It was an unbelievable moment in Irish Fest history and no one who witnessed it will ever forget it."

After looking at the past, Tommy set his eyes on the future; of the song tradition, Irish music, and the saving of the culture that is so glorious and so precious to him: "The Song Tradition, well, I've been pushing very hard, and it's a struggle, I can tell ya. Certainly, the young people in Ireland are being deprived of it. On *Radio Eireann*, you won't hear any Irish music at all. You'll hear a lot of Rock-n-Roll, and you'll hear a lot of fairly bad punchy music.

"Sure, it never ceases to amaze me that our Irish music left Ireland, crossed the Atlantic, and it came over here [to the U.S.] and became very much a part of American bluegrass music and then country music. So, it was a watered down version of Irish music. Then it went back across the Atlantic and then some people in Ireland very foolishly started to do a watered down version of a watered down version of their own music. I could never understand why. Couldn't understand it. Still can't understand it. How they can't see the power and the beauty of their own culture?

"[The creative edge or the drive was lost], it must have been.

"But it is ironic, also, that most of the old music that has survived, both instrumental and songs, was saved by a bunch of Presbyterian businessmen in Belfast, in 1792. The Harp Festival in Belfast, these businessmen, thought that the culture was in danger of being lost, so they came up with the money and they hired all of the remaining itinerant harpers and brought them into Belfast for July 12th and 13th, 1792. They hired a man called Edward Bunting, from Armagh, to write down all of the tunes that these people played.

"These were itinerant harpers, who roved around the country. That is where most of O'Carolan's music was saved, because Bunting wrote it all down. And it was paid for by these businessmen, who figured out that the culture was in danger and something would have to be done to save it. Wasn't that wonderful?

"So with all their divisions and trying to blame it on religion, the whole situation in the North of Ireland, they got it all wrong. It was those men did their phenomenal jobs. [People can work together, regardless of religion].

Those who financed and developed the Harp Festival were businessmen, patriots, arts enthusiasts, in short, Irishmen, no matter their religion. "One was a man called Henry Joy, and the Joy family were big business people, in Belfast. And Henry Joy would have had a nephew, called Henry Joy McCracken, who was one of the leaders of the United Irishmen in 1798, there is a couple of good songs about it [him, Tommy recorded one himself, simply called *Henry Joy*, on *The Archives* CD].

"And Dr. MacDonnell was another. He also had a sister, MaryAnn McCracken, who was one of the most remarkable women I have ever read anything about, remarkable woman. She was a great patriot woman and on about women's rights, which at that time that was never heard of. And she was in love with Thomas Russell. There is a great poem written about *The Man From God Knows Where*. I used to do it on stage and I have recorded it on Ancient Pulsing. Thomas Russell was the man [about which] God Knows Where was written. He was involved in the 1798 Rebellion with the United Irishmen and he later was involved in Robert Emmet's Rebellion in 1803. He was caught and hanged in Downpatrick Gaol.

"So because of these businessmen, our culture was saved then, and I wish there was a few of them around today. Because it really, badly needs saving again. Seamus Ennis did a tremendous amount; wonderful collections (Seamus Ennis, the piper) and he knew all the songs, of course. He did tremendous work for the Irish Folklore Commission, as did a number of other people as well. They have a sort of a library, in Dublin, a library of wonderful music and song and dance there, preserved and readily available.

"Most of it has been collected [but not made readily available to the average young person growing up outside of Dublin]. I think we're losing a lot of it. Radio and television have a lot to answer for as well. Through it being suppressed, the young people have nothing to base it on, because you can turn on Radio Eireann and not hear any Irish music at all, mostly Rock-n-roll and sometimes country music. Where are they going to hear this music if it is not being performed and you can't get people who are performing it because they can't get any work singing or playing?

"There was a competition for bands from all over [the world] competing, and *Danu* was the only band from Ireland to win any prize. They won the best traditional band, and when they got back to Ireland, they wouldn't have them on the *Late Late Show* [Irish TV] because they played Irish music.

"What I have been on about the music and the song and the poetry, it's just criminal, and the people who made the money in the Celtic Tiger, they're not interested in saving the culture. There needs to be a national program.

"Irish America has done a phenomenal job in saving our culture. There is more Irish music in Cleveland or Milwaukee or Dublin [Ohio], than you would find in Ireland, all over the country. And the people there [in Ireland] are crying out for it [the music], but they cannot get it.

"I did a tour in Ireland last October. They were jam packed, every one of them, People asking why can't we have more of this? When I had the Pavilion [Tommy Makem's Irish Pavilion] in New York, people would come in from Ireland and ask the same question. Why can't we have this kind of entertainment in Ireland?"

Can there be recognition of the problem before there is no problem left to recognize?

"Long ago," says Makem, "some wise but forgotten man wrote that 'history is the propaganda of the victors.' But it is in folk song that you'll find the real history. In folk song, the truth will out."[5]

"I hope to leave an awareness of the songs of Ireland. I had it handed down to me from my mother and she had them handed down to her from her mother, her father, her uncles. So she passed it on to me. I've tried to pass it on to my family - and anyone who will have it."

Tommy has had many hit songs, most sung all over the world. But *Four Green Fields* is recognized as Tommy's signature song. He wrote it, and no one sings it so passionately, so perfectly. The inspiration for the song came on an ordinary day, as Tommy was driving down the road to Newry, in the County Down.

"I was traveling along the road from Dundalk, in County Louth, in the Republic of Ireland, to Newry, in the North of Ireland. I had already passed through the Irish Customs hut on the Dundalk side and about a half mile or mile further along the road was the British Customs hut. There was a woman driving cattle out of a field, in between the two huts. I was well aware of the old adage in Ireland that in bad times, Ireland was always referred to as an old woman, and in good times, of course, she was referred to as the beautiful young queen. I had been thinking about that prior to this, but it came to my mind again.

"I saw the woman driving cattle out of a field, sort of in No-Man's Land, in between the two customs huts, and it struck me. I saw hard times coming. This was in 1967. I had sort of, it struck me, watching this woman driving the cattle out onto the road. There she was in No-Man's Land and she just wanted to be left alone, to the care of her land, her cattle. Then I got the idea that this is what Ireland is all about. The Four Provinces, and one of them was - all four were threatened, but we had settled three of them. The fourth was in danger. I saw very dark times coming.

"So I started to think about the song and I got a part of it, maybe the first verse, before I got to Newry. I did whatever business I was doing in Newry. Then, on the way back, I got more of it and that night, or maybe the next day, I finished."

And Four Green Fields, the anthem of the Irish Diaspora, was created, finally offering an outlet for expression of the hurt and hope of generations of Irish emigrants.

"By the way, Michael Flatley is using the song in his new show, *Celtic Tiger*. I saw it in Madison Square Garden," said Tommy. "I enjoyed it thoroughly. He didn't hold back, he put all his cards on the table and he gave the history of Ireland, he didn't pull any punches with it. He wasn't afraid to stand up, he had something to say and he said it. It was really great."

Rory Makem, Tommy's youngest son, also shares a thought on *Four Green Fields*, "The imagery, lyricism, and simplicity of the melody remind me of another of my favorite songs by another of my favorite writers; *This Land is Your Land* by Woody Guthrie. Both writers had intimate knowledge of their subject and put their thoughts into words that are so disarmingly and deceptively simple. And though I feel Guthrie's should be sung to the rafters by anyone and everyone, I feel Four Green Fields is best sung by only one man... Tommy Makem. This song isn't just sung. It isn't just performed. It comes from the core of his being. It is who he is."

The Makem family legacy continues on as The Makem & Spain Brothers are performing with great success across the U.S. and Ireland. "I'm hoping they will be able to go on and certainly survive [make a living] singing," Tommy explains. "I'm hoping enough people will wake up and realize that these young men are preserving our culture, or doing their damnest to do it, and doing it very well I would think.

"I have a notion that, they have been at it a little while now, but it is very difficult to bring them to a bigger audience. Once they get there and perform, that's great, they'll do well. But it'll be a tough row to hoe. But, sure I had a tough row to hoe myself and I think they're well fit for it."

Tommy has blazed a path for the boys and they are carrying on the hard work, and brilliant legacy, of their father. They are shining in their own right.

Liam Clancy is quoted several times in this window into Tommy Makem, mostly from Liam's own biography. I asked Tommy if he would ever write a biography himself as there is great interest in him and his story.

"When I was a kid, I wanted to be a newspaper man. Maybe I would take to writing or something [if I wasn't a performer], but no, I wouldn't write a biography.

It would take a lot of … I could fill twenty books with stories. I have never thought about it. You never know if it would work [if it could come alive in print compared to on stage or verbally recounted]. He mentioned all the great storytellers who were no where near as funny when they tried to write it all down.

"Writers I am very fond of – Flann O'Brien, I think is a genius. I like Paddy Kavanagh, I like Yeats. I like Seamus Heaney, the poets. There's a man called Joseph Campbell, the poet from Ireland [not the philosopher]. I think he is an astounding poet. He's written songs that a lot of people think are traditional songs. Songs like *My Lagan Love* and the *Gartan Mother's Lullaby*. He's written a lot of wonderful stuff. People like that I admire. Short story writers, I love Ben (Benedict) Kiely."

Tommy answers the question of his own legacy as "The Godfather of Irish Music" in his usual way, humor first, then eloquent answer, explaining and teaching in the same response: "As long as they don't call me a thief or a lazy bugger or anything like that. I don't know whether it is good bad or indifferent. I suppose it is not going to hurt.

[You must realize that you had a huge impact on Irish music and on people]: "I would like to think that I had, at this point in the game, that I had some thing, some sort of an impact and that I was still doing it and helping young people to get a grip on their own culture. It has been a terrible struggle, because all the forces are against you, being able to do anything [TVs and computers and video games and other less than mind stimulating distractions]. But I feel like those businessmen out in 1792, that the culture is in peril and something needs to be done to save it.

"It is never going to die because it is too powerful. It is too powerful. Like Shakespeare's plays, they can battle them and thump them and raise them up and down and go to town on them but they cannot destroy them no matter how hard they try.

"I feel the same way. The culture really has been really battered and pounded for the last twenty to twenty-five years and it's taken a terrible pounding. It is all part of the dumbing down of society that people are losing whatever bit of taste they had and sense of propriety and not realizing what the phenomenal legacy that has been left to all of us, culturally. It is not taught in the schools and this may be a persecution complex but I think that there was set out [a philosophy of], let's pound this into the ground, we don't want any of that. We're too modern a country.

"This is the whole thing in Ireland, Modern! And I'm not that sure that modern is a very good thing. In certain instances, it certainly is, I like the progress that has been made, for instance in health, in medicine, and so forth and what you can do for your health, this past fifty years. I am all for that kind of progression.

"But in other areas, the cultural areas, what they would be calling progression, I would have very grave doubts that it is progression. It is not going to kill our culture but it is doing damage to it.

"America has done themselves very proud in the Irish music tradition. They have preserved it much better than it has been preserved in Ireland. I [cite] the example of the Irish music coming across the Atlantic and then being used in country music and bluegrass music and going back to Ireland and it's a watered down version of a watered down version of stuff that they could do much better if they'd do their own music. But that's been downsized and sneered at and pushed down. 'You're not modern, you have to have Rock-n-Roll to be modern.'

"And I don't know if any of them have ever stopped to listen to the majority of Rock-n-Roll. I think Rock-n-Roll, in its own circumstances, is great, but it's an American phenomenon, and as a matter of fact, the poor English, even worse than the Irish are about it, they think Rock-n-Roll is English. It has not at all to do with English culture, including the Beatles. The Beatles were doing something different. They were coming up with music of their own, which was not Rock-n-Roll. The Rolling Stones, they were doing Rock-n-Roll.

"And still, I'll take somebody like Bruce Springsteen; I listen to some of the songs that he has written, his hard Rock-n-Roll things. But I would regard a number of them as folk music. He's done an acoustic tour. I believe his *Tom Joad* record was just superb.

"I did a lecture one time, which I'm going to do at the school in Milwaukee again [at Milwaukee Irish Fest Summer School] this year. I call it *The Music Road* and it is showing how American music came to be, and to be what it is. It was the influence of the Celtic-Anglo music, plus the religious music of the pilgrims who came over, plus, the work songs and the music from the slaves who were brought in from West Africa and brought their culture with them.

"Some of them settled down around the sea coast, down south. And then there was the great influence of the Spanish and the French down around New Orleans. Well they had this all mixed up and they all borrowed from each other and you had, up in the north, the northern half of the United States, the great Celtic-Anglo influence and you had some other European things like German and even Israeli music, that kind of stuff. Down the southern half of the United States, you had the influence of the slaves, which was a completely different form altogether, the Celtic thing was all decorated notes, because they didn't have instruments, it was all, like *sean nós* singing, but the people from West Africa, they had a big booming voice and a very rhythmic chorus answering them.

"So you put that together with the Celtic thing and the religious music of the pilgrims who had brought it over and a bit of spice of the Spanish and the French around the Mississippi Delta, around New Orleans and this is where Rock music was born. And that is what Elvis Presley, for instance, grew up hearing, this great amalgamation. They all borrowed from each other.

"Lead Belly, the great singer and songwriter, he wrote wonderful songs. For instance, *Kisses Sweeter than Wine*. The other day, I heard somebody singing it at a party. So we keep borrowing from each other, that is the American process. But also, I think it is very sad that, in

Ireland, and in England, I must add, they have forgotten about their own culture and contributing to it instead of being imitators. They're not innovators anymore. They're imitators. And you have to innovate. I'm convinced if you're going to dilute the culture with what you are doing, don't do it. If you can add to it, that's great, without taking away the essence of the music and poetry itself. That's what I'm always harping about. You must not allow any dilution, or revision, of what your culture is."

To give an example how to improve, not dilute, the music and the culture, I asked Tommy who he admired: "I have a lot of CD's. A lot of them shouldn't have been made, including some of my own. That is a very difficult question for me. I am very impressed with Mícheál Ó Súileabháin, [pron. *Mee haul O'Sullowhine*, Director, Irish World Music Centre, University of Limerick]. He has done something that I thought was an impossible [task]. He has made a traditional instrument of the piano. Phenomenal stuff.

"He has a CD out that I think is one of the most brilliant things that I have ever heard. It is called *Dolphin's Way* and it is just piano and bodhran. He'll take Irish, a reel or jig or whatever, and he can play it, and then he changes the chord patterns on it and it becomes a very intricate, almost jazz, thing, but then he'll take it back into its original.

"So he does not lose the flavor of what the original was but he is showing you the potential of it. But he would be adding to it but still you have the basis that's still there. Oh, he's phenomenal, very impressive.

"You can take a degree in Irish music at the University of Limerick, and in performing, and there's a girl called Aine [*Ahn yah*], she's from around the Boston area, she plays the harp. And she went back last year and studied at the University of Limerick. I think she's got herself a Masters degree. And she's wonderful. She's two or four CD's out. She has this little voice but she knows her music, inside and out. Aine Minogue is her name.

"And then I like a girl group out of Galway, called *Dordan*. Mary Bergen plays the whistle in it [Mary Bergen is a world class whistle player who had tremendous impact on many whistle and flute players, including Cherish the Ladies', Joanie Madden]. Now Dordan, I think there are four of them in the group. They do a mixture of Irish and Baroque music. They both lend [musically, both styles lend] to each other, they're superb.

"[I enjoy] some of the newer trad groups, I'm very fond of Altan. She's [Mairead Ni Mhaonaigh] a great singer as well. Danu is a very good group. I think Solas is a very good group. They add to it but they don't lose the flavor of it."

Others that Tommy sites who have done much to preserve and improve the culture include: "The 1792 Harp Festival in Belfast saved our music, and then the renaissance in the early 1920's [of all the great poets; Yeats and Lady Gregory and John M. Synge, Behan, Joyce, Wilde, Kavanagh, Shaw, etc...] and people like that."

"[Although it is not Irish music] it is the culture. I think Sean O'Riada did a phenomenal job in the 1950's, early 60's [founder of Ceoltoiri Eireann, precursor to The Chieftains]. Those are the people that I like."

"I read. Mythology would be my big thing [outside of music]. Experiencing a lot of things is important to me. I found in Ireland, that it's a very spiritual country. I'm not talking about religion now. There's a whole spirituality in Ireland that is very, very shallow, under the surface, and you don't have to dig very deep to get it, you just have to have your heart open and your mind open and you'll gain phenomenal stuff.

"I was lucky enough to fall into this singing thing and it covers a multitude of sins. I get to perform and make a living doing something I really like to do. And I know I can do a good job of it. Putting a show together is not a matter of getting up and singing eight or ten songs. You have to watch what song is going to complement the one before it or the one coming after it. The song will have much more impact [if there is a story presented with it]. But it also takes care of the acting sort of thing. You're on stage and you're telling a story with your song. Every one would be a little vignette, every song."

Through at least today, Tommy's fifty-five plus years as a performer, an ambassador, and a shining beacon of all that the Irish culture has to offer, is leaving a lasting legacy, one that is unparalleled, unquantifiable and international in its scope. His influence and impact are certainly immeasurable, but the stories are heard in every corner and field, of those affected by him, his contributions, and his efforts. Tommy is truly a gift that keeps on giving, and will continue to do so, generations from now. The seeds have been planted and, year after year, keep bearing new fruit, new branches and spread wider and deeper with each new season. As Stephen Pedersen of the Halifax Herald says,

> "If there are Old Masters in the world of Irish Folk Music,
> Tommy Makem is Rembrandt."

We will continue to learn from him, be inspired by him, and treasure our Rembrandt.

Tommy

by John O'Brien, Jr.

The baritone guidance among the whispers of creativity
History walks, hammering with pillows,
with verse and song - and laughter.
Bubbling forth in a man, a bard, The Godfather.
In passionate action is a legacy delivered to a new generation,
An heirloom, made more precious, more prolific, with each passing day,
With each new inspired poet, songwriter, singer and musician.
This is Tommy Makem, This is Ireland.

"I was born in Keady, the Hub of the Universe."

No, Tommy, you were born in the soul of Ireland itself.
A giving tree of immortal life; to tradition, to the rich heritage
and the powerful ballads that will never die.
You altered history, instilled a pride, planted the seeds.
The Giving Tree Makem has spread its roots.
And flourishes, in the songs and stories of The Bard

Just a few of the multitude of Highlights and Awards that Tommy has earned:

Gold Medal - awarded April, 1957 by the Eire Society of Boston for his contributions to Irish culture.

Obie Award (Village Voice Award) - to Tommy Makem and The Clancy Brothers for Off-Broadway Theatre work.

Performed at the White House - with The Clancy Brothers for John F. Kennedy in 1963.

Genesis Award - awarded to Tommy and Liam Clancy by Stonehill College in Massachusetts at their last dual appearance in 1988, for their promotion of Irish culture.

Doctor of Humane Letters - awarded to Tommy by The University of New Hampshire in May of 1998.

Placed in the Congressional Record - On August 4th 1998, the Honorable Nancy L. Johnson of Connecticut placed Tommy officially in the Congressional Record with her wonderful remarks and words of praise for him.

Lifetime Achievement Award - presented by The World Folk Music Association in 1999.

Awarded - one of "The Greatest Irish Americans of the Century," Irish America Magazine. Others awarded that night included; Maureen O'Hara, Gregory Peck and former Senator and Northern Ireland Peace Process Negotiator George Mitchell.

Awarded - the first ever Aer Lingus/Irish America Lifetime Achievement Award.

Awarded - Honorary Doctorate of Letters from the University of Limerick in December 2001, for his role in representing his country, its people, culture and traditions.

Awarded - Honorary degree from The University of New Hampshire.

Presented - Honorary Decree from Milwaukee Irish Fest on the occasion of his 50th year in Irish music and his contributions to preserving and promoting the Irish culture.

Presented - Honorary Decree from Cleveland's Irish Cultural Festival on the occasion of his 50th year in Irish music and his contributions to preserving and promoting the Irish culture.

A *few* of Tommy Makem's Signature Songs:
Four Green Fields

by Tommy Makem

"What did I have?" said the fine old woman
"What did I have?" this proud old woman did say
"I had four green fields, each one was a jewel
But strangers came and tried to take them from me
I had fine strong sons, they fought to save my jewels
They fought and died, and that was my grief," said she

"Long time ago" said the fine old woman
"Long time ago" this proud old woman did say
"There was war and death, plundering and pillage
My children starved by mountain valley and sea
And their wailing cries, they shook the very heavens
My four green fields ran red with their blood" said she

"What have I now?" said the fine old woman
"What have I now?" this proud old woman did say
"I have four green fields, one of them's in bondage
In stranger's hands, that tried to take it from me
But my sons have sons, as brave as were their fathers
My fourth green field will bloom once again," said she

Gentle Annie

by Tommy Makem

"I wrote this song for my wife, whose name is Mary, but I had written
so many songs that included the name Mary that I thought I needed
a different name. She understands."
- Tommy Makem

Fair and lovely Annie, your gentle ways have won me.
You bring peace and joy and laughter ev'rywhere.
Where you go the sunshine follows, you're a breath of spring in winter
And my heart and soul are always in your care.
Chorus: Gentle Annie, Gentle Annie,
And my heart and soul are always in your care.

When you touch me with your fingers, my cares and worries vanish
Like the morning dew before the rising sun,
When your eyes tell me you love me, then my soul is filled with wonder
And my love for you will live when life is done.

Chorus: Gentle Annie, Gentle Annie,
And my love for you will live when life is done.

You're the flower among the flowers, you're the birdsong in the morning,
You're the laughter of the children at their play.
You're my hope and joy and wisdom, you're my reason just for living,
You're my treasure, you're my very night and day.

Chorus: Gentle Annie, Gentle Annie,
You're my treasure, you're my very night and day.

When the mountains all come tumbling
and the earth has stopped its turning,
When the winds don't blow and stars refuse to shine,
When the moon has left the heavens, and the seven seas are empty,
I will still have Gentle Annie on my mind.

Chorus: Gentle Annie, Gentle Annie,
I will still have Gentle Annie on my mind.

Winds of Morning

by Tommy Makem. (air: Dumbarton's drums)

I've walked the hills when rain was falling
Rested by a wide oak tree
Heard a lark sing high at evening
Caught a moonbeam on the sea

Chorus:
Softly blow ye winds of morning
Sing ye winds your mournful sound
Blow ye from the earth's four corners
Guide this traveler where he's bound

Chorus

I've helped a ploughman tend his horses
Heard a rippling river sing
Talked to stars when night was falling
Seen a primrose welcome spring

Chorus

By foreign shores, my feet have wandered
Heard a stranger call me friend
Every time my mind was troubled
Found a smile around the bend

Chorus

There's a ship stands in the harbour
All prepared to cross the foam
Far off hills were fair and friendly
Still there's fairer hills at home

Chorus

Farewell to Carlingford

by Tommy Makem

When I was young and in my prime
And could wander wild and free
There was always a longing in my mind
To follow the call of the sea

Chorus:
So, I'll sing farewell to Carlingford
And farewell to Greenore
And I'll think of you both day and night
Until I return once more
Until I return once more

On all of the stormy seven seas
I have sailed before the mast
And on every voyage I ever made
I swore it would be my last

Chorus

Now, I had a girl called Mary Doyle
And she lived in Greenore
And the foremost thought was in her mind
Was to keep me safe on shore

Chorus

Now, the landsman's life is all his own
He can go or he can stay
But when the sea gets in your blood
When she calls, you must obey

Chorus

The Winds Are Singing Freedom

by Tommy Makem

In the battered streets of Belfast
Can't you hear the people cry?
For justice long denied them
And their crying fills the sky
But the winds of change are singing
Bringing hope from dark despair
There's a day of justice coming
You can feel it in the air

Chorus:
And the winds are singing freedom
They sing it everywhere
They sing it on the mountainside
And in the city square
They sing of a new day dawning
When our people will be free
Come and join their song of freedom
Let it ring from sea to sea

Too long our people suffered
In their misery and their tears
And foreign rulers used our land
For about eight hundred years
It's a long road has no turning
And I know that soon we'll see
That day of justice dawning
When our people will be free

Chorus

There's a time laid out for laughing
There's a time laid out to weep
There's a time laid out for sowing

And a time laid out to reap
There's a time to love your brother
There's a time for hate to cease
You must sow the seeds of justice
To reap the fruits of peace

Chorus

Just a few of: The Original Songs by Tommy Makem:

(He has written more than 400)
"If you know the names of all the tunes,
you don't know enough tunes." - Anon.

Awaken MaryAnn
Better Times
Boys of Killybegs
Brendan
Bright Eyed Girl From Keady
Canada My Own Land
Cape Breton of the Welcomes
Clean Air Clean Water
Clear Blue Hills
Darkley Weaver (The)
Don't Go Down to the Big Green Sea
Enniskillen Dragoons (The)
Farewell My Friends
Farewell to Carlingford
Fare Thee Well Enniskillen
Four Green Fields
Freedoms Sons
Gentle Annie
Give the Woman in the Bed More Porter
Goin' Home to Mary
Grey October Clouds
I Wish I Was a Big Red Apple
I Wish I Was Hunting
If You Should Ask Me
In Newry Town
In the Dark Green Woods
In the Time of Scented Roses
Johnny is a Rovin Blade
Jolly Roving Swag Man (The)

Keady is a Sporting Place
Kinsale
Listowel Blackbird
Liar (The)
Long Winter Nights
Long Woman's Grave (The)
Lord Nelson
Marvelous Peak (The) (rewritten song)
Men of No Conscience
Morning After Blues (The)
Music in the Twilight (The)
No Irish Need Apply
Old Heel Ball
Paddy Kelly's Brew
Peace and Justice
Pretty Maggie O'
Pretty Saro (1967)
Rambles of Spring (The)
Rambling River
Rape of the Gael (The)
Redmond O'Hanlon
Rolling Home
Rosie
Sally O'
Sargony
Seven Shades of Sunday
Ships of War
Sing Me the Old Songs
Smiling Mary
Song For the Children (not the same as Tom Sweeney's)
Ever The Winds
Sweet Dromintee
That Land I Love So Well
There Was an Old Woman
This Dusty Road
Town of Ballybay (The)

Town of Rostrevor
True Love and Time
Vancouver
Water Sings (The)
Winds Are Singing Freedom (The)
Winds of Morning
Wonderful Ram (The)
Hunting the Wren   (rewrote – not the one recorded with the Clancys. Wrote the words and a different tune to it).

Others:

The Ballad of Lady Jane   (music, written by JB Goodenough)
Battle of Benburb   (music, words written by Robert Dwyer Joyce)
Apples in the Basket   (put tune to it, words written by JB Goodenough)
Bonny Bladdy   (resurrected song)
Shores of Botany   (brought from Australia)

Added to:

I'll Tell Me Ma   (written by Dave Hammond – "Davie only had 2 verses and we were going to record it and we all decided it needs a little bit more. So I wrote the last verse but no one knows about that: *(Let the wind and the rain and the hail low high and the snow come traveling from the sky. She's as nice as apple pie and she'll get her own lad by and by).*

"People say, ahh no, no, I didn't learn that from you, … my grandfather used to sing that song (but they're singing my verse). So that's not a well known thing."

Leaving of Liverpool   Tommy added the final verse to this song, now accepted the world over as part of the original.
> Oh, the fog is on the harbour love
> And I wish I could remain
> But I know it will be some long time
> Before I see you again

Tommy's Song

by John O'Brien, Jr.

Awaken Mary Ann, for
The Liar,
The Man of No Conscience, cries,
That No Irish Need Apply
Peace and Justice disappear
in *the Rape of the Gael*
In *That Land I Loved So Well,*
True Love and Time.
have stopped.

There Was An Old Woman.
among the *Four Green Fields,*
She entreated me,
Brendan, The Darkley Weaver,
Don't Go Down To The Big Green Sea.
Contrast,
from *Clean Air, Clean Water,*
to the *Ships of War* ready,
even *The Water Sings* out -
to the march of
The Enniskillen Dragoons
Where Ever The Winds?
The Winds of Morning?

The Winds Are Singing Freedom!
And call for *Better Times.*
I went anyway.
And so,
Farewell My Friends.
Farewell to Carlingford,
Fare Thee Well Enniskillen
Let there be none
of *The Morning After Blues.*
Fear, but hope again to walk

This Dusty Road.
when next again, in victory
we are *Rolling Home.*

But now, as we enjoin
The Boys of Killybegs
Toasting farewells,
sipping *Paddy Kelly's Brew.*
Freedom's Sons are singing;
singing sad songs,
to their love, songs.
Pretty Maggie O', Sally O',
Pretty Saro and *Rosie.*
for some,
a *Song For The Children.*

In The Time Of Scented Roses,
let they be not black,
The Long Woman's Grave.
Rather *Sing Me The Old Songs;*
of *Rambling Rivers*
in *The Rambles of Spring,*
Clear Blue Hills
or *Grey October Clouds,*
among *Long Winter Nights.*

If I should return,
If You Should Ask Me,
I'm Going Home To Mary,
Smiling Mary
I can see her, as she holds
our *Gentle Annie* in her arms,
listening to
The Listowel Blackbird sing;
Music In The Twilight,
In Newry Town

I will return again.

Tommy Makem Discography:

(Memories and "approximate" dates, re-releases, often
under different names and/or covers, and lost information
– this list is as good as I could make it, despite the
unknown redundancies, compilations and re releases.)

CD's and LP's:
Tommy Makem:

- Newport Folk Festival   (1959)
- Newport Folk Festival   (1960)
- The Folk Music of the Newport Folk Festival
  1959-60 Vol. 1   (1960)
- Songs of Tommy Makem   (1961)
- Songs For a Better Tomorrow   (1963)
- Tommy Makem Sings Tommy Makem   (1968)
- In the Dark Green Woods   (1969)
- Bard of Armagh   (1970)
- Lord is Love of All   (1971)
- An Evening with Tommy Makem (Also called Listen
  For the Rafters Are Ringing, two different titles and
  jackets)   (1972)
- Tommy Makem Recorded Live, "A Room Full of Song"(1973)
- In the Dark Green Wood   (1974)
- 4 Green Fields   (1975)
- Ever the Winds   (1975)
- Four Green Fields   (1975)
- Lonesome Waters   (1985)
- An Evening with Tommy Makem   (1985)
- Song of The Working People   (1988)
- Rolling Home   (1989)
- Songbag   (1990)
- Irish Pipe and Tin Whistle Songs   (1992)
- Live at the Irish Pavilion   (CD & Cassette)   (1993)
- From the Archives   (CD & Cassette)   (1995)
- Christmas   (CD & Cassette)   (1995)

- Ancient Pulsing Poetry with Music   (CD Only)   (1996)
- The Song Tradition   (CD & Cassette)   (1998)

Other titles, year of release unknown:
- Songs for a Better Tomorrow with Tommy Makem (w/ The Tarriers)
- Tommy Makem and Friends In Concert
- Tommy Makem

𝕿𝖍𝖊 𝕮𝖑𝖆𝖓𝖈𝖞 𝕭𝖗𝖔𝖙𝖍𝖊𝖗𝖘 & 𝕿𝖔𝖒𝖒𝖞 𝕸𝖆𝖐𝖊𝖒:
𝕮𝕯'𝖘 𝖆𝖓𝖉 𝕷𝕻'𝖘:

- The Rising of the Moon (two different jackets, Also called *Irish Songs of Rebellion*)   (1956, 1998)
- Come Fill Your Glass with Us (Also called *Irish Drinking Songs* and *Irish Songs of Drinking and Blackguarding*)   (1959, 1998)
- The Clancy Brothers and Tommy Makem   (1961, 1996)
- Spontaneous Performance   (**Out Of P**rint)   (1961)
- Hearty & Hellish   (1962)
- The Boys Won't Leave the Girls Alone (OOP)   (1962)
- Super Hits (re released in 1963, '64, '66, '69, '97, 2000) (1962)
- In Person at Carnegie Hall   (1963, 1992, 1997)
- BBC Concert   (1964)
- The First Hurrah   (OOP)   (1964)
- Recorded Live in Ireland   (OOP)   (1965)
- Isn't it Grand Boys   (OOP)   (1966)
- The Irish Uprising/ 1916 - 1922   (OOP)   (2 different labels)   (1966)
- Songs of Ireland and Beyond   (1966, 1997)
- Freedom's Sons   (OOP)   (1967)
- In Concert   (1967, 1992, 1997)
- Home Boys Home   (OOP)   (1968)
- Sing of the Sea   (OOP)   (1969)
- The Bold Fenian Men   (OOP)   (1969)
- Irish Folk Airs; The Clancy Brothers & Tommy Makem and Their Families (also called The Clancy Brothers & Tommy

Makem With Their Families or Irish Folk Songs & Airs)   (2
different Jackets)   (1969, 1992)
- Flowers in the Valley   (OOP)   (1970)
- Green In the Green   (1971)
- I'm A Freeborn Man   (1972, 1989)
- Greatest Irish Hits   (1973)
- Seriously Speaking   (1975)
- Every Day   (1976)
- Reunion   (1984)
- Luck of The Irish   (1992)
- Irish Drinking Songs   (1993)
- The Best of The Clancy Brothers and Tommy
  Makem   (1994, 2002)
- Ain't It Grand Boys   (1995)
- Home to Ireland; 28 Irish Favorites   (1996)
- 28 Irish Pub Songs, The Clancy Brothers & Tommy
  Makem   (1996)
- Irish Revolutionary Songs   (1999)
- An Essential Collection   (circa 2000)

Other titles, year released unknown: May be compilations
- Welcome to Our House
- Show Me the Way
- Save the Land
- Live on St. Patrick's Day
- Clancy Brothers and Tommy Makem (4 Box LP Set)
- From Ireland with Love
- The Clancy Brothers and Tommy Makem
- The Best of the Clancy Brothers and Tommy Makem
- So Early in the Morning
- Presenting The Clancy Brothers and Tommy Makem
- Fine Boys You Are (two different titles and jackets)
- At Home with The Clancy Brothers and Tommy
  Makem & Their Families (also called At Home
  with The Clancy Brothers, Their Families &
  Tommy Makem, 2 different jackets)

- Celtic Classic Treasures: The Clancy Brothers and Tommy Makem and Friends
- The Clancy Brothers and Tommy Makem (3 different labels)
- Newport Folk Festival, Vol. I, 1959
- Newport Folk Festival, Vol. I 1960
- The Folk Music of the Newport Folk Festival, 1959-1960, Vol. I
- Boolavogue
- Wrap the Green Flag
- Tunes & Tales of Ireland
- In The Dark Green Wood (NOT the same as "In the Dark Green Woods")
- Farewell to Nova Scotia
- Shine on Brighter
- Collection
- Pete Seeger's Rainbow Quest; The Clancy Brothers and Tommy Makem w/ Tom Paxton and Mamou Cajun Band

EP's/45's:

- Songs From the Irish Uprising
- In Person
- The Clancy Brothers & Tommy Makem No. 1
- The Clancy Brothers and Tommy Makem No. 2
- The Moonshiner
- Irish Rover/Brennan on the Moor
- The Whistling Gypsy & The Moonshiner
- Tim Finnegan/Reilly's Daughter
- Wild Rover/Weela Wallia
- The Rising of the Moon/Young Cassidy
- Isn't It Grand Boys & Nancy Whiskey
- The Good Ship Calibar & The Lowlands Low
- Jennifer Gentle and Beer, Beer, Beer
- The Rising of the Moon/The Wild Rover
- The Rising of the Moon/Green In the Green
- O'Donnell Abu/Freedom's Sons

- Green in the Green/Isn't It Grand Boys
- You're Always Welcome to Our House/
  Time Gentleman, Time
- Streets of London/Dandelion Wine
- Finnegan's Wake/The Wild Colonial Boy
- Irish Rover/Courtin' in the Kitchen
- Jug of This/Johnny McEldoo
- Whiskey You're the Devil/Mountain Dew
- When I Was Single/God Bless England
- The Rising of the Moon/Mr. Moses Ri-Toora-I -Ay
- Bring Home the Oil
- The Band Played Waltzing Matilda/The Town of Rostrevor
- Four Green Fields/Mary Ellen Carter

Cassettes:

- Wrap the Green Flag
- Irish Drinking Songs
- Greatest Irish Hits
- Older But No Wiser
- It's About Time
- Isn't It Grand Boys
- Tunes and Tales of Ireland
- Songs of Ireland and Beyond
- Best of the Vanguard Years
- Tiananmen Square
- Four Green Fields/Come by the Hills
- Waltzing with Bears/Courtin' in the Kitchen
- Vancouver/Better Times
- In the Dark Green Woods/My Father
  Loves Nikita Khrushchev
- Irish Piping and Tin Whistle Songs
- The Song Tradition
- Shine on Brighter

Makem & Clancy:
CD's and LP's:

- Makem & Clancy   (1976)
- The Makem & Clancy Concert   (1977)
- Two For the Early Dew   (1978, 1992)
- The Makem and Clancy Collection   (1980, 1992)
- Live At the National Concert Hall   (1983, 1991)
- We've Come a Long Way   (1986)
- Tommy Makem & Liam Clancy   (1987)
- Makem & Clancy In Concert
- Tommy Makem & Liam Clancy
- In Person at Carnegie Hall
- Sing of the Sea

Singles:

- The Band Played Waltzing Matilda/Town Of Rostrevor & Maggie Pickens (1976)
- The Town Of Ballybay/Kitty From Baltimore   (1977)
- The Dutchman/The Lowland Sea   (1977)
- Red Is The Rose/Cruiscin Lan   (1979)
- Morning Glory/Bower Madden   (1979)
- The Garden Song/The Tombstone   (1980)
- A Place In The Choir/Sliabh Gheal Gua Na Feile   (1980)
- Waltzing Matilda/Red is the Rose   (1981)
- The Ballad Of St. Anne's Reel/Sliabh Galleon Braes (1981)
- Rainbow Race/Dear Dark Eyes   (1981)
- Dandelion Wine/We Are The Boat   (1985)
- The Tale Of Bridie Murphy And The Kamikaize Pilot/The Newry Highwayman   (1985)
- Four Green Fields/New Mary Ellen Carter

Other Makem Family Recordings:
Sarah Makem:

- Sarah Makem
- Ulster Ballad Singer by Mrs. Sarah Makem

74

- May Morning Dew by Mrs. Sarah Makem

Makem Brothers:

- Outstanding In A Field (w/ Brian Sullivan)   (1994)
- Outstanding In A Field (cassette)   (1994)
- On The Rocks   (1995)
- On The Rocks (cassette)   (1995)
- Who Fears To Speak   (Songs of the Rebellion of 1798)(1997)
- Stand Together (CD)   (2001)

Makem & Spain Brothers:

- Like Others Did Before Us   (2004)

Other Makem Family Recordings:

- At Home with The Makems by Jack Makem

Barley Bree (with Jimmy Sweeney, pre-Tom Sweeney)

- Ireland's International Folk Tom Sweeney (With Barley Bree):
- No Man's Land (re released in the States in 1986)   (1983)
- Castles in the Air
- Barley Bree Live, Here's to Song
- Speak Up For Old Ireland
- Anthem For the Children
- Best of Barley Bree   (compilation CD)
- Love is Teasing (self-released LP and cassette)   (1993)

Barley Bree Live Show:

- The Wind That Shakes The Barley, An Evocation of
  The Uprising of 1798 in Prose, Poetry and Song

Barley Bree Video:

- Let's Have an Irish Party (with Anna McGoldrick, Carmel
  Quinn and Paddy Noonan Band w/ Ritchie O'Shea)

Tom Sweeney Solo:

- The Bard of Ireland   (1990)
- Fair Hills of Ireland   (1992)
- Songs of Ireland   (1994)
- Live @ Fernagh Cottage   (1996)
- Little Isle of Green
- Daisy A Day   (1999)
- Favorite Irish Poems   (2001)

Tom Sweeney Videos:

- The Fair Hills of Ireland   (1995)

Tom Sweeney's Children's Albums:

- I'm In The Mood for Singing   (1997)
- Happy Songs For Children   (1999)
- Sleepytime   (2001)
- A Family Christmas   (2003)
- All Together Again

New Children's Series, with Book and accompanying CD, debuting 2005:

- Book 1: Nine Penny Fiddle; Irish Songs for Children (2005)
- Book 2: In The Mood For Singing
- Book 3: Happy Songs For Children
- Book 4: Sleepy Time
- Book 5: A Family Christmas
- Book 6: The Animal Fair
- Book 7: Nursery Rhymes
- Book 8: Songs For The Car
- Book 9: Songs Of The Season
- Book 10: Alphabet Soup

Videos:
The Clancy Brothers & Tommy Makem:

- The Story of The Clancy Brothers and Tommy Makem

- Reunion Concert
- Bob Dylan 30th Anniversary Concert
- Farewell to Ireland
- Seeger with The Clancy Brothers and Tommy Makem
- Rainbow Quest

𝕿𝖔𝖒𝖒𝖞 𝕸𝖆𝖐𝖊𝖒:

- A Christmas tradition with Tommy Makem
- Tommy Makem's Ireland Vol. 3 & 4, The Road Less Taken
- Tommy Makem & Friends In Concert
- Tommy Makem In Concert with Pete Seeger
- Tommy Makem In Concert with Odetta
- A Time To Remember (movie with Tommy Makem)
- The Mouse (movie with Tommy Makem)

𝕿𝖍𝖊 𝕸𝖆𝖐𝖊𝖒 𝕭𝖗𝖔𝖙𝖍𝖊𝖗𝖘:

- Slainte, The Makem Brothers and Brian Sullivan   (1994)
- Live in Concert (w/ Soibhan Egan)   (1997)

𝕭𝖔𝖔𝖐𝖘:
𝕿𝖍𝖊 𝕮𝖑𝖆𝖓𝖈𝖞 𝕭𝖗𝖔𝖙𝖍𝖊𝖗𝖘 𝖆𝖓𝖉 𝕿𝖔𝖒𝖒𝖞 𝕸𝖆𝖐𝖊𝖒:

- The Clancy Brothers and Tommy Makem Songbook

𝕿𝖔𝖒𝖒𝖞 𝕸𝖆𝖐𝖊𝖒:

- The Tommy Makem Songbook
- Tommy Makem's Secret Ireland

𝕾𝖕𝖊𝖈𝖎𝖆𝖑𝖘 𝕱𝖔𝖗 𝕿𝖁 & 𝕿𝖍𝖊𝖆𝖙𝖗𝖊:

- Tommy Makem & Friends (w/ Cherish the Ladies & BarleyBree)   (1992)
- Tommy Makem in Concert (w/ Pete Seeger and the Egan-Ivers Band)   (1994)
- Tommy Makem in Concert (w/ Odetta & the Barra McNeills)   (1994)
- Tommy Makem's Ireland   (1994)

- Invasions and Legacies (A one man show at the Irish
  Repertory Theatre)   (1999)
- The Road Taken (Parts III and IV)   (2001)
- Songs of The Sea (w/ Judy Collins, The Shaw
  Brothers, The Makem Brothers)
- The Tommy Makem Children's Show (w/ Tom Sweeney)
- A Christmas Tradition (w/ Schooner Fare and Cathie Ryan)
- Tommy Makem's Ancient Pulsing (w/ Seamus
  Connolly, Aine Minogue & Rory Makem

www.makem.com

II.

Danny Doyle

"After a while, people started drifting in and soon I was singing Irish
ballads for Ms. Sinatra, Robert Stack, Robert Mitchum, Henry Mancini,
James Coburn and God knows who else. They loved Finnegan's Wake,
and as I sat there teaching them the chorus, I suddenly thought, 'what
the hell am I doing here, I'm Danny Doyle, a coal-man's son from the
back lanes of Dublin.' All I could do was laugh." - Danny Doyle

One of the greatest Irish ballad singers to ever play an Irish festival, a
concert hall or a palace, Danny Doyle has captured audiences throughout
the world with his songs and stories, stories often told to him by his
mother and his great-grandmother, or learned in the back room of some
distant pub. His great-grandmother's bright memories of the strike and
lock-out in Dublin 1913, the violent drama of the 1916 Easter Rising
and the following War of Independence, 1918-1922, fascinated the
young Dublin man who soaked up the tales that now make up much
of his stage presentation.

Kathleen Fitzgerald Doyle and Frank Doyle, Danny's parents, were
Dublin born but with rural ancestry. Danny, born in Dublin in 1940,
is one of three boys and five girls. They lived in a damp two room
basement flat on Herbert Place, by the banks of the Grand Canal near
Baggot Street Bridge. "A somewhat Bohemian area," Danny says," of
whom someone wrote 'no small area of any city anywhere has been trod

by so much genius.' Something of an exaggeration perhaps, but still, there is a great deal of truth in it."

Renowned literary personalities and neighbors Brendan Behan (1923 – 1964) and Patrick Kavanagh (1904 – 1967), who heard the young Doyle singing in the church choir in St. Mary's, Haddington Road, Dublin, encouraged his interest in Irish song. Behan's appreciation was often expressed with the occasional shilling or two.

Danny avers he was fortunate to be born into an Ireland still immersed in the Irish oral tradition. This tradition had flourished since the arrival of the Celts, five hundred years before the coming of Christ. The new nation, one that had survived the centuries old attempts to subjugate it, was emerging into a dramatically changing new world and "the national radio service, *Radio Eireann*, did much to foster the folk tradition and celebrate the new nationhood with programming that reflected the Irish heritage and character," said Danny, "But forty years later, this heritage would be hard to find on Irish air-waves, subsumed and almost swamped by a deluge of 'rock & roll drivel and pop pabulum.'"

Danny is eternally grateful to the radio of his childhood, which helped him to learn of the depth and richness of Irish culture. He remembers that, "There was for me excitement in the discovery of every new song, play, poem and story."

As a teen-ager Danny became intensely interested in folk songs. Since his early childhood he had heard much of these songs sung around his home in Dublin, from his mother and especially his great-grandmother, Bridget Fitzgerald, from Kilrush, County Clare. But now, through the songs, he developed a fierce curiosity about Irish history, for he had learned little of it while in school.

"They gave us a litany of dates, a broad overview and not much else; they served us up the big picture, never the small stories that collectively make up the whole-cloth of our past. But my curiosity for the living, breathing history, the heart-beat of the incredible characters who make up our Irish story, was found at home," Doyle recounts.

Danny tries to bring his past and even the generation's before that; to bring all of Irish history, to the stage. He presents a broad, meticulously researched show, so that we may understand where our ancestors came from, what made them what they were and therefore, who we are. Danny doesn't just transport his listeners, he engulfs them. Danny strives, as Sam Ferguson, a 19th century poet says: "to link his present with his country's past, and live anew in the knowledge of his sires."

"I loved the songs then, as I do now, for many reasons. They are a fascinating window into the past, into the social, personal and political life of the people. They were the poor man's newspaper and gave powerful expression to the emotional aspirations of a downtrodden people, and were a potent force in our nationalist history. They can be beautifully lyrical and musically sumptuous, often full of a wild, soft sadness. As weapons, they were as lethal as any the invader had ..." - from Danny Doyle, The Classic Collection, 2003. Doyle Music. Liner Notes.

While bringing the songs to the stage, Danny also shows us much more than just singing; he brings to life the milieu, the social, political, joyous, humorous and tragic events and times in which the songs germinated - all in a way that grips the audience and takes them on an emotional time machine, right back to the days written about in the songs and poetry. Danny's voice is enough to make you take note - here is a phenomenal singer – but the presentation of his songs and stories is like a sumptuous, endless multi-course meal, full of surprises and wonderful tastes and memorable, often humorous conversation.

"Danny Doyle is a great singer and a good guitarist as well, and a man who pays attention to what he is doing and does the research. I think he is rather neglected [not appreciated]. Danny is a phenomenal performer and singer. There are very few that would stand out like Danny Doyle does." – Tommy Makem

Danny's great-grandmother, Bridget Fitzgerald, had been involved in the awful eight months long strike and lock-out in Dublin in 1913, the curtain-raising event that led directly to the rebellion in 1916.

Doyle's mother and great-grandmother sang the songs and told the stories, always explaining the related background, and young Danny listened well, "in," he explained, "a permanent state of quizzical wonder and intense curiosity."

At that time Dublin presented the most extra-ordinary contrast in poverty and magnificence. The once fashionable Georgian mansions, built for 18th century aristocrats, now housed more than one third of the city's population, each mansion housing more than one hundred people, one family per room. The death rate was the highest in Europe, exceeding that of even Moscow and Calcutta. This was the domicile of the laboring class, who, for a pittance in wages, worked a seventy hour work week.

Behind the once stately facades, now crumbling and decaying, lay a hidden city of desperation and disease. There was also anger, and a defiance of unjust authority. Too often stricken, the laboring class in 1913 struck back. Irish Transport & General Workers Union bosses James Connolly and Jim Larkin called a general strike. The intransigent masters of Dublin, the employers, declared; "Let them submit or starve." Larkin shouted back his now famous line: "If they want revolution, then God be with them."

Danny's great-grandmother was in the thick of the violent events of the time and told him about that awful and often violent period in Dublin history. The strikers meetings and demonstrations were declared unlawful and riots broke out daily without warning. She told him how the police attacked the strikers and with their heavy batons, they beat savagely on flesh and bone. The dead and injured lay in scores on the streets of the city. She remembered one man being dragged to jail and although his jaw was shattered, he roared; "Up Jim Larkin! Bayonet nor baton can stop us now. The workers are loose at last."

The strike lasted eight months. The men, beaten by the hunger of their wives and children, were forced to renounce the union, but the resentment of injustice, the scheming and brooding, would continue, indirectly even leading to the point where a fresh blow would be struck on Easter Sunday 1916, when the liberation of the world's oldest political prisoner, Ireland, would commence.

During the dark days of that rebellion, Danny's great-grandmother, a member of *Cumann na mBhan* (The Organization of Women), would act as a courier, carrying messages between the rebel positions, or ferrying the seriously wounded to the hospital, running the gauntlet of burning buildings and British machine guns.

Others of Bridget's family were also involved in the extraordinary events of 1913 and 1916. Her sons, particularly Eddy, were later involved in the War of Independence, 1918-22, and she knew many of the rebel personages that would dominate those dramatic periods, such as Michael Collins, Patrick Pearse, James Connolly, The Countess Markievicz and more. "She was a woman of great spirit," Danny says, "she disliked Dublin people, claiming, quite rightly, that they were too pro-British."

"She sat in the chimney corner of her one-room flat in the Dublin slums, regaling us with songs and stories of those remarkable times. She taught me many songs of rebellion," Doyle remembers. Danny is able to capture the emotion and atmosphere of the experiences with his grandmother in song.

> "Her Galway shawl around her shoulders
> We'd gather close, she'd start the tale
> Of times and places, loved and lost now
> Beyond the meadows and the vale
> On her loom of life she wove her story
> Songs and poems, timeworn, still told
> The warp and weft of toil and struggle
> A patch-work weave of Green and Gold
>
> Songs from out the chimney corner
> Rowdy rhymes of a by-gone age
> With turf-smoke drifting all around us
> Her songs made Ireland come alive,
>
> *-Songs From Out the Chimney Corner*
> *by Danny Doyle & Terence Folan*

"Granny Fitz thought that any songs other than rebel songs were not worth singing. 'She was a fierce, implacable, rebelly woman,'" he said, with palpable pride.

The Doyle family occupied the lowest possible rung on the social ladder in Dublin. Danny's father was a coal man, selling coal, logs and turf from the back of a horse and cart. Out in all weathers, ill-clad and hardly nourished, he was often sick, sometimes for a month or more.

Even though he was a very young man/child, Danny would have to step in and make the deliveries. This Dickensian existence made a deep impression upon the young teen-ager: "I determined there had to be a better life than the one my father was forced to follow. On a day in 1953, I got an inkling of what that life might be. An unusual and unexpected event brightened up the grey, drab, colorless lives, we often lived," Danny explains.

One day in Herbert Lane, just across from his father's coal yard, an Irish Army truck pulled up outside a crumbling coach house. An officer and soldiers of the Second Field Engineers proceeded to unload materials that looked suspiciously like Irish Army supplies: timber, toolboxes, ladders, cement, paint of a camouflage hue, rolls of latrine canvas and more. For months and months the sound of hammering, sawing and drilling could be heard until finally the work was finished.

The Irish Army officer, Captain Alan Simpson, invited Danny and his father in to have a look. They couldn't have been more astonished at the sight that greeted them, Doyle recalls:

"We were standing in what looked like an early Victorian theatre seen through the wrong end of a telescope, a strange combination of a doll's house and an opera house. The moon-lighting Irish soldiers had built a theatre with a tiny stage and seating for fifty-three people. The walls were painted maroon and Irish Army green. The seats were covered with latrine canvas. The stage lights were large tin cans that had previously carried ammunition. There were gilt pillars and a tiny coffee bar in the corner."

The elder Doyle became caretaker and Danny "was appointed general factotum" (jack-of-all-trades), moving scenery, raising the curtain and running the box office. Here he met the traveling players, learning songs and recitations from them. It was from this experience that he got his first inkling of what an uneducated teen-ager with no academic qualifications might do with his life.

The Pike Theatre would create a sensation and shake up Irish conservative moral attitudes. It would also land Captain Simpson in jail on obscenity charges. Although the play, *The Rose Tattoo* was banned in Ireland as being "obscene," and "immoral," Simpson was determined to stage the Tennessee Williams work. At the first and second performances, members of the Vice Squad were in the audience. Simpson was warned that if the play proceeded on the following night or anytime thereafter, he and the cast would be arrested and charged under the State obscenity laws.

The Captain and cast decided to go ahead with the play the following night. Danny relates what followed; "The play had hardly commenced when the Vice Squad detectives rushed in and stopped the play. I was assistant stage manager that night. They grabbed Alan Simpson and carted him off to prison. Myself, and some of the cast were briefly detained. The cops were particularly shocked and offended that a child, myself, should be subject to "such profanity," muttering that that would not go well in court for Mr. Simpson.

"Outside in the lane, my neighbor and playwright, the somewhat tipsy Brendan Behan, was having a grand old time jeering and sneering at the cops. As he staggered off he roared at them; 'Just wait here. Don't go anywhere, yis Cromwell's bastards. I'm goin' home to get me gun.' He never came back. He probably went to a pub.

"At thirteen years [old], the Pike Theatre gave me an education in European drama. At that tender age I saw the works of Ionesco, Beckett, Ugo Betti, Diego Fabbri, Ibsen, Shaw, Sartre, and the gritty plays and songs of my neighbor, Brendan Behan."

On leaving school at age fourteen, Danny decided it was time to satisfy a burning need to explore the world beyond his hometown. "For as long as I could remember I had gazed longingly at the Dublin Mountains, wondering daily what exotic locales lay beyond them, what new songs and strange stories were waiting to be savored out there in 'the wilds' as we called them."

Danny was soon able to answer those questions, for he would shortly go to work as a messenger boy to help out with the family finances. So, with camping gear packed on his bike, he set off to explore the world outside of Dublin. "In the local library I had seen black and white photos of County Kerry. The pictures depicted magnificent scenery and mile long deserted beaches. Kerry it would be. Pedaling like a mad Dervish, I reached Rossbeg Beach near Glenbeigh [this is about two hundred miles from Dublin] in three and a half days."

In the local Kerry pubs at night, Danny would drink lemonade, intoxicated with the strange talk and wondrous songs of love, loss, war, death and marriage. Ballads about bacon and cabbage, pints of porter, tales of murder and of a de-frocked priest and another concerning a mad goat, filled his ears and touched his soul. He was hooked. "I realized that Irish folk song would become the unrelenting quest of my life."

Then in the early 1960's, the Irish music scene took a dramatic turn and all was changed. Four "Hearty & Hellish" Irish troubadours burst onto the world stage and by themselves created an international audience for Irish folk song which, in turn, prompted the beginning of a recording industry in Ireland.

"There is not an Irish ballad singer alive today that does not owe the Clancy Brothers & Tommy Makem an enormous debt. I was in abject admiration of them, never missing their wonderful concerts in Dublin. They were heroes who became my friends. When I was a raw recruit they treated me as if I were an old friend, and an equal. The Clancy Brothers & Tommy Makem didn't simply open doors for all of us, they kicked them down!"

Despite the popularity of The Clancy Brothers & Tommy Makem, the folk music revival in Ireland was as yet in its infancy. This was not the case in Great Britain, where the resurgence of folk song was at full throttle. All over England, Scotland and Wales there were hundreds of folk clubs presenting music every night. Doyle simply couldn't stand not to be part of it. In 1964, he left Dublin and went to live in London, becoming a regular guest at the many clubs there. Soon after, they began to pay him and his London day job went the way of his Dublin one. "In London I had talked my way into an interior design job, decorating people's homes, in spite of the fact that I came from a two-room Dublin slum and knew absolutely nothing about the trade. It was a very stressful job and it put me off work forever," he teasingly recounts.

One day Danny noticed an advertisement for a folk club in the grimy London district of Clapham Junction. The name in Gaelic, "*The Crubeen Club* [Crubeen: Pigs Foot] told me this was an Irish club. I went and it changed my life," says Doyle.

"The *Fear An Ti*," 'Man of the House,' and club founder, was a larger than life Kerryman named Sean McCarthy, from Listowel," Doyle recalls. That night he sang songs Danny had never heard before. Several of McCarthy's compositions, like *Red Haired Mary*, took Danny's fancy and the very trusting Kerryman gave them to Doyle. Another of them, *Step It Out, Mary*, would launch Danny's musical career in Ireland.

Traveling around the folk clubs of Great Britain, Doyle learned literally hundreds of esoteric songs, many of them Irish. When he arrived back in Ireland in September 1966, the country was in the grip of the folk song revival. With his repertoire of little known songs, Danny became an immediate and significant success. Sean McCarthy's song, *Step It out Mary*, Doyle's first number one hit, was followed by two more in the same year, the second of which, *Whiskey on a Sunday*, was, for many years after, the best-selling single in Ireland. It was another life altering moment for the young Dublin man. The hit records and best selling albums kept coming; a partial list of them include; *Step It Out, Mary* (1967); *The Irish Soldier* (1967); *Whiskey On A Sunday* (1967); *Lizzie Lindsay* (1968); *The Mucky Kid* (1968); *The Green Hills Of Kerry* (1971); *A Daisy A Day* (1972); *Leaving Nancy* (1978) and *The Rare Auld Times* (1979). The Rare Ould Times is often considered Danny's signature song or anthem. None does it better than the passionate and gifted Dubliner. Other trademark songs that once heard, belong only to him, include; *The West's Awake, Grace, The Foggy Dew, Dublin Me Darlin', The Band Played Waltzing Matilda* and *Down By the Glenside*.

At the start of this burgeoning success, circa late 1966, Danny had struggled to make a living, and began doing bit parts in movies filmed in Ireland. He was hired to play in a period piece being shot in a mansion in County Dublin, titled *Rocket to the Moon*. There were hours and hours of waiting before they would shoot a scene so Danny brought his guitar and would sit off in a room practicing.

"Just as I finished a song one day somebody applauded. I looked up to see the star of the film, Burl Ives. He said he had never heard the song before and asked me did I know any more. I told him I knew hundreds. He invited me to dinner at a Dublin steak house and we drank brandy and swapped songs into the wee small hours. As a fledgling ballad singer very nervous about his abilities, or lack of them, this was a great confidence booster. If Burl Ives could listen to me three nights in a row, well then I might not be as inept as I imagined, maybe I could even make a living from my passion. The kindly Mr. Ives paid for the food, wine and brandy. He also taught me to eat my steak rare, not well done, or destroyed, as my Mother cooked it."

Soon Danny was touring the world from Romania to Moscow; Monte Carlo to Malta, Rio de Janeiro to Sydney, New Zealand to Canada, as well as the United States, and many points in between.

Danny has lost count of how many times he has been on television. Twice he had his own series on RTE (*Radio Telefís Eireann* – Irish Television), and two series on UTV (Northern Ireland television). He has performed on countless BBC shows and more in Scotland where *Step It Out, Mary* became a minor hit. He was permanent musical guest on the BBC show, *Pebble Mill at One*, and the *Tommy Cooper Show* on ITV. Cooper was the funniest man in Britain.

Pam Ayres was a West of England poet and raconteur. Although she at first fiercely opposed his participation in her series *The Pam Ayres Show*, nonetheless Danny won her over and she agreed he would be her weekly musical guest.

Doyle was also a guest of Princess Grace, in Monaco, at a music festival and appeared on TV there every morning for a week. Romanian Television was the most arduous TV filming he ever did. Starting in the morning they began taping every song he knew. He finished singing at 11 p.m. In Moscow the following week he went through the same all-day wringer. Maltese television was amazing, he says. "No rehearsal, just sing the song and goodbye. It took all of ten minutes."

Danny's appearance on Brazilian television in 1969 is a bizarre and hilarious story. "I was invited to appear on the biggest talk-entertainment show in the country, to be interviewed and sing a couple of songs. The show was broadcast live from a beautiful theatre in Sao Paolo. When I was introduced I stepped out to a great round of applause. The format was awkward, to say the least. I sat on this couch facing the audience. Sitting beside me were two of the most beautiful women I've ever encountered. One would ask me a question in English and the other would then translate it into Portuguese.

"I sang an Irish ballad and when I finished, the two ladies were in tears. This was very disconcerting. It had never happened before. Then one of them, still visibly upset, said, (and this is where I nearly cracked up), 'You must have suffered terribly to be able to sing like that.' They are a very emotional people. While the audience was applauding this observation I could hear my manager, Noel Pearson, laughing hysterically in the wings.

"There was more to come. My 'English' interviewer said; 'Our audience will be thrilled to know that our wonderful guest today, Danny Doyle, is a nephew of the great English detective, the great Sherlock Holmes.' The audience went crazy at this, whooping and hollering for what seemed like a long time. I'm sitting, utterly stiff with shock at this revelation, and thinking; this is going out live; what the hell am I going to say? In the wings I can see Noel Pearson, helplessly bent over with laughing. I came to the conclusion that he had put them up to this and as soon as it was over I was going to kill him. But now the audience is quiet and I have to say something, so what the hell, I thought, why not play along and off I went into a riff about my 'uncle,' Sherlock Holmes. I told them that he had bequeathed to me a few items I treasured greatly; his magnifying glass, his deer-stalker hat and one of the hypodermic needles with which he used to inject himself with illegal drugs.

"'But what was he like as a person' they wanted to know. My brain was now in turmoil and I'm on the verge of a maniacal laughing fit, so I said, 'Let me sing you his favorite song' and I lashed into *Molly Malone.*' The beautiful girls were soon crying again and the audience went wild. I finished my song and got to hell out of there. Noel Pearson swears to this day that he had nothing to do with setting me up. And I believe him. I have not the foggiest notion how those women connected me with Sherlock Holmes."

Danny has made at least thirty TV appearances in all in Australia and New Zealand, where his sister Geraldine is a big star. In February 2004, for the seventh year in a row, Geraldine was voted Australia's #1 Stand-Up Comedian. It is obvious Danny is very proud of her.

Doyle would have another encounter with Hollywood in 1968. Paramount Pictures was filming *Where's Jack?* in Wicklow, and were having a reception to publicize the movie. Danny was invited to the reception and there he met the film's composer, the Oscar winning Elmer Bernstein, who has written some of the most memorable film music ever produced, including; *The Man With the Golden Arm, The Magnificent Seven, Thoroughly Modern Millie, Ghostbusters, My Left Foot* and more.

"It turned out he loved folk music, so I took him to *The Old Sheiling Pub* in Dublin to hear a new group called *The Chieftains.* He was fascinated with the uileann pipes playing of Paddy Moloney. I introduced them and they had a long technical conversation on the pipes."

Bernstein had written a song for the movie, the story of Jack Sheppard, an 18th century English convict famous for his many escapes from prison. Stanley Baker, actor and producer, and director James Clavell, (author of *King Rat, Whirlwind, Shogun, Taipei, Noble House* and many other novels), were not sure that an Irish voice would fit into a purely English story, but after an audition for them in London, Danny got the assignment.

"I was flown first-class to Hollywood and we recorded the score and song at the Paramount Recording Studios with the Los Angeles Philharmonic. But Mr. Bernstein didn't like the sound. So off we went to Rome a week later, where we recorded the whole thing again with the Rome Symphonic Orchestra, on St. Patrick's Day, 1969. Again, Elmer rejected the recording and a few days later we found ourselves in a London studio with yet another orchestra. This time the sound was to his liking. I had flown half way around the world, from Dublin, to Los Angeles, to Rome, to get to London!

"It was a thrill to attend the premiere in London. When the credits rolled, there up on the screen was my name in huge letters, my London pals in the audience roared their approval. One of their own had made it to Hollywood."

Danny and Elmer Bernstein became very great friends. Over the years, Danny spent many weeks and months as Elmer's guest on his ranch in the Ventura hills above Hollywood, riding Bernstein's magnificent Arabian horses across the hills, all the way to the Pacific Ocean.

"For such a famous, accomplished, wealthy man, he was as down to earth as one could possibly be. He treated everybody equally, he spoke to the person in the street, the working man or woman, exactly as he did to the powerful movers and shakers and Hollywood stars. He had been heavily involved in the labor movement of the 1930's and '40s in the United States and was black-listed for it back then. He was a lovely man and a true democrat, class and status were utterly irrelevant to him," recalls Danny.

The celebrated composer brought Danny to dinner at Gregory Peck's house; another time he took him to Burt Lancaster's home. Danny discovered that the acrobatic Lancaster was also a terribly bright and intelligent man. "Lovely people, they treated me as if I was the most important person in the room."

On another occasion, Elmer brought Danny to a party at Nancy Sinatra's place. All the stars were there, in groups, discussing the movie business amongst themselves. Danny wandered down the hall to the music room where he found a guitar and began singing and playing to himself. "After a while, people started drifting in and soon I was singing an Irish ballad for Ms. Sinatra, Robert Stack, Robert Mitchum, Henry Mancini, James Coburn and God knows who else. They loved *Finnegan's Wake*, and as I sat there teaching them the chorus, I suddenly thought, 'what the hell am I doing here, I'm Danny Doyle, a coal-man's son from the back lanes of Dublin.' All I could do was laugh."

Elmer was instrumental in getting Danny invited to the Brazilian Song Contest in Rio de Janeiro in 1969. Phil Coulter wrote an original song for him, *Roundstone River*, and Danny and Phil both flew off to Brazil.

"It was an experience I'll never forget. We performed for six nights in a stadium that held 50,000 people each night!! We had a sixty-five piece orchestra, plus a choir, and when we sang, the Brazilians, the most demonstrably passionate people you'll find anywhere, just jumped up and down and roared and shouted with joy. Elmer had warned us to include at least one key change in the song. When we got to the key change, all hell broke loose. They went mental with excitement."

There were forty-seven countries competing and Phil's song came in sixth. Amazingly, they had only been in Brazil for about a week, when "Coulter was engaging in conversations with the locals, in Portuguese! A very quick study," says Doyle.

"My old friend Elmer Bernstein passed away late in 2004. I learned a great deal from him and he confirmed my belief that the music is more important than the performer. Although he lived to his mid eighties and wrote music for more than fifty films and had two Oscars sitting on his mantle, he would scoff at the notion that he was some kind of legend."

Danny expressed sad regret that he and Elmer never got to make the album they worked on together and planned to record. Bernstein's soaring career and Danny's incessant wanderings intervened and the album never got made. Bernstein's favorite Irish song, and Danny's for a long time, was, *The West's Awake*. "What wouldn't I give," Doyle says, "to hear his arrangement of that stirring piece."

"I feel that the song is more important than the singer and I consider myself merely a servant of the songs, a conduit for passing them on to others. The focus should not be on us performers, what we ballad singers and musicians do should not be a 'show-business ego trip.' The focus should be on the history, the people, the sufferings, sacrifices and joys from which the ballads and music came."

In the late 1970's, Danny had "a discussion with myself," as he put it, and came to a career altering decision. Tired of the lighter musical fare he had been singing since the beginning of his career in "show-business," he avowed, that from that point on, he would only do work he absolutely believed in. He promised himself that he would only work with people he admired and could learn from, people who would expect a lot from him, in terms of performance and honesty.

He found a young Limerick musician and budding record producer, Bill Whelan, who had never been involved in Irish folk music. They would go on to collaborate on seven albums, one of which, *The Highwayman*, was described by the magazine, *In Dublin*, as "One of the best folk albums of all time."

"The recordings I did with my old friend Bill Whelan, especially 'The Highwayman,' are the best things I have done in my career. As one who can usually only find fault with my own performance, I have to say that I'm immensely proud of the work we did together. Bill brought out the very best in me. He taught me that you must always work with superior artists. It brings your game way up."

Working with Danny in the studio, Whelan was introduced to the extraordinary talents of Donal Lunny, Liam O'Flynn, Andy Irvine, Davy Spillane and others. It would be a life changing time for the brilliant Whelan as well, who absorbed every note and nuance played by these superb artists. Out of this immersion would eventually come Whelan's incredible success, *Riverdance*.

Liam Clancy offers a glimpse, "Danny Doyle has been a friend since the Ballad Boom of the sixties in Ireland. I wore out his first few records. Danny is a master storyteller but you should never be deceived by his humor. There is a serious historian behind the mask. My favorite gem from Danny comes from an early morning encounter in a hotel lobby while we on tour together in Ireland. 'Good morning Danny. How are you this fine morning?' I asked him. He looked around to make sure no one was listening and said conspiratorially 'Liam - after last night, I feel like a stunned mullet!'"

Starting in the 1980's, Danny researched and wrote a series of one-man shows based on dramatic periods of Irish history. His first, *"A Terrible Beauty, The Songs, Story & Poems of the Irish Rebellion, 1913-1922"* was described by the New Orleans Times Picayune as, "A heroic story. A brilliant performance."

In 1998, with co-author Terence Folan, Danny wrote a book entitled, *The Gold Sun of Irish Freedom*, to commemorate the 200th anniversary of the failed rebellion of 1798. It became a best-seller in Ireland, and surprisingly, also in Great Britain.

Doyle's next one-man history and song concert was, *The Wild Geese,* the forgotten tale of the extraordinary 17th and 18th century Irish Diaspora to the European continent. The little known songs and poetry of this time in Irish history made the story intensely interesting.

The latest concert Doyle has authored is *The Glee-Men Sing, The Songs & Stories of Yeats, Joyce, O'Casey, Kavanagh & Behan,* in 2005. The latter two writers were neighbors of Danny's in Dublin when he was growing up. Their tale is tragic and oftentimes very funny.

Doyle's next concert will showcase his hometown of Dublin. Highlighting its' marvelous history and its' deeply eccentric characters.

"Danny had a huge hit when I was a young boy. He won't like me saying this but he is brilliant, a great, great singer. I have all his albums in the house. He always records great songs. Danny Doyle, even to this day, chooses his material so, so carefully, sings so magnificently, and recites great poetry. The history, his knowledge of the songs, his love of it, is unsurpassed." - Tom Sweeney

When asked about his favorite Irish song, Danny related that he didn't have one since "it would be impossible to pick one as better than a thousand other equally great ones."

On whom he admires he replied, "Most of my heroes are either rebels, [or] musicians, writers, actors and artists and I think the true heroes are the regular men and women who go out to work year after year to provide for their families. That may sound corny, but I hold them in great admiration." Musically, he counts The Dubliners and The Clancy Brothers & Tommy Makem as major influences. Favorite singers include Liam Clancy, Luke Kelly, Al O'Donnell, Harry Belafonte and Delia Murphy.

On the personal side, the people who have influenced Danny most are his great-grandmother Bridget Fitzgerald, and his own mother, Kathleen, now eighty-four years old, still hale, hearty and feisty in Dublin.

An "angelic singer," whom Danny still listens to, is the early 1900's Irish tenor, John McCormack, from Athlone, County Roscommon. He also loves the Carter Family from the Appalachians, since first hearing them in the late 1950's. Their music "took him to times and strange places he'd never heard of," he said.

"Without the Clancy Brothers & Tommy Makem I wouldn't have a career," he continues earnestly. "I loved the original Dubliners, especially Luke Kelly. Although dead more than twenty years [Luke Kelly passed away in 1984 of a brain tumor], he is still head and shoulders over all of us and the best Irish ballad singer ever."

Listening to Joan Baez in the early sixties taught Danny how to play the guitar and Doyle is a great admirer of the superb and intricate musicianship of Andy Irvine. But it is with sorrow that Danny talks of the Dublin ballad singer Frank Harte, friend, mentor and national treasure, "Frank Harte, was one of the greatest repositories of folk song in Ireland, the Johnny Appleseed of Irish folk music, scattering with great passion and generous profusion, wherever he went, the songs of his country. He would call me from Dublin and sing me songs over the phone. [Danny has been based in Manassas, Virginia since 1986]. It made my day.

"In 1998, the bi-centennial year of the rebellion of 1798, I sat with Frank outside his cottage by the river Liffey, where he sang me two dozen ballads from that rebellious time. I had only heard two of them before. He selflessly gave me the songs for my planned '98 book and album, despite the fact that even as he sang he was planning a 1798 CD himself. When it came to the songs he was utterly selfless about passing them on. It's what he lived for. He is my all time folk song hero. We'll never see his like again," Doyle recounts with both obvious pleasure and sorrow. "But those days are now gone." [Frank Harte passed away on June 27th, 2005].

Doyle loves the man, and the songs and devilish humor of Andy M. Stewart, from Scotland, who has written an "astonishing" catalogue of great lyrics. Mick Moloney is another artist he holds in high regard, because, "Every time I listen to him I learn something."

And the Daddy of them all, Danny says, and the only one to whom he would apply the term "legend," is Pete Seeger.

When asked what singers he listens to now, he gave an interesting answer: "There are many fine singers out there and I enjoy them, but I find that at this stage in my life I learn more about expressive singing from watching really good actors than I do by listening to vocalists. That may sound puzzling and even paradoxical, but let me explain. What a really good actor does is; he internalizes the emotion of the piece he or she is playing. Instead of engaging in scenery chewing histrionics, the actor shows the emotions of the moment through subtle facial and body language, thus making the moment powerful. It is a very intricate art and I constantly strive to incorporate it into my singing. The late, great Luke Kelly was a master of this. He measured the meaning and intent of a lyric then sublimated the feelings it expressed. The performance and song were the more powerful for it. Some Irish ballad singers would do well to learn this technique instead of just roaring out a song from start to finish."

"I became an Irish folk singer because I'm not qualified to do anything else. Leaving school at age fourteen in 1954 was an economic necessity, and besides, they weren't teaching me the things I cared about, the music and history. But thank God for folk music, it saved my life. I am forever grateful for the rich gift handed to me by our culture. It is something I discovered when very young, and more than fifty years later, the gift is still giving. It constantly reveals itself, bringing again that excitement I felt as a youngster at the discovery of a new song or story."

"I was born and raised in Ireland, a place of memories and plentiful ghosts, in Dublin town hard by the banks of the Liffey's Guinness-coloured waters. The city was a great teacher, giving me history and legend, stories of the commonplace and heroic, legends more real than dull facts; the bawdy, rowdy grist of the ballad maker's mill."

"The poet Brendan Kennealy wrote that 'All songs are living ghosts and long for a living voice.' I sometimes visualize the living voice of my great-grandmother sitting in the chimney corner of her single room in the fetid slums of Dublin, conjuring into spectral life, through song and poem, heroes, rebels, rogues and lovers, the song-time history of Ireland.

"Our ballads are an expressive reflection of the people who gave them voice - a folk symphony of melody and lyric, full of sly humour, wild and soft sadness, gentle defiance, roaring resistance and a raucous longing for life. They bind us to our past. I've spent a lifetime being shadowed by this Spirit of the Gael. What a rich musical haunting it has been."[1]

"I don't wish to be churlish but I don't consider myself a 'legend.' I'm just a working folk singer who loves what he does. Just because someone has attained longevity does not, in my opinion, make him or her a legend. There has to be great stature and much accomplishment along with it to even think about applying the term. As well, 'legend' is not an objective expression, in my opinion, and it may in fact be meaningless since it is mostly applied subjectively and differently. One man's legend, methinks, could easily be another man's hack.

"As I said, the song is more important than the singer, so when I am long gone and forgotten, the songs and stories will still be reverberating down the years. Although the voices that inform the lyrics may fade away, the song lives on."

"In Ireland, our ancient fatalism has been spurned by a new generation of dynamic young men and women. The racial memory has well and truly awakened from its usual state of slumbering inferiority to find a country now infused with pride and self-reliance, evidenced in the bustling joy of life and riot of colour that is modern Irish life. Pete St. John's anthemic *Spirit of the Gael* speaks eloquently to these exciting new times.

'Ireland, Oh, Ireland.
Our Nation will prevail
Forever free through all eternity
Lives the Spirit of the Gael.'"[1]

Danny may think he is not qualified to be called a "Festival Legend," but most of the tens of thousands of people who have been blessed enough to hear him sing and see him perform live, see the effect and inspiration he has provided in his very distinguished career, would greatly disagree. Even by his own definition, "*There has to be great stature and much accomplishment along with it to even think about applying the term,*" Danny more than exceeds the meaning, and the intent, of his own definition.

The legacy of Danny's body of work will continue to educate and inspire future generations - long may it live. For just as he was inspired by singers before him, Danny has inspired a whole new generation; to pick up a guitar, to learn the songs and to spread the love of Irish music and history through song, thorough research and the passing on of our rich heritage, the whole world over. Doyle's performances – not just the gorgeously sung song, but the relating, with drama or great humor, of the people, places and events related to it, cause the song, and performer, to be emblazoned in our memories. He is a gift that keeps giving. Danny Doyle is a Legend, through and through.

Danny Doyle Discography:

(I believe this to be complete but make no promises)

CD's/LP's:

- Expressions Of Danny Doyle   (1967)
- Danny Doyle   (1968)
- Whiskey On A Sunday   (1969)
- Mary From Dungloe   (1970)
- A Daisy A Day   (1972)
- Three Drunken Maidens   (1975, UK release only)
- The West's Awake   (1976)
- Raised On Songs & Stories   (1979)
- The Highwayman   (1981)
- Twenty Years A-Growing   (1985)
- Dublin, Me Darlin'   (1988)
- Emigrant Eyes   (1991)
- Emerald Encore, Vol. 1   (1994)
- Folk Master's Ensemble   (1996)
- Under A Connemara Moon   (1997)
- Rebels! 1798   (1998)
- Live In New Orleans   (2000)
- Spirit Of the Gael   (2002)
- St. Brendan's Fair Isle   (2003)
- Classic Collection   (2003)
- Wearing Of The Green   (2005)

#1 or Top Hit Singles:

- Whiskey on a Sunday   (1967)
- Step it out Mary   (1967)
- The Irish Soldier Laddie   (1967)
- Whiskey on a Sunday   (1967)
- The Mucky Kid   (1968)
- Streets of London   (1968)
- Lizzie Lindsay   (1968)
- A Daisy a Day   (1972)

- The Green Hills of Kerry   (1976)
- Dublin in the Rare 'Ould Times   (1979)
- Maid in a Calico Dress   (1979)
- Year of the French   (1987)
- The West's Awake   (1989)
- The Highwayman   (1989)

Books:

- The Gold Sun of Freedom, Songs 1798 in Song & Story (w/ Terence Folan)   (1997)

Videos:

- "No videos yet. I will wait until after I get the plastic surgery. Break out the scaffolding and the spackling." - Danny Doyle

www.dannydoyle.org

III.

Liam Clancy

"Liam was for me. I never heard a singer as good as him, ever. He was just the best ballad singer I ever heard in my life, still is probably." – Bob Dylan

Liam Clancy met his waiting destiny head on, at his front door, on an August day in 1955, in Carrick-on-Suir: "I answered a knock at our door on Williams Street. There stood two American women: one narrow-waisted, big bosomed, sallow, and soft-spoken, the other huge, gaudy, and loud. They were glaringly American against the drab, gray backdrop of an Irish town of the time. They looked to me like two exotic birds that had been blown off course in some storm and had come to earth in the wrong place.

"The slimmer of the two said in a soft, refined American accent, 'Hi, my name is Diane Hamilton and this is my friend Catherine Wright. We're in Ireland collecting folk music. This is the Clancy's, isn't it? We were told to come see Mammy Clancy by her sons Paddy and Tom in New York. They said she had some wonderful children's songs.'"[1]

Diane Hamilton (Guggenheim), an affluent American song collector who came to Ireland to collect as many songs, lyrics and music of the Irish song tradition as she could find, became a flashpoint, mostly good, of many of the life-changing incidents in Liam Clancy's life. She had changed her last name to hide her wealth, being the daughter of Harry Guggenheim, known as the 'Father of American Aviation,' as well as to give her better access to the treasure troves of songs and stories that she was seeking out, especially children's songs, a special love of hers. She met Liam Clancy, formed a friendship and they traveled together all around Ireland, collecting these Irish ballads, mostly in their natural settings, the kitchens and parlors of farmers, tradesmen, shop keepers and their families and friends. Many neighbors would gather for impromptu *sessiuns* (sing-alongs), when they heard that collectors were at work nearby.

"… Dianne, with all her problems, had a very important talent: she was a catalyst. Never mind her singing or playing or collecting. That was just covered ground that others had traveled before, but she had an uncanny instinct for bringing people together whose combined energies and interests made a magical new element. She saw the potential in a situation, and she had the money to make it happen," said Liam.[1]

Another fateful day soon followed later that year, when on one such excursion in search of songs, they went to visit legendary source singer and song collector, Sarah Makem, and her son, Tommy, in the Makems' hometown of Keady, County Armagh.

As Liam tells it, "The recording sessions at the Makem's house were memorable. Peter, the man of the house, with his pipe and fiddle…and Jack, his son…Tommy, the youngest son, in the corner nearly as shy as myself…. And they all buzzed around the queen bee herself, Sarah Makem, as she sat placid in the eye of the hurricane.

"It was so much like the Clancy household it was uncanny, in our case Mammy Clancy being the queen bee. All that was different was the accents.

"Sarah Makem has a vast store of songs which the Clancy Brothers and Tommy Makem would later plunder. Sean O'Boyle, too, the great musical scholar and folklorist, was a regular at the sessions. From him I got the beautiful Gaelic song "Buachaill on Eirne." It was later 'Englishized' by a journalist from a Glascow newpaper and became quite famous as an Irish 'folk song' renamed 'Come by the Hills.'

"The young Tommy Makem and I struck up an instant friendship. Our interests were so similar: girls, theatre and singing, in that order. He was heading to America soon, he told me, to try his luck at acting. We agreed to keep in touch."[1]

Liam and Tommy hit it off, and about a year after they met, each headed for America (separately) to try their luck at acting – both on stage and on television. But the legendary *Clancy Brothers & Tommy Makem* seeds had been planted and would blossom and multiply beyond anyone's dreams.

The deep love that Liam has for singing, actually presenting, a song, the just-right ballad, has always existed in him. The presentation talent deep within him first found expression in acting, but the ever present song tradition that was as much a part of his daily life as breathing, stayed hidden, for lack of recognition and realization that it was something special.

"I did not know how rich a lode of song and music existed in Ireland until 1955, when I had set with Diane Hamilton and Catherine Wright to record the *Lark in the Morning* - although I was mostly lugging the tape recorder, taking the photographs and getting us from place to place, through the Irish countryside. It was an amazing journey, full of good fortune: I found both Tommy Makem and the songs that became the cornerstone of my career." - Liam Clancy from *The Lark in the Morning,* (1956, Tradition Records) Liner notes.

"The Clancy Brothers with Tommy Makem have already, in their own lifetimes, attained legendary status in the world of Irish music. They have changed forever the way in which Irish folk songs are arranged and performed in public, and they have drawn a whole generation of folk music fans into a musical culture that until their arrival languished in obscurity."[7]- Mick Moloney.

In a story by Rambling House's Ronan Nolan, in 2000, about the impact these first appearances of the, at the time, unknown *Clancy Brothers & Tommy Makem*, "Utilising their instrumental armoury and the store of songs from the Clancy and Makem families, songbooks and Ewan MacColl tapes, they added stage banter to manly harmonies and passionate choruses to create a unique repertoire for the American folk audience. Their acting days helped shape their stagecraft and their trademark Aran ganseys made them stand out."[2]

Prior to the Clancy Brothers and Tommy Makem, there was very little Irish music coming from Ireland, most of it actually came from New York. Explains Liam, "Tin Pan Alley was a factory for turning out music. It was written for a specific purpose: to sell sheet music. And schmaltz was very popular, very saleable, but it certainly didn't represent the authentic Irish music, which came out of the history. It came out of the hardships, it came out of the joys and loves of the people themselves."[3]

"The Dance Hall Act of 1935, which had dealt such a blow to traditional music by banning the house dances, could not outlaw family occasions and parties. It is significant that come the ballad boom, a large volume of songs flowed from families such as the O'Domhnaills of Donegal, the Tunneys and McConnells of Fermanagh, the Clancys of Tipperary, Sarah and Tommy Makem of Armagh and the Keane sisters of Galway. Added to this were the wonderful and often ribald Dublin street ballads and the songs of Dominic and Brendan Behan.

"In England and Scotland in the late 1950s, the number of folk clubs were growing, the most influential being Ewan MacColl's Singers Club in London.

"At the beginning of the 1960's the Irish State was emerging from the cultural and economic stagnation that marked its first 40 years. The Abbey Tavern in Howth, on the outskirts of Dublin, introduced the first ballad sessions and the country's first television station, *Radio Telifis Eireann*, was launched in January, 1961.

"Barely beneath the surface of a young nation craving respectability, there existed, as ever, a vibrant sub-culture of traditional music and song in rural homes, at fairs, sports events and in some pubs. Peggy Jordan was one of the early organisers of the Dublin ballad sessions. Interested in Irish music since her youth, the home of Peggy and her husband Tom in Kenilworth Square saw many late night sessions of musicians and singers. By chance Liam Clancy was staying in [her] ... Dublin home, [when she] was asked to bring singers and musicians out to the Abbey Tavern, so he became one of the first performers at those early sessions at the Abbey Tavern which marked the start of the Irish ballad boom.

"Soon sessions cropped up in Dublin at the Old Sheiling, the International Bar, the Hollybrook in Clontarf, and the 'Ballads at Midnight' Saturday night session in the old Grafton Cinema."[2]

From singing solo in tiny pubs and ballad houses, Liam's singing career got a boost when *the Clancy Brothers & Tommy Makem* began a series of appearances on the most popular television show in the world. *The Ed Sullivan Show* was one of the highest rated shows on television, drawing over eighty million viewers, huge audiences each Sunday night. Irish music began to come into its own.

"I knew we had established something new - a new way of singing old songs," recalled Liam.

But it was not their first appearance on the Ed Sullivan Show that shook the foundations of Irish Music in America, as most believe. The Clancy Brothers and Tommy Makem appeared on the Ed Sullivan Show four times. Saving the best for last, the final appearance is the episode that altered history.

The first appearance was on March 12, 1961, when they sang *Brennan on the Moor.* Other entertainers included actors Tammy Grimes and Pat O'Brien and Irish singers Brendan O'Dowda and Mary O'Hara.

Their second appearance was on December 16th, 1962 and included Liberace, Abbe Lane, Xavier Cugat and Barbra Streisand, who would go on to open for The Clancy Brothers & Tommy Makem, on their own tour. They performed *Whistling Gypsy* and *South Australia.*

March 14th, 1965, the Clancy Brothers and Tommy Makem made their third appearance, where they sang *Wild Colonial Boy.* Other guests on that show included Petula Clark, Nancy Walker and Burt Lahr.

But it was the fourth appearance, on March 13th, 1966, that altered the future, the prestige, and the acceptance, of Irish music in America, and eventually back in Ireland too. It also did well for The Clancy Brothers and Tommy Makem! Other guests included Wayne & Shuster, the McNiff Dancers and Mary O'Hara. Pearl Bailey was scheduled to be the headliner, but did not show.

Liam recalls the producer coming to them, the next act, in a panic.

"'We've got a problem. Could you guys improvise three extra songs?'

{Liam thought to himself...] That would leave us with about fifteen minutes out of a one hour show. ...

'Be good gentlemen. Remember – there's eighty million people watching you!'"[1]

The group had rehearsed two songs, which turned into five. For sixteen minutes (an Ed Sullivan Show record that not even the Beatles or Elvis ever surpassed) they held the stage – and most of the television tuned world, in the palm of their hands. The young performers didn't waste the opportunity. Their careers were already successful and growing, but their performance on Ed Sullivan sent the Clancy Brothers & Tommy Makem on a path to world recognition, sold out concerts and gigs in White Houses and Royal Theatres the world over.

The group did more than revolutionize Irish music. There were the sweaters, too.

"My mother felt sorry for us," says Liam. "She got three sweaters made to send out to us as Christmas present -- to her sons, so that they wouldn't get cold. And then she thought, 'Poor Tommy Makem is going to be cold as well.' So she got a fourth one made.

"Their manager saw something else in the sweaters: a signature look. He said, 'That's it.' He said, 'That's it. We got it.'

"I said, 'Marty, we're going to die in the heat.'

He said, 'Die then. It'll keep your weight down. This is perfect.'"[3]

In his book *Luke Kelly, A Memoir* (1993 Attic Press/Basement Press), Des Geraghty recalls The Clancy Brothers turning up at a Fleadh [*Flah* - festival] in Co Clare: "They were a new sight for regular Fleadh-goers and had a dramatic impact on all of us - this family from Carrick-on-Suir, in their bainín jumpers, bringing a sense of polished entertainment to some very old worn songs."

"There is no doubt that the unexpected and enormous success of the Clancys fuelled a new professionalism among Irish musicians and gave a great impetus to the movement that was emerging; but of course there was also a lot of uncertainty about this commercial and obviously well-organized and rehearsed group back from America. They didn't fit either the old or the new stereotypes but they were clearly a force to be reckoned with. They had great stage presence and exuberance and were definitely going places."[5]

- Ronan Nolan, from his interview, *The Clancy Brothers and Tommy Makem*, 2002.

A bit of a different story: In Ireland, a Christmas tradition involved celebrating St. Stephen's Day in a unique way, going back generations. In the days leading up to Christmas, young boys would gather, find a big stick and then kill a small bird, called the Wren (*pron. Wran*). They would place the bird's body in a Holly Bush and then decorate the bush. On the day after Christmas, they would place the corpse into a box, get themselves all mussed up in the dirt and put on crazy bits of clothing. Going door to door, they would sing a song called *The Wren Song*, hoping to get a penny from the landlord, "for the funeral" of the wren. Multiple groups of boys would be doing this at the same time, often yielding a mad flurry of noise and shouting voices. The Clancy Brothers and Tommy Makem (certain "ethnic folk types," as they called themselves) tell this story with a bit of an ironic twist at the end, in their 1963 concert, *In Person at Carnegie Hall*, recorded live, on Columbia Records.

"On St. Stephen's Day, you'd hear all the different groups of Wren Boys, some of them singing as fast as they could, to get from one door to another, to get more money. But then there was always the *ethnic folk types*, who sang it slowly and deliberately. They never made any money, of course. [... after a long pause] But they ended up in Carnegie Hall."

The audience roared their approval.

Sean McGuinness, founder and leader of the Dublin City Ramblers: "The Clancy Brothers and Tommy Makem started it all. They took Irish Folk Music out of Ireland and made it known and loved throughout the world. And they did it with passion and charm, whoops and whistles and leg slapping spontaneity, their trademark Aran sweaters, and songs like Holy Ground, and The Irish Rover. Yet never compromising the integrity of the material. They were a huge influence to a whole generation of Irish musicians and singers and they showed us that to sing the songs of Ireland was something to be proud of. ...The story of the Clancy Brothers is the story of the ballad revival in America and the rebirth of ethnic folk music across three continents. If it wasn't for them, we wouldn't be performing all over the world, as we do now."[6]

Tommy left the group to go solo in 1969. The final show, as The Clancy Brothers & Tommy Makem, was in Sacramento, California that year. All members of the group felt that it was time to move on and that the breakup was final. "We were beginning to bog down back then. We needed to do other things,"[1] recalls Liam.

Paddy, Tom and Liam recruited Finbar and Eddie Furey, who would later be part of *the Furey Brothers*, along with their own brother, Bobby, to join the group for the next years tour, as well as two albums (*The Clancy Brothers Christmas* and *Flowers in the Valley*). From 1971 into 1976, Louis (Lou) Killen joined the Clancy Brothers. Tom Clancy decided to return to acting, so The Clancy Brothers only toured sporadically, with Liam working solo or touring as a duo with Lou Killen. The group continued as The Clancy Brothers until Liam went solo in 1976, moving to Canada, where he intended to retire.

But the pull of the stage wouldn't let Liam go. In Canada, Liam did a lot of acting, television, and a bit of singing too. He was based in Calgary, where he became an established television performer. Liam had his own series called *The Liam Clancy Show*, which won a Canadian

Emmy Award. Tommy Makem was a guest on Liam's show in 1976. That episode won *The Best Canadian Variety Show* of the year.

The success of the show and a chance meeting at a folk festival in Cleveland, Ohio, where they decided on the spot to go on stage together and do a few of their old songs, led to the duo deciding to reunite, as *Makem & Clancy*, ("we pulled the names out of a hat to see whose name would go first,") with the television show becoming *The Liam Clancy - Tommy Makem Show*. Makem & Clancy recorded several albums; including *We've Come A Long Way, Two For The Early Dew, Live at The National Concert Hall, In Person at Carnegie Hall, Sing Of The Sea, Tommy and Liam*, which went Gold, and the platinum selling *Tommy and Liam in Concert*.

They also won international recognition for their recordings of Peter Michael Smith's *The Dutchman* and Eric Bogle's *The Band Played Waltzing Matilda*.

Liam again went solo in 1988, until he eventually joined with his brothers and nephew, Robbie O'Connell, in 1990, as *The Clancy Brothers & Robbie O'Connell*. From 1996 to 1999, Liam joined with his son, Donal, and Robbie O'Connell, to form *Clancy, O'Connell & Clancy*.

"Working with Liam on stage is unbelievable," says Robbie O'Connell. "His stage presence is just so powerful, more so than anybody that I've ever been on stage with. He just kind of radiates it. It is phenomenal really to watch him. It is just so natural to him. If he was down at the local pub he couldn't contain himself, he had to sing, it just has to burst out of him somehow.

"We were doing some tracks on an album about the 1798 Rebellion, back in 1998, and we were doing it with the Irish Philharmonic Orchestra. We were recording in a big studio in Kildare, in Manooth. Liam was singing *The Croppy Boy*. These people were sitting around reading the newspaper, musicians, eating their lunch and such. Then Liam sang *Aghadoe*. When he finished there was just stunned silence for about ten seconds. Then all of the musicians, they all stood up, and they gave him a standing ovation. It was, it would give ya goose bumps! I had never seen anything like it.

"That was a moment in time, that's so rare, I'm sure those people probably never did anything like that. They were so, so moved by it, so, kind of overwhelmed by it. It was spectacular." - Robbie O'Connell, of *Clancy, O'Connell & Clancy, Green Fields of America* and *Moloney, O'Connell & Keane.*

Liam has also played with his own group, the *Fayerweather Band* and with the *Phil Coulter Orchestra.* He plays the guitar, bodhran and concertina.

The Clancy family musical legacy extends beyond just the Clancy Brothers. Paddy, Tom, Bobby and Liam Clancy are joined in that legacy by sister Peg Clancy Power, who sang in both English and Irish and recorded an album on the Folk Legacy label, nephew Robby O'Connell (son of Cait, *pron.* Cawth, Liam's sister), niece Aiofe Clancy (daughter of Bobby), son Donal Clancy, and many more – all successful in their own right.

Tom Clancy passed away in London in November 8, 1990. Paddy Clancy bought a farm and with his wife, Mary, raised Charolais and Simetal cattle for more than twenty years. He passed away in November 11th, 1998 of cancer.

Said Roanan Nolan, [There is a famous] "… RTE newsclip, showing the graveside ceremony as Liam and Bobby Clancy, Ronnie Drew, Finbar Furey and Paddy Reilly, accompanied by John Sheehan, sang the Parting Glass."[5]

Bobby passed away on September 6th, 2002.

"Liam was a folk song hero who became a friend. In the early sixties when sound amplification equipment was not as sophisticated as it is today, I saw him in the National Stadium, in Dublin in 1965, quiet down to a bare hush, a raucous, roaring crowd of two and a half thousand fans, and sing softly 'The Patriot Game.' It took great courage in those days to be quiet onstage in front of a Dublin audience." - Danny Doyle

Liam (Willie) Clancy was born on September 4th, 1935, on Williams Street in Carrick-on-Sur, County Tipperary, to Joanna (called Hannah) McGrath and Robert Joseph Clancy. Both parents were singers and reciters, and met at a hooley around 1910. Hanna had a relative living in Arlington, outside of Boston, who owned a boarding house and had a housemaid job held for her. She went to America to make money to pay for Robert to come over but not too long after, the Titanic sank. Robert wrote for the extremely homesick Hannah to come home. She gladly did and they married in 1913, in Ireland.

Willie was named after his mother's hero, Fr. Willie Doyle, a chaplain of the First World War Willie became Liam when during a walk-on part in *The Playboy of the Western World,* with Cyril Cusack and Soibhan McKenna, in 1954, Cusack asked his name. When told Willie, replied that it was a very English sounding name: "From now on, on this production, you'll be Liam. A good Irish name, Liam." And it stuck.[1] [Liam is Gaelic for Willie].

Liam is the youngest of the Clancy Brothers band and also the youngest of eleven children. Teasingly called "The shakins' of the bag," by his family, he was born to his mother when she was forty-seven years old. Robert and Hannah's first child, Alice (called Lally), died at two years old of pneumonia. May, their second, died in 1936, at age twenty-one, after a poorly set ankle that she had twisted getting off a train in Dublin became infected with tuberculosis and gangrene. Liam was six months old at the time. Leish and Cait (twins) were followed by Paddy, Tom and another set of twins, Bobby and Joan. Then came Peg and finally, six years later, Willie.

The Clancy name has a long history of being Brehon lawyers and Bards, since medieval times. James Butler, the "White Earl," granted a tract of land called Cregg, outside Carrick-on-Suir, to a Donal Clancy in payment for his services as a lawyer who could interpret both the Norman and Brehon laws. This was in 1428. Donal's responsibilities were to act as intermediary between those within the Carrick walls, the Butlers and Powers, and those outside the walls, like Hannah

McGrath's family, generations previously. Five centuries later, Paddy Clancy, without even being aware of the history of Cregg, bought the land from the Anglo-Irish Beary family. In another twist of history's connection on the little island, Joan Clancy married a Butler and Peg Clancy married a Power."[1]

Times in Carrick-on-Suir, just outside of Slievenamon (*Sleeve nah mon* - Gaelic for *Mountain of the Women*, The mountain is a gorgeous green backdrop to the town), were typical of the times in all of Ireland. Things were not scarce but they weren't in open abundance either. Liam recalls his time in elementary school with his typical humor, laced with a touch of nostalgia: "We brought our own lunch to the school yard, hot milk in a bottle with a cork wrapped in greased paper to make it tight and bread thickly spread with beaded, salty country butter and a sprinkling of course sugar. The smell of warm milk always transports me to the little lean-to shed with its wooden bench where we had our lunch.

"My mother and her sisters had gone to the same school in their time, but the McGrath girls were brought up in a pub on Main Street and they were given ale instead of milk to take to school for lunch. Ale was cheaper and easier (and probably healthier, it didn't carry TB). The nuns couldn't figure out for a long time why the McGrath girls fell asleep on their desks after lunch. Finally, one of the nuns noticed the smell. "Oh My God! The child is drunk!" [1]

But soon the war had arrived, even in Carrick-on-Suir. Food was rationed and every family was issued the hated ration books (the very words bring on a flash of depression for Liam) with their stamps for sugar and tea, bread, butter and other basics.

"The people of the town started to experiment with all kinds of alternatives to tea. One substitute for the big tea leaves we had then was toasted carrot slivers. We had a cousin around the corner from William Street, Mrs. Walsh, a big, loud woman. I heard her calling her son Jack in for his 'tea' one evening when he was out playing on the street. 'Jack, come in here for your carrots!' she shouted. The saying caught on all around the town." [1]

The war eventually ended, and after being demobilized from the RAF, Paddy and Tom Clancy left Ireland, first immigrating to

Canada in 1947, then to Cleveland, Ohio. The Clancy's had an aunt in Cleveland, who sponsored Paddy and Tom into America. Among their employments were house painting and driving a taxi. Tom joined the Cleveland Playhouse for a spell, and then went to New York's Greenwich Village. Paddy followed and the two brothers, with Noel Behn, formed *Trio Productions* at the Cherry Lane Theatre, in New York, just as the Folk Revival was gaining some steam. It was difficult to make enough money to live on solely as an actor, so they rented out space for concerts, then earned more by promoting the concerts themselves. When Tom Clancy returned to Ireland, he carried the passion for acting with him. There he joined *Andrew MacMaster's* famous troupe and then joined *Shakespeareana Internationale*.

"Tom ferried back to us cargoes of wonderful tales of the goings-on in a touring 'fit-up' company of the dying days of the barnstorming Shakespeareans," said Liam [1]

Besides numerous television and off-Broadway appearances, Tom also starred in the Broadway Production of *A Moon for the Misbegotten*, alongside Jason Robards and Colleen Dewhurst.

Liam's father, Robert, was an opera aficionado and occasionally played the accordion. After working in a toffee factory, he started R.J. Clancy and Sons Insurance, with the hope that his sons would follow in his footsteps. "My mother was the quintessential Irish mother; she wanted a son a priest," [recalls Liam]. "All hope was gone for Paddy, Tom and Bobby; she had written them off as pagans. That left me." [1]

The reality of the world forced its way between Liam living out his dreams of being an actor, and actually needing to make a living. So, for a while, he worked with his sister Leish's husband, Lory Keily, delivering bread. "I loved the job with Lory; taking the hot yeasty rows of Carrick loaves from the ovens in the morning and loading them into the little Austin delivery van. The fresh crusts were so sharp we had to wear coats with long tweed sleeves, and even then our forearms were often cut and sore. But making deliveries was what I loved, to all the remote country shops and houses around the Comeraghs and Slievenamon and little townlands I'd heard of in my father's insurance office but had never been to. I felt at home with all the place-names: Crehana, Mothel, Rathgormack, Curraghballintlay, Ninemilehouse,

Faugheen, Mullinhone, Skough, Tullahought, Windgap. Big names for small places." [1]

But time moved on, and so did Liam. The last son of Robert Clancy felt some pressure to live up to the title on R.J. Clancy *and Sons* Insurance, which so far, had only R.J. Clancy. So he began a training program in Dublin with the Zurich Insurance Company, provider for his father's agency.

"As to the 'and Sons' my fate was decided for the time being. It suited me well enough to bide my time, avoid argument, even take up employment in the Zurich Insurance Company on Dawson Street in Dublin as a trainee insurance broker." [1]

Thank God that didn't stick.

The internal struggle of acting and living out his dreams against the reality of earning a wage and taking a place in R.J. Clancy & Sons Insurance continued for young Liam. He had an affinity and an affection for the theatre, but he also enjoyed painting and writing.

"Now that is the secret! Loving a song, or loving what you're doing –it's infectious,"[4] said Liam

This enthusiasm and passion for acting, especially the works of J.M. Synge, wouldn't loose its grip on Liam, and within his mind, they urged him to find some way to give outlet to them. Before he was twenty years old, Liam, his sister Peg, and Liam's former English teacher, Liam Hogan, began the *Carrick-on-Suir Dramatic Society*, in 1955. Despite his father's concern for Liam's future, Liam began a production of *The Playboy of the Western World*, produced, directed and starring Liam Clancy, as *Christy Mahon*. He also performed at the renowned Gaiety Theatre in Dublin.

"... It was a time for me of intense spiritual awakening. I had a deep baptismal immersion in the world of poetry, of ideas, music and writing as well as the joyous upwelling I experienced at the unfolding of the beauty of the world around me.

"All I wanted was to be on stage. Not because I was extroverted. In fact, the opposite! The stage was a place where I could hide behind makeup, behind a character. In character I could get away from being me, from the shyness, from wanting to fade into the wallpaper.

"The real magic for me was that I'd found a path that could lead me out the world of Willie Clancy's head into the great broad places where the inner, the nameless inner me, wanted to pitch my tent. Behind makeup and stage lighting, I could be anything I wanted.

[The success of the show was gratifying] "... But it was my father's reaction that most surprised and delighted me. He was aglow with pride. He seemed almost eager for me to pursue the career that he had scoffed at a short time before.

"When I left for America not long afterward, under circumstances I couldn't possibly have foreseen, all the bills for the production were paid and there was twenty pounds credit in the bank, a profit not to be sniffed at in those days. Peg Power and Liam Hogan started on a new production almost immediately. They even ended up buying their own theatre, the Brewery Lane Theatre. Both the Theatre and the Dramatic Society are still going strong forty-some years later." [1]

Those unforeseen circumstance were the arrival of Diane Guggenheim at his front door on Williams Street. "Meeting the Conlon family through her brought me to a love of the sean nós singing, to Joe Henry to Seamus Ennis, to Willie Clancy, the piper, people who were to become friends and teachers. She brought the Clancys and Makems together, then started the record company, Tradition Records, which would be the launching pad for Paddy, Tom, Tommy Makem and myself, as The Clancy Brothers & Tommy Makem." Diane introduced The Clancys to Josh White (Liam's favorite singer): ..."whose managers would guide us onto the world's stages." [1]

Diane spread her wealth, often without thought or reason. She and Liam toured all over the countryside as Liam fought an internal battle between immersing himself in music and the old stories, and trying to keep Diane's advances from ensnaring him.

Liam came to the U.S. in January, 1956. Diane paid his way and for a course in film at New York University. He tried several different back up jobs while he pursued acting, including stacking books at Harvard's Widener Library, working at a tree farm in Connecticut - for one week, and rowing a boat in Central Park. But then Diane arranged a job for him. Liam was hired as an assistant camera man, to learn film making.

"On the way up to ski country in North Conway in New Hampshire's White Mountains [where they were assigned to recreate a calendar of New England winters. In those days, it was cheaper to try to film a scene again than it was to purchase copy rights], we stopped off in Dover in Southern New Hampshire to visit Tommy Makem, who had come out there in December of 1955 and now lived with the Boyle family [his mother's brother and sisters].

"Tommy's Aunt Annie put on the tea for us and Tommy and I got into a huddle to talk about our common ambition, acting in New York. He had a job at the time in a printing works, and his plan was to save enough money to buy time in New York to break into theatrical work. It seemed to me that it could take a long time in Dover wages. But fate took a hand in things. Shortly after our get-together in Dover, Tommy's left hand was crushed in a printing press, severing all the tendons to his fingers. His job was finished, and it looked as if his days of playing the pipes and pennywhistle we're over too."[1]

Tommy eventually recovered and Liam began singing with his brothers at fund-raising events for the Cherry Lane Theatre and the Guthrie benefits. "When we returned to New York, Diane set in motion the plan she had been hatching ever since we took the Irish recordings back to America…. The name Tradition Records was quickly agreed on…. 'The Lark in the Morning' was the name of our first release. On it was the best of the material we had collected in Ireland…. We wanted Tradition to be a record label that would specialize in folk music but also open up to poetry and the spoken word… What we needed was a catalog."[1]

Soibhan McKenna was still in New York, after starring in G. B. Shaw's, *Saint Joan*. She agreed to record *The Countess Cathleen*, by W.B. Yeats. It was recorded at Town Hall, in New York in March, 1956. Others signed to Tradition Records included Josh White, Sr., Odetta (Odetta Felious Gordon, a fantastic singer of that time), Oscar Brand and Carolyn Hester.

Kenny Goldstein, a professor of folklore at Columbia University, suggested an album of Irish Rebel songs. Tommy Makem was in the midst of a series of surgeries to repair his hand and figured he could do that in New York as easily as in New Hampshire.

The Clancy Brothers & Tommy Makem began recording on the Guggenheim and Paddy Clancy "Tradition" label in the late 1950's. The quartet enjoyed great success during the 60's folk revival but actually got their beginning in New York's Greenwich Village, where the folk music revival was just kicking off in the late 1950's.

"There in the back room of the Whitehorse we took our first tentative steps at performing in front of a real, albeit drunk, audience. Out of that experience came the offer to sing at a benefit for Woodie Gutherie at the Circle in the Square Theatre. It was shortly after the [Woodie Gutherie] concert that I went to confession for the first time since leaving Ireland. Intimations of immortality perhaps.... I confessed to a big, beefy man whose accent and demeanor reminded me more of a banker than a priest. [I did my confession and penance and] I went to a barber and had a haircut. I had to shed something. I haven't been to confession from that day to this, nor to a barber. That day, I decided it was time to cut my own hair and tend to my own soul." [1]

When he left Ireland for the first time, in 1956, Liam had promised his mother that the time in America would only be six months. It was now almost a year since he had left to go to New York and take the film class. "The trip was now coming to an end. I was in love with it all; the land, the seasons, the amazing light, the people, the freedom. My mother was right. I had been seduced. The dark attic of my soul, with its dust collecting baggage of other generations, had its windows flung open and a giant fresh breath of sunlit air swept through it." [1]

[Just before Christmas, 1956] "Bobby had picked me up at the airport...He had obviously...gotten himself a girlfriend, judging by the smile on his face...It was one of those sharp clear frosty day you often get in Ireland just before Christmas, not a hint of a cloud in the winter blue of the sky and the filigree of bare hawthorn trees along the hedgerows etched against the low December light. [I arrived home after almost a year, what was supposed to be six months, to the door of the house] ... "my father clearing his throat and my mother biting her lip and holding back the tears. *'Oh Sha, Willieboy, You're home.'"*[1]

But Liam's time in Carrick could not last. For not only were things as his mother had predicted; he had been seduced, but other forces were demanding to be heard, within Liam as well. This inner sentiment, or passion for fulfillment in expression, is best expressed in the liner notes of *Liam Clancy* (Liam's first solo release, in 1965). Liam quotes Sean O'Casey, in his *Rose & Crown:*

"The chants of an odd bird, the lowing of cattle, the whistling of the wind, the patient patter of falling rain, the brave, meritorious tinkle of the Abbey Theatre orchestra, were all of the sweet sounds that the ear of Sean knew. Oh, and the folk-song, the folk-song, the gay and melancholy strains of the Irish folk-song, on fiddle, on harp, and on fife. And no folk-art is there but is born in the disregard of gain, and in the desire to add a newer beauty and a steadier charm to God's well-turned-out gifts to man; and so, out of the big love in his heart for all things comely and of good shape, the great poet Yeats exclaims:

"'Folk-art is indeed, the oldest of the aristocracies of thought, and because it refuses what is passing and trivial, the merely clever and pretty, as certainly as the vulgar and insincere, and because it has gathered unto itself the simplest and most unforgettable thoughts of the generations, it is the soil where all art is rooted.'"

Liam returned to the U.S. on March 24th, 1957. As the year went on, *The Rising of the Moon* was selling well. Paddy Clancy phoned Liam to suggest that they do an album of drinking songs. After a vacation home, Tommy Makem returned to the U. S. in March, 1958, and set about to find work as an actor.

" … Almost immediately after Tommy arrived, we started work on another album, this time a collection of drinking songs [which eventually was called *"Come Fill Your Glass With Us"*]. We rehearsed by day at Traditions office on Christopher Street and belted out the songs by night at the White Horse Tavern." [1]

"[Come Fill Your Glass with Us] was to be a turning point. We had never really thought of ourselves as a group before, but now the concept was starting to sink in….Friends of ours, Izzy Young and Tom Prendergast, had opened a folk club called the *Fifth Peg,* which had a free-for-all hootenanny every Monday night. Tommy Makem and I would get up and sing, trading solos initially, but as we got more songs together from the recording gigs, we also became more of a duo... Prendergast and Izzy offered us a singing gig at $125 a week each. It was a staggering amount, considering that an off-Broadway actor made only forty dollars. Needless to say, we jumped at it.

"Tom [Clancy] was playing on Broadway at the time, and on his nights off, he and Paddy would join us. This was the way, bit by bit; the group took shape, even though in our heads we were actors first and foremost. It would be a while yet before we'd face the fact that the money was in the singing business." [1]

Liam and his band mates signed to play a gig at *The Gate of Horn,* a popular live music location in Chicago. The owner called, "I need a name to put on the billboard. What are you going to call yourselves?" The thought had never occurred to the four guys just getting the idea of singing for a living into their heads. "A name for the group? Yes. We needed a name.

"[Upon arriving in Chicago], we still hadn't been able to come up with a name... When we arrived at the club, the decision had been made for us. The Marquee simply had on it, 'The Clancy Brothers and Tommy Makem.' Just like that." [1] The name of what was to become one of the most famous Irish performing groups of all time was decided, for them.

Recalling their start, Liam tells how things were received, "The reviewer for the *Chicago Sun-Times* commented the day after we opened, 'Three of the worst haircuts in show business opened at The Gate Horn last night, The Clancy Brothers. Their partner, Tommy Makem seems to have a better barber,'

Liam recalls, "Our opening song was 'O'Donnell Abu,' [*O'Donnell Onward*] a raucous, ballsy rebel song. This, we figured, would knock 'em dead, all twenty people in the audience. We were choked up with neckties and the sweat pouring off of us. But we stood up manfully and I struck a cord on the guitar. 'O'Donnell Abu' was supposed to be in the key of A. I had the capo on the wrong fret. I hit a D. Suddenly, we were four sopranos. I was going to try to bluff it out but Tom let us down. He stopped after the first line and turned to me. What a look! We all stopped.

"'You can keep goin' if you like but I'm not going to castrate myself singing in that fuckin' key!'

"That was the first, and the last, attempt we ever made at formality. Off came the coats. Up went the sleeves. Off came the ties, never again to go on. The audience fell about laughing; we suddenly realized how ridiculous it was trying to be serious and proceeded to re-create the atmosphere of the White Horse [Tavern, in Greenwich Village].[1]

The debut of The Clancy Brothers & Tommy Makem at Manhattan's most posh and prestigious nightclub, *the Blue Angel*, in 1959 was received in a much better way. But it was after a few more gigs at the Blue Angel that the Clancy's agents got the Ed Sullivan folks in to see them. After what would figuratively prove to be like opening a window to change the future, the Clancys and Tommy Makem took a giant leap. The folk music awakening, the deeply ingrained passions for both acting and singing that each of the boys struggled to master and succeed in, and the talent scouts for the Ed Sullivan show, all collided. After a show at the Blue Angel, the talent scouts asked the performers to join them for a few drinks.

"Guys, that was class. We'd love to have you on the Ed Sullivan Show,"[1] they told the Clancys and Tommy. History altering shows for the Clancys and Tommy Makem led to a history altering for Irish music -- and its ripple effect was felt worldwide. It still is.

These days, Liam is touring the Irish Theatre circuit with occasional forays to America for concerts and festivals. A documentary of his life is in the works as well as a written retrospective, as he enjoys his 70th year. The documentary is being made by *Crossing the Line Films,* with the financial help of the Irish Film Board and RTE. The first filming was done in Milwaukee. "We plan to retrace my steps through Ireland, New York, the Southern Appalachian Mountains and where ever else the story takes us. The plan is to make a start in the next couple of weeks and let the film grow organically."

Liam is an award winning author, actor (winning a Canadian Emmy for his own series), producer, director and, of course, performer. His planned two part autobiography/retrospective of his life is in fine form. The first, *The Mountain of the Women, Memoirs of an Irish Troubadour* was published in 2001 and the second, as mentioned, is in process. "The second book is in the works. It covers the CBTM [Clancy Brothers & Tommy Makem] heyday years, my years in Canada, where I had my own TV series, the Ballad Boom in Ireland, lots of anecdotes, snatches of philosophy and who knows what else. Right now I'm mostly doing my one-man show in theatres all round Ireland. I've limited my shows to two a week so I don't burn out again as I did in the Makem and Clancy era," recounts Liam.

But Liam still keeps very busy. He runs his own recording studio, designed by Irish architect Duncan Stewart. This eco-friendly seven-acre solar powered complex is attached to his home overlooking Dungarvin Bay, in Ring, Co. Waterford. Such notables as *The Chieftains* and *Joanie Madden* have recorded there.

Liam's influences are varied and include: Pete Seeger, Dylan Thomas, W.B. Yeats, Patrick Kavanagh and Shakespeare. "Bob Dylan has said that he had learned much from the Clancys, and was a frequent visitor at Clancy performances where he heard them sing Dominic Behan's *Patriot Game*. He borrowed this tune and added his own lyrics for his song *With God on Our Side*. Behan was furious but, ironically, the melody is of American origin.[5]

In the early 1960's, while still a young man scurrying about Greenwich Village, Dylan was heard to proclaim, "I'm going to be as big as the Clancy's." The Clancy Brothers performed at Bob Dylan's 30th Anniversary concert at Madison Square Garden in 1992. Liam will also appear in Dylan's film biography, *No Direction Home*, which is in post production for PBS and BBC. It is directed by Martin Scorsese.

"I'll never forget the night we were playing for Bob Dylan's anniversary in the music business at Tommy Makems' Irish Pavilion in New York City," Cherish the Ladies' Joanie Madden recalls. "I think it was a great nod to the impact of the Clancy Brothers & Tommy Makem on Dylan's musical development and career that he invited them to partake in the show at Madison Square Garden and then follow it up with the after party at Tommy's restaurant. Needless to say it was the who's who of the music business....George Harrison, Joe Cocker, Emmy Lou Harris, Eric Clapton, Kris Kristofferson, members of the Rolling Stones, Nancy Griffith, etcetera. And there was Dylan, roped off in a little corner of the place.

"Anyway, of all those stars in the place - he asked for Liam and the two of them talked for hours in the little roped off area. I was then sent for and he told me that Liam is the greatest ballad singer he ever heard. I agree with him."

Liam and wife Kim have four children; Eben (a video editor with the BBC in London), Fiona, Donal (as mentioned above as well as singing with *Solas* before leaving to tour with *Danu*) and Soibhan, (married to *sean nos* singer Cartagh McGrath – they have two daughters Alilidh and Mein). Liam also has one daughter, Anya, from a previous marriage.

"Liam - well, there's not much you can say about himself. Liam and his brothers and Tommy Makem, they threw a bash in the world of music. They started the whole thing off. I always maintain, that when we sing, *The Rare 'Ould Times*, *Mountain Dew*, or a couple of those songs, I always dedicate it to them, to the Clancy Brothers and Tommy Makem. If it wasn't for them, I honestly don't believe I would be where I am today. I could be sitting, still, repairing telephones.

"He is [Liam] similar to Johnny [McEvoy] in that Liam would sit on a stool and hold the audience, completely enthralled, for two hours. Whole monologues and stories, very natural stories, things that actually happened." - Sean McGuinness, Dublin City Ramblers.

Liam, Paddy Reilly and Luke Kelly are recognized as the best balladeers to ever sing a song. It is all in the presentation - and the honesty. When Luke passed away in 1984 of a brain tumor, the Irish ballad tradition lost a great singer and songwriter, long, long before his time. Liam was asked to do a tribute at an anniversary of Luke's death. He was out on the road at the time and could not attend but he wrote a tribute to Luke anyway and sent it on for one of the other fellas to read at Luke's graveside. It went like this:

Lukey

by Liam Clancy

Luke – How glad I am that our paths crossed
in that brief window of consciousness
that is given to us between the two great mysteries.

You came into my life through a window – the men's room window –
in the Central Hotel at the Fleadh in Miltown Malbay back in 1964.
They wouldn't let you in the front door
because they said 'twas after hours and you weren't a resident –
but it was really because they didn't want a
Dublin Jackeen upsetting their session.

Willie Clancy was there, in the parlour, and Jimmy Ward and
the great Seamus Ennis who shares this piece
of ground with you now forever.

You startled us all that night when you sang.
You were no self-effacing rustic
waiting to be coaxed to sing soft sad love songs.
You were as strident as a street in Crickelwood,
as brash as a Dublin hackney driver
and you took delight in what you sang.

Joy and anger mixed in a powerful blend –
that was your hallmark – then as always –
joy in the act of singing – anger in the words that spoke of injustice.
You came from the mold of the great commune-ists
who knew that it was right to rail against
the tyranny of class and privilege.

Look at us now Luke, here in this cemetery,
a small huddle of the living, amidst a vast throng of the generations
that marched through before us and, coming fast behind,
the generations waiting to be born.

So what signifies? What signifies is that you fulfilled your destiny –
that you did not stint in the giving of the
talent that was uniquely yours.
Had you been a blade of grass
you would have been very green and very tall and very pointed –
because all things must be what they are to their fullness.

Since we laid you down here – how many years ago? –
you have been joined in the long silence
by so many of those we knew –
by Kieran Burke and Seamus Ennis
and Joe Heaney and Willie Clancy –
and by my own brothers Tom, Paddy and Bobby.

But are ye really silenced? No, No and never will be.
It's all preserved isn't it – in reality as well as in memory.
And when in the future there are those who want to hear,
not the froth of fashion in the pop song of the month,
but the timeless vision of the true story told,
they will listen to you Lukey – you and your likes, if there are such.

And even though we understand all this with our heads,
we still lament that you will, as the song says –
no nay never – never no more –
will you play the wild rover
–no never no more.

One last Liam Clancy story;
"Well, you know, I once got myself into a very dangerous situation one night at an Irish festival. We had a crowd out on the street – millions of dancers – the pubs were all closed – and this other fellow and I started singing, started out down the street, and everybody joined in, and they all followed us, because they figured we knew what we were doing, and where we were going. And by the time we got to the other end of town, we had an army! We tried to stop them, and there was no way, and I could see that it was getting a bit dangerous. Somebody got hit on the side of the head by the skin of an orange – it was a small thing, but it

could get sour in a minute. And I knew we had to get back to the hotel, which had big iron gates in front of it.

"So we started into the songs again, and got back into the mood one more time. And by the time we got back to the hotel gates there were several hundred people following us. I tried to get through the gates – the old Brown Hotel in Ennis – they would have torn the gates out of the cement, if I had gone in there then and they couldn't get in after me. I thought, 'What in the name of God am I going to do?'

"So what I did was, I stood up on the wall, and very quietly I started singing, 'The Parting Glass.' Slowly, bit by bit, the audience – it was an audience by now – all started joining in. And some people carried it, and, at the end of the song, I was able to step off the wall, slip in through the gates, and the crowd quietly dispersed."[4]

"Liam Clancy is the luckiest man I know," said Tommy Makem's wife Mary, "If he fell off the Empire State Building, there would be a truckload of mattresses going by."[7]

Liam Clancy, one of Ireland's, one of the world's, greatest balladeers, exemplifies, with passion and humor, all the beauty, inspiration, emotion and history of Irish song and story. Whether in prose, poetry or ballad, Liam's body of work stands as a beacon. There is none better.

Liam Clancy Discography:

(Memories and "approximate" dates, re-releases, often under different names and/or covers, and lost information – this list is as good as I could make it, despite the unknown redundancies and re releases.)

The Clancy Brothers & Tommy Makem:
CD's and LP's:

- The Rising of the Moon (two different jackets, Also called *Irish Songs of Rebellion*) (1956, 1998)
- Come Fill Your Glass with Us (Also called *Irish Drinking Songs* and *Irish Songs of Drinking and Blackguarding*) (1959, 1998)
- The Clancy Brothers and Tommy Makem (1961, 1996)
- Spontaneous Performance (**O**ut **O**f **P**rint) (1961)
- Hearty & Hellish (1962)
- The Boys Won't Leave the Girls Alone (OOP) (1962)
- Super Hits (re released in 1963, '64, '66, '69, '97, 2000) (1962)
- In Person at Carnegie Hall (1963, 1992, 1997)
- BBC Concert (1964)
- The First Hurrah   (OOP) (1964)
- Recorded Live in Ireland   (OOP) (1965)
- Isn't it Grand Boys   (OOP) (1966)
- The Irish Uprising/ 1916 - 1922   (OOP)   (2 different labels) (1966)
- Songs of Ireland and Beyond (1966, 1997)
- Freedom's Sons   (OOP) (1967)
- In Concert (1967, 1992, 1997)
- Home Boys Home   (OOP) (1968)
- Sing of the Sea   (OOP) (1969)
- The Bold Fenian Men   (OOP) (1969)
- Irish Folk Airs; The Clancy Brothers & Tommy Makem and Their Families (also called The Clancy Brothers & Tommy

  Makem With Their Families or Irish Folk Songs & Airs) (2
  different Jackets)   (1969, 1992)
- Flowers in the Valley   (OOP)   (1970)
- Green In the Green   (1971)
- I'm A Freeborn Man   (1972, 1989)
- Greatest Irish Hits   (1973)
- Seriously Speaking   (1975)
- Every Day   (1976)
- Reunion   (1984)
- Luck of The Irish   (1992)
- Irish Drinking Songs   (1993)
- The Best of The Clancy Brothers and Tommy
  Makem   (1994, 2002)
- Ain't It Grand Boys   (1995)
- Home to Ireland; 28 Irish Favorites   (1996)
- 28 Irish Pub Songs, The Clancy Brothers & Tommy
  Makem   (1996)
- Irish Revolutionary Songs   (1999)
- An Essential Collection   (circa 2000)

Other titles, year released unknown: May be compilations

- Welcome to Our House
- Show Me the Way
- Save the Land
- Live on St. Patrick's Day
- Clancy Brothers and Tommy Makem (4 Box LP Set)
- From Ireland with Love
- The Clancy Brothers and Tommy Makem
- The Best of the Clancy Brothers and Tommy Makem
- So Early in the Morning
- Presenting The Clancy Brothers and Tommy Makem
- Fine Boys You Are (two different titles and jackets)
- At Home with The Clancy Brothers and Tommy
  Makem & Their Families (also called At Home
  with The Clancy Brothers, Their Families &
  Tommy Makem, 2 different jackets)

- Celtic Classic Treasures: The Clancy Brothers and Tommy Makem and Friends
- The Clancy Brothers and Tommy Makem (3 different labels)
- Boolavogue
- Wrap the Green Flag
- Tunes & Tales of Ireland
- In The Dark Green Wood (NOT the same as "In the Dark Green Woods")
- Farewell to Nova Scotia
- Shine on Brighter
- Collection
- Pete Seeger's Rainbow Quest; The Clancy Brothers and Tommy Makem w/ Tom Paxton and Mamou Cajun Band

EP's/45's:

- Songs From the Irish Uprising
- In Person
- The Clancy Brothers & Tommy Makem No. 1
- The Clancy Brothers and Tommy Makem No. 2
- The Moonshiner
- Irish Rover/Brennan on the Moor
- The Whistling Gypsy & The Moonshiner
- Tim Finnegan/Reilly's Daughter
- Wild Rover/Weela Wallia
- The Rising of the Moon/Young Cassidy
- Isn't It Grand Boys & Nancy Whiskey
- The Good Ship Calibar & The Lowlands Low
- Jennifer Gentle and Beer, Beer, Beer
- The Rising of the Moon/The Wild Rover
- The Rising of the Moon/Green In the Green
- O'Donnell Abu/Freedom's Sons
- Green in the Green/Isn't It Grand Boys
- You're Always Welcome to Our House/ Time Gentleman, Time
- Streets of London/Dandelion Wine

- Finnegan's Wake/The Wild Colonial Boy
- Irish Rover/Courtin' in the Kitchen
- Jug of This/Johnny McEldoo
- Whiskey You're the Devil/Mountain Dew
- When I Was Single/God Bless England
- The Rising of the Moon/Mr. Moses Ri-Toora-I -Ay
- Bring Home the Oil
- The Band Played Waltzing Matilda/The Town of Rostrevor
- Four Green Fields/Mary Ellen Carter

Cassettes:

- Wrap the Green Flag
- Irish Drinking Songs
- Greatest Irish Hits
- Older But No Wiser
- It's About Time
- Isn't It Grand Boys
- Tunes and Tales of Ireland
- Songs of Ireland and Beyond
- Best of the Vanguard Years
- Tiananmen Square
- Four Green Fields/Come by the Hills
- Waltzing with Bears/Courtin' in the Kitchen
- Vancouver/Better Times
- In the Dark Green Woods/My Father
  Loves Nikita Khrushchev
- Irish Piping and Tin Whistle Songs
- The Song Tradition
- Shine on Brighter

Makem & Clancy:
CD's and LP's:

• Makem & Clancy	(1976)
• The Makem & Clancy Concert	(1977)
• Two For the Early Dew	(1978, 1992)
• The Makem and Clancy Collection	(1980, 1992)

- Live At the National Concert Hall (1983, 1991)
- We've Come a Long Way (1986)
- Tommy Makem & Liam Clancy (1987)
- Makem & Clancy In Concert
- Tommy Makem & Liam Clancy
- In Person at Carnegie Hall
- Sing of the Sea

Singles:

- The Band Played Waltzing Matilda/Town Of Rostrevor & Maggie Pickens (1976)
- The Town Of Ballybay/Kitty From Baltimore (1977)
- The Dutchman/The Lowland Sea (1977)
- Red Is The Rose/Cruiscin Lan (1979)
- Morning Glory/Bower Madden (1979)
- The Garden Song/The Tombstone (1980)
- A Place In The Choir/Sliabh Gheal Gua Na Feile (1980)
- Waltzing Matilda/Red is the Rose (1981)
- The Ballad Of St. Anne's Reel/Sliabh Galleon Braes (1981)
- Rainbow Race/Dear Dark Eyes (1981)
- Dandelion Wine/We Are The Boat (1985)
- The Tale Of Bridie Murphy And The Kamikaize Pilot/The Newry Highwayman (1985)
- Four Green Fields/New Mary Ellen Carter

Liam Clancy:

- Liam Clancy (1965, 1989)
- The Dutchman (re release of Farewell to Tarawaithe (Yr unknown) (1993)
- Irish Troubadour (same songs as *Liam Clancy* but additional 9 tracks recorded the same day, previously unreleased, added to the original 14 tracks). (1999)

Clancy, O'Connell & Clancy:

- Clancy, O'Connell & Clancy (1998)

- Wild and Wasteful Ocean (2000)

Other Clancy Family Recordings:
The Clancy Brothers:

- Hootennany / Bar Harbor (1963)
- The Clancy Brother's Christmas (w/ Finbar and Eddie Furey) (1969)
- Flowers in the Valley (w/ Finbar and Eddie Furey) (2 different Jackets) (1970)
- Welcome to Our House (1970)
- Show Me the Way (1972)
- Save the Land (1972)
- Live on St. Patrick's Day (1972)
- Greatest Hits (1973)
- The Clancy Brothers Live (Tom, Pat and Bobby Clancy) (1982)
- Traditional Folk Songs (1993)
- Tunes & Tales of Ireland (1994)
- The Clancy Brothers & Dave Hammond (1996)
- The Clancy Brothers and Lou Killen
- The Clancy Brothers Greatest Hits
- Show Me The Way, (The Clancy Brothers) with Lou Killen
- The Best of the Clancy Brothers with Lou Killen
- The Best of The Clancy Brothers (1997)

The Clancy Brothers and Robbie O'Connell:

- The Clancy Brothers Live w/ Robbie O'Connell (1982, 1991)
- Tunes 'n' Tales of Ireland (1988)
- Older But No Wiser (1995)

Robbie O'Connell:

- Close to the Bone (1982)
- Love of the Land (1989)
- Never Learned to Dance (1992)
- Humorous Songs, Live (1998)

- All On A Christmas Morning (as Aengus, with Jimmy Keane) (1998)
- Recollections, Vol. I (1999)

Robbie O'Connell - as part of Moloney, O'Connell & Keane:

- There were Roses (w/ Liz Carroll) (1985)
- Kilkelly (1987)

Robbie O'Connell - as part of Green Fields of America

- Green Fields of America, Live (1989)

Aoife Clancy:

- It's About Time (1994)
- Soldiers and Dreams (1997)
- Cherish The Ladies with Aoife Clancy, Live (1997)
- Cherish The Ladies with Aoife Clancy, Threads of Time (1998)
- Silvery Moon (2002)

Donal Clancy:

- Donal has extensive recordings with *Solas* and with *Danu*

Others:

- The Lark in the Morning (Liam Clancy, Tommy Makem, Family and Friends) (1956)
- The Clancy Children, So Early in the Morning. Irish Children's Songs, Rhymes and Dance
- The Quiet Land (cassette by Bobby Clancy)
- Clancy Sing Along Songs (cassette by Bobby Clancy)
- Make Me a Cup (cassette by Bobby Clancy)
- Songs From Ireland (also called "Songs of Ireland" and "Traditional Songs of Ireland") by Peg and Bobby Clancy (3 different jackets)
- Good Times When Bobby Clancy Sings
- As We Roved Out by Peg & Bobby Clancy

- Down by the Glenside by Peg Clancy Power
- So Early In The Morning The Clancy
  Children,   (1962, re released, 1997)

Videos:
The Clancy Brothers & Tommy Makem:

- The Story of The Clancy Brothers and Tommy Makem
- Reunion Concert
- Bob Dylan 30th Anniversary Concert
- Farewell to Ireland
- Seeger with The Clancy Brothers and Tommy Makem
- Rainbow Quest

Liam Clancy:

- Liam Clancy In Close Vol. I
- Liam Clancy In Close, Vol. 2
- Kerry Gold, Irish Cheddar commercial by Liam Clancy

Books:
The Clancy Brothers and Tommy Makem:

- The Clancy Brothers and Tommy Makem Songbook

Liam Clancy:

- Liam Clancy, The Mountain of the Women. Memories of an
  Irish Troubadour,   (2001)

www.liamclancy.com

IV

Johnny McEvoy

"Ballads will never die out. People have been singing ballads since the beginning of time; ballads of the American Civil War, ballads of Irish Rebellion, going back hundreds and hundreds of years. The ancient man sang about hunting, and slaying animals. He told stories about the old people that lived before them and the happy hunting grounds and where they would go when they died. They sang of the battles and wars with the enemy. They sang and they told their stories in their tents and around their campfires. Ballads were there since time began, and will go on forever. - Johnny McEvoy

The legendary Johnny McEvoy has sung songs and thrilled audiences the world over for more than forty years. He started professionally in 1964, at age nineteen, with the folk explosion, moved into country music and then returned to live performances in the ballad tradition, his true love. He has guested on many television shows in the U.S. and in Europe and had his own shows on RTE, UTV, BBC Northern Ireland and UK Network TV. Johnny has given stunning performances in the Mecca's of the music world, including multiple performances in Albert Hall, London and Carnegie Hall, New York. He has so many trademark songs and, when you remember songs that you heard long ago, it was often Johnny's voice that you were singing along with.

"Johnny is all poetry, a fantastic character and songwriter. There is an album he has, called *All Our Wars Are Merry, All Our Songs Are Sad*. It's all monologue and poetry, a story leading into each song. I think

Johnny has very powerful songs, a lot of great songs over the years that he has written himself. Johnny's great with storytelling. He has a lovely voice, a haunting voice, a classic voice, to go with it. It's one of my favorite albums of all time, a beautiful album." - Sean McGuinness, Dublin City Ramblers.

Johnny Joseph McEvoy was born in Banagher, (*Ban ah her*) County Offaly, on April 24th, 1945, to County Galway parents Emily Ryan McEvoy, from Colmfert, and John (Jack) McEvoy, from Eyrcourt. He was born between two sisters, Marie and Emily, and has an older brother, Tom. Tom plays the accordion and sings locally in St. Louis, where he lives. Marie also lives in St. Louis.

"My first years at home were spent with my mother and my brother and sister. My older sister Marie was away. She had gone to America. I went to Convent School in Banagher, Co. Offaly. I have a very vivid memory of; I think I was about three years of age, I remember a fair in Banagher. The town was full of cattle, thousands of farmers. I remember, I had a very vivid memory of cows that looked like the size of elephants. And they were terrifying. I was absolutely terrified. They were huge because I was so small.

"I remember Banagher very well. I remember winters sliding down the street, streets with no cars, just horse and cart at the side of the street. Everybody walking, and people going to mass, walking up the town. Ice at the side of the road and snow. And lovely hot summer days, smell of tar on the road. Going to the bog, and playing in the hay. Going out to my grandmother's in Clonfert, in Galway, which was only about four miles away. Great memories of that time. I had a lovely childhood and I'm grateful for that.

"We left Banagher when I was six and I then went to the National School, in Milltown, Dublin. I played in a Pipe Band at that time, when I was in school. Started when I was eleven and left when I was fifteen - *Donnybrook Boy Scouts Pipe Band*, called the *Sacred Heart Unit Pipe Band*. My first band - a long time ago. It was great fun." Johnny and The Sacred Heart Unit Pipe Band were also in a movie, 1960's *The Big Birthday*, starring Barry Fitzgerald.

"My memories of home are like that of a fatherless house. I had no father living with us. Banagher was a very poor region. There was no work around the town so my father worked in Dublin. He worked for CIE, working on the buses. It was around 1947 and the company was just formed. So he was living away from home.

"He would come down on an odd weekend, or at Christmas, but only for a short time. So I never knew my father until I went to live in Dublin. That was part of the excitement of living in Dublin, in having my father there every day and every night. He had a great love of Irish music. He loved ceili music. Couldn't sing a note himself, never heard him sing in my life.

"It was a big house (in my mind only) in Clonskeagh, on the south side of the city. They were hard times, for my parents. We weren't well off. We were poor. [Then] my family came to live in Dublin. We had a two story house and electricity and a backyard. We had really come up in the world. Great memories.

"My father and I didn't get on very well when I was young, mainly because he hadn't lived at home for the first few years of my life and we didn't know each other. He worked a lot. He worked very hard. It was a bit difficult. He was very close to my brother. He was heartbroken when my brother went to America. He was inconsolable.

"At that time, going to America was like dying. You were never going to come back. My brother had gotten married, and he decided instead of buying a house here, he would use whatever money he had and buy a one-way ticket to the States, himself and his young bride. He took the deposit for the house and flew to America, going to St. Louis. My sister was a nun stationed there, and he's been there ever since. I see him in Cleveland when I play there. It's nice to meet him there, we reminisce and he can tell me things that I didn't know; about my mother, and father, and how hard things were in Banagher.

"My father lived at home when my brother was growing up. There's ten years between my brother and myself, there were twins born between us. They didn't survive childbirth, my mother was very ill for many years after that. So there was ten years of gap. He knew my brother better than he knew me. They had more in common.

"I was very much a loner, very much into reading books, drawing, sketching and painting, doing model aircraft building and that kind of thing. He never understood it. He thought I was wasting my time. He was a bit of a workaholic himself and he thought that reading books was idle work.

"It was hard on me, that I couldn't communicate with him during those years, the teenage years. And then it was too late. I started singing, because I had to develop, myself. I started to develop personally. I grew up into a man. I had become independent. I was earning money. I had a house. I was singing, performing, getting this adulation. I didn't need anybody else then. I was my own man. I was independent.

"It was only in later years, when I became famous, that we started to go out and have a drink together and talk, and when I got married and my children came along, it was only then that we became close. But by then, I suppose to a certain extent, that it was too late. We had missed the best years. I was shattered when he died. It took me along time to get over it."

"Back when I was going to school, during the whole Rock-n-Roll era, I was only into Rock-n-Roll to a certain extent. I liked Buddy Holly, the Everly Brothers. I was more into people like Woodie Guthrie, Ramblin' Jack Elliott and the Weavers. Everybody thought that I was crazy. But I love the word. And I loved the songs they sang. I loved the stories the songs told. So when someone like Bob Dylan came on the scene, I was knocked over. He was a guy, standing up on his own, singing his own songs. Nothing but a guitar and his own voice and a harmonica. He made the biggest impact on me, when he first came on the scene (1962), I was seventeen. Later on, when I branched out on my own, I used the harmonica myself, but I was singing Irish songs, up on the stage.

"It was the time of the Space Race and Kennedy and there was a big American thing happening at the time. The fact that Kennedy was Irish-American, good looking, Irish Catholic, the leader of the free world, mostly because he was Irish, I suppose. I remember when he visited Ireland. I remember him being driven down O'Connell Street in a big limousine, so tanned and healthy, larger than life. There was a very pro-American feel to the time, because so many of the people had relations in America. He was humble enough to come back to his native land and go down to Wexford, meet his own relations there. I'm sure he had other things on his mind. The Berlin Wall was only after going up. Things were set to pop in Germany and Russia."

The Space Program was in full flight with great pride, hard work - and President Kennedy's challenge to go to the moon. Johnny's interest in astronomy and watching for streaking satellites across the nighttime Irish sky was boosted by the reports of Alan Shepard's rocket to space and especially John Glenn, circling the earth. "I remember lying on the floor and listening to every moment of it on the radio. So proud of it, it was so exciting. The Russians were so secretive. The Americans wore everything on their sleeves. They were doing it not because it was easy, but because it was hard."

Even today, Johnny and the Irish American link stands strong. Johnny had a cousin trapped for five hours in the tower on September 11th and a nephew who worked on rescue for days after.

"My life is totally different than what I imagined it would be in school. I left school thinking I was going to become an advertising man. I wanted to get into advertising to become a commercial artist [graphic artist]. At the time I knew it was going to be very difficult to do that sort of thing in Ireland. Ireland in the 1960's, Ireland was only beginning to blossom, beginning to open up, and opportunities like that were few and far between. But that's what I wanted to do and that was my goal in life, to get into advertising and become a nine-to-fiver. Have a nice, secure job with the suit and the tie and the pencils in the pocket and going to the job and doing my job and coming home, loving the weekends free. Buy a car and drive off on the weekends and come home and watch TV, listen to the radio and smoke a pipe. That's what I thought I was going to be."

Music wise, Johnny was not involved in anything for a few years after leaving the pipe band and National School. But while enrolling at the Rathmines College of Commerce, in Rathmines, Dublin, as part of his plan to become a commercial artist, he met another ballad lover, Mick Crotty, from Waterford. Johnny was seventeen and working in the advertising agency at the time and the two got to talking.

"We discovered we liked the same music. We discovered that neither of us was into pop music. I loved the ballads. And then I discovered The Clancys, who were all the rage at the time, and I realized we had folk songs of our own, and they were Irish. I recognized a lot of these songs. I had heard them before, from my childhood, but I hadn't given them much thought. I heard the Clancy Brothers singing songs that I could sing.

"Mick Crotty used to some down to the house, after college, on a Tuesday night and we'd play records. I was after buying a couple of the Clancy Brothers albums. We played them and thought, 'this is really the thing for us.'

"We would go to the folk clubs around town, in the city center, clubs like the *Coffee Kitchen* and *The Old Triangle, Piper's Club, O'Donoghue's Pub*, famous old clubs in Dublin at the time. We used to go and listen to people like Luke Kelly, and Ronnie Drew, people who would come in off the street and sing their songs and we'd jot down the words to the songs, learn them and go home and sing them in my bedroom.

"I was very good at picking up a melody; I could learn a melody very quickly. I'd hear it once and I'd have it. We bought a guitar for £2. It was a lot of money; as much money as I was earning at the time. We learned the songs in my bedroom at home purely for our own pleasure, with no intention of doing them anywhere else, just to pass the time. We eventually started going to folk clubs ourselves and getting up and singing. There was a tradition in Dublin, in pubs, where people would go in and give their name to an emcee and he'd call out the name during the evening and you'd go up and do a song. You only got to sing one song, and then it was somebody else's turn.

"We used to go to a place called the *Ardmore Bar*, in Bray, in County Wicklow. We'd give our name and then we'd go up and sing. That was the first time we got up to sing in front of anybody. Then we'd go down to the bus station, and get the last bus home. We'd sit on the window ledge of the bus station and sing. It was about half past twelve and there was nobody around, the place was deserted, there was nobody on the bus and we used to sing on the back seat of the bus, with a guitar and a tin whistle.

"After doing that for a few months, we decided that we really weren't too bad. So we started to go to the folk clubs then and sing and we were surprised that people would ask us to sing particular songs that we used to do. One of the first gigs was a *Hootenanny Folk Session*, as they were called, a folk concert. It was in the Cinerama Theatre in Dublin, about 1963 [The Cinerama was a movie theatre occasionally converted for use as a concert hall]. I was working in an advertising agency and I was doing the ads for this concert. The promoter asked me did I know anyone who would go on in the first half and do half an hour. There was no money in it. I said 'I'm your man, I'll do it.'

"The two of us went on, as brazen as could be. It was the biggest crowd we had ever played to, about 1,200 people. We went on the first half of the show and we strolled on with our guitars, and I sang a song on my own, the first solo song I ever sang. It went great, it went down very well. It was a treat!

"And that was where I first got the bug. I never got such a kick in all my life. I was bitten on that night. I never felt anything like it. That's when I knew that this was the road I wanted to take. When I eventually left my job, I didn't tell my father for four weeks. My father would never have approved of singing for a living. He would never have approved. It was hard enough to get him to approve of me as a commercial artist, let alone a singer."

But sustaining success in the field when the field is saturated is a difficult task, until Johnny got a break. "My first television appearance, I was - terrified, frightened to death. It was July, 1963, on the RTE television program called *Ballad Session*. It was the only television station in Ireland at the time, so everyone was watching. It was very powerful. We hadn't been singing very long together, Mick and me. We were asked to appear on this television show, with Bobby Clancy, the Dubliners, and a few others. 'Course we thought we were made [had made the big time]. That stands out in my mind because of the terror - the sheer terror - of being on live television. So I've hated live television ever since. Live television terrifies me but I love live stage performances. RTE have it in their archives. I've seen it a few times since."

With a laugh Johnny recounts, "That was the beginning of the *Ramblers Two*, we had to get a name, for the television show. It was not very original, but the best we could come up with."

"We eventually got a permanent residency in the *Abbey Tavern*, out in Howth, the north side of the city. I got a phone call one day; to see would I fill in for *The Wolftones*, at the Abbey Tavern, which was one of the top ballad houses in the city. All the coaches [tour buses] used to go there; you had an international audience, Irish, Americans, English. It was *the* place to get into because it offered you regular work.

"We stood in for the Wolftones and Minnie Scott Lennon, who owned the place; she asked me would we like to do it full time. We played there maybe three, four nights a week. It worked as sort of a co-op, where all the musicians who played would take whatever came in at the door and divide it up amongst themselves. There was no star system. No matter who you were or how good you were, you got the same as the guy who was playing the spoons, or the guy who was singing on his own or playing the fiddle or the banjo. This was a bit before the bodhran, there was no bodhran then.

"We sang from about half past eight to about half past eleven. We were there up until 1966. We were doing well. We had that three, four nights a week and then we were working the folk clubs in Dublin. We also had a residency at *The Embankment* out in Tallaght. We were doing very well, working six or seven nights a week. We found our selves, and turned professional."

This was early 1964; Johnny was 18 and about to celebrate his 19th birthday, with a party there at the Abbey. "We were better than we thought. I used to sing the song and Mick would sing the harmonies. We had two guitars and a tin whistle and mouth organ. We were pretty serious about it, very professional. We went to all the folk clubs and sang and rehearsed. While we were at the Abbey Tavern, we did all the folk clubs in England. We did some tours, of England, especially in the north of England, around the Leeds area, Bradford, Halifax, Lancaster, Liverpool, Manchester, Newcastle, all around that area, all the way down to London. We played at the *Troubadour* down in London, about a week after [Bob] Dylan was there and about two weeks after Paul Simon was there. So it was a top club in London to play in.

"We were spotted there by an agent and he arranged an audition for us with Pye Records. The song we auditioned with was *The Merry Ploughboy*, a song about the IRA, and we got the audition. So they brought us over about three weeks later and we recorded a song called *Today Is the Highway*, which was a contemporary folk song. It wasn't the type of song we were singing, which was a mistake. It never did any good because the situation in Ireland was that anybody who wanted to have a record played on the radio in Ireland, you had to record at Eamon Andrews Studios. It was the only way of getting your record played, on radio. We had broken the rules. We had gone to England and recorded. So we didn't get played and our record died. It was too commercial, we sang with an orchestra. It didn't go over, especially in Ireland.

"That relationship with Mick lasted from age seventeen until I was about twenty-one (1966), and then we went our separate ways. Mick went with a group [to be] called the Dublin City Ramblers and I went off on my own."

Johnny had already served his apprenticeship in the Dublin ballad houses and city folk clubs by the end of his teen years. Mick went on to join with Sean McGuinness, Kevin Geraghty and Patsy Watchorn, forming the Dublin City Ramblers. Mick also originated the name, *Dublin City Ramblers*, when the four founding members joined together to form that group. The Ballad Boom was in full swing, The Clancy Brothers & Tommy Makem were creating noise, and Johnny was in perfect position to grab the opportunity presented.

"The pipe band and Ramblers Two were the only musical introduction I got. Apart from my own, I didn't play in any other bands. I worked on my own from '66 on. I traveled all over Ireland and England. I toured America on my own with just the guitar and the harmonica."

"Mick and I sang together up until Easter of 1966. I was beginning to get itchy feet. I wanted to go on my own, take my own road. He was not as ambitious as I was. I wanted to go to the top, I wanted to go right to the top, and the only way to do that was to get a hit record. We just sort of drifted apart. We remain friends, there was no disagreement. We just sort of drifted apart. Each of us continued to play at the Abbey Tavern, I on my own and he was with one of the other groups that played there.

"It was put to me by Minnie Scott Lennon that if I didn't get my haircut, I needn't come back. I had a Beatles haircut. That was a very dangerous thing to say to somebody of those years of age. I said, 'I'm not cutting my hair Minnie, I'm leaving it as it is.' So I lost my job. So I went out on my own, I was going around Dublin, doing ok playing the folk clubs in Dublin."

The apprenticeship that all performers with staying power go through was now in full swing for Johnny. But he was about to receive a helping hand to get over the hump on the learning curve. "I was spotted by an agent and asked would I appear on a summer variety show which was going on at the Gaiety Theatre in Dublin, in the summer of '66, a program called *Gaels of Laughter*, run by and starring Maureen Potter."

Maureen Potter, called *The Queen of Irish Comedy*, was the preeminent comedienne in Ireland. She starred in Gaels of Laughter for an unbelievable eighteen consecutive seasons and also appeared in more than fifty pantomimes at the Gaiety Theatre.

Johnny continued, "I was terrified for the first night but after that I was fine. It changed my life. Up to that time, I was only going around singing in pubs. I was only another ballad singer. Now I was taken from that and brought into the theatre. I was working with professional theatre people, like Danny Cummins, Milo O'Shea, Maureen Potter, John Molloy, people like that, who were prominent national performers. I learned an awful lot from them.

"It was a big break for me and it changed my outlook on the business completely. It was a defining moment. They became friends, they didn't act the star. After the show, we would all go up to the pub and unwind. I learned so much from these people, stagecraft, the importance of being on time, at the theatre for make up, and to be on your spot before the curtain came back. And I learned the importance of playing to the whole audience. So that lasted about sixteen weeks. I had great experience from it. I was also playing the ballad sessions out at The Embankment, so I was working seven nights a week, I was doing fine.

"When the run finished, I was approached by Pye Ireland to go into the studio and record a couple of songs. I was in my bedroom at home, going through every song I knew. I didn't know which way to turn. But my mother was outside the room in the kitchen and she heard me sing *Muirsheen Durkin*. And she came into the room, which she would never do.

"She said, 'That's a good song, you should try and do that one.' So I took her at her word and I went in the next day and recorded Muirsheen Durkin and a song called *Those Brown Eyes*, a Woodie Guthrie song. It was all over in about half an hour. All I used was my guitar and harmonica. I went away and forgot all about it. About six weeks later, I got a call from John Woods, from Pye Ireland to come into the office, and he said, 'Listen to this, you've got a hit on your hands.'

"I didn't believe that for a second, until it came out and I saw it go to #1 on the charts."

At twenty-one years old, Johnny achieved instant fame with his 1966 hit record *Muirsheen Durkin*, the biggest selling Irish recording at the time. Muirsheen Durkin earned Johnny a *Silver Disc*, the first ever presented to an Irish artist. He had first heard the song at a local club, took note of the words and then hit #1 with his recording of it less than a year later with the singles release. This led to tours in America, the UK, Germany, Holland, Belgium and Canada. Johnny is one of the first Irish artists to tour the Gulf States.

He also had three other #1 hits; *Boston Burglar, Nora* (A poem written by Sean O'Casey for his play *Plough and Stars*, set to the tune, *Maggie*) and *Long Before Your Time*; Johnny's own composition about a father explaining the passing of his wife to their own child.

Johnny recalls when Muirsheen Durkin reached #1 on the Irish Top 20, hosted by Brendan Balfe, on Radio Eireann. It was one of the biggest moments of his life. The song debuted at number three the week before.

"The night that happened, I was sitting at home with my parents and my sister and we listened to the charts [on the radio]. The Beach Boys song, *Good Vibrations* had been #1 the week before and when they announced it as the number two song for the week, the tension rose. It came on 'Number 1, the boy from Banagher, John McEvoy, singing Muirsheen Durkin.' I wasn't even called Johnny at the time.

"I knew that that was going to change my life completely, and it did. Within the space of two weeks, I went from singing to forty to fifty people a night, to two thousand and three thousand, and that was mind boggling, for myself as well. But I managed; I coped with it all right.

"My parents were over the moon. My father didn't believe it had happened at all. Never saw it happening in the first place. [Now], he never got in my way, he didn't try to stop me, but he didn't understand what I was doing. The plan was that I was going to give singing professionally a few months to see how it would go, see if I got anything out of it, and if I could make a living out of it and if not, then go to America and join my brother in the States. That was the plan.

"But they were all over the moon when the announcement said that I was #1. My mother started crying. My sister started to cry. My father was speechless. And I got up and got a taxi and went off and did a gig, in Clontarf Castle, that night, for much less money than I was earning a week later!

"That was a very big moment. It changed me mentally, as well. It changed my outlook on my life because my life changed. I was getting fan mail from all over the country. I was getting sacks and sacks of mail. It was impossible to read them all. I had a fan club and someone used to open every single letter and reply to them but it was unbelievable.

"I was having screaming kids, screaming in front of me while I was on stage, tearing my hair, tearing my jacket. It was Beatlemania for the best part of three or four years. That was hectic - way out of this world all together. I doubt if any of them heard a word I sang.

"I used to have to get bodyguards to bring me up on stage, to bring me down off the stage and to guard the dressing room, to lead me to my car and to drive away as fast as we could because I was mobbed, not just by girls, but young fellas as well. That was happening every night, all over the country. I traveled something like 400,000 miles in about three years. Literally from Donegal to Cork, Galway to Dublin. And all over Ireland, screaming teenagers. I was a pop idol and all I was singing were ballads; I wasn't singing anything pop!

"The showband would go off the stage and I would go on in the Ballroom and there would be two thousand and three thousand people in the ballroom and jammed to the doors. You couldn't get near the place, and screaming - you couldn't hear the singing. I'd go through a forty-five minute program and nobody heard a word I sang, because of the screaming. It seems like a dream now, but it was a nightmare when I look back on it. But it did happen, and it happened big.

"It lasted up until I started the band and that was the beginning of the end of the screaming adulation. The band had stopped the screaming. The scene had changed anyway. The Beatlemania had passed, there were no more stars like that. It lasted for four years. Four years of playing before screaming audiences, who didn't hear a word I sang. Then I started the band and it continued for about a year, then the screaming died out. The scene had changed. People started to resent the interruption to the dancing."

At that time, in the mid and late 1960's, showbands played for an hour or so, with everyone dancing. Then the showband would leave the stage and guest singers; such as Johnny McEvoy, Johnny Cash, The Clancy Brothers, Tom Jones or The Everly Brothers, would come and do their guest spot, perform for an hour. People would just stop dancing and watch, before the showband returned to finish the night with dancing. But by 1970, people started to resent that interruption in the dancing. Dancing was the more popular activity and people no longer wanted to stop for the guest singer.

It was the end of the showband era and the birth of the Country and Western era in Ireland. There were over 500 ballrooms around Ireland at that time and Johnny had a young family to watch out for. If you wanted to work, you had to change with the times. He was looking for security, which playing six or seven night a week, in steady gigs, would give him. He started *Johnny McEvoy & His Country Band* in March, 1970, with seven other members in the band, composing of rhythm guitar, fiddle, base guitar, lead guitar, drums, piano and Johnny on guitar as well. The rehearsed for seven weeks, then hit the road. He performed country favorites along side his own hits, using an electric set up. His country album, *Johnny McEvoy Sings Hank Williams* (1976) is a highly prized collector's item and cherished by country and Irish music fans the world over.

"It was hard to get used to, a readjustment. It caused a lot of resentment in the band [because Johnny was drawing so much individual attention].

"My manager at the time, Tom Costello, suggested that I should forget about the ballads and start the country band, and I allowed myself to be talked into it, much to my regret, and my wife's too. It caused a lot of problems at home, she didn't like it. But I was looking for the security.

"From the first night, I knew that this was not what I wanted to do. I wasn't happy with it, and with that many members, with the noise of the band on stage, resentments from some members of the band [of Johnny's popularity from all the hit songs]."

When asked if the screaming would have continued if he hadn't started the band, Johnny hesitated, showing a little uncertainly at first, before expressing surely, "No, I think it was just a trend that was going on at the time. Not every artist was getting it but I used to go out and get a decent haircut and wear flashy clothes. I was unique in that I was the only one standing up on the stage on my own. Danny Doyle followed shortly after that - he was doing the same sort of thing. But I was getting screams and the adulation [because of the uniqueness of the performance, and the performer]. I was getting the attention that the Beatles were getting when they came to Ireland. It was very hard to keep your feet on the ground.

"I was lucky that I was surrounded by good people. I had met my wife to be. It was very hard on her and she was very steady and she kept my feet on the ground. I had close friends who also treated me as one of the gang, although, away from my friends, I was a loner as well. When I was young, up on stage, I was very much alone and before hand, before going on stage, used to be quite terrifying, and you hear the screaming and they used to take chunks of my hair, tearing jackets, and I'd lose watches and rings and bracelets, and things out of my pockets. It was crazy."

After about ten years, the music scene in Ireland changed again, going from American Country to Irish Country, Irish songs with a country flavor. Johnny drew a line and refused to perform this kind of music. Ten years of unhappiness was enough and he folded Johnny

McEvoy & His Country Band. Keeping a few musicians from the country band, Johnny turned to performing in the new cabaret style, which was drawing well in Ireland and was taking the place of the Country & Western and Irish Country Showbands, as well as the dance halls.

There was only one musicians union in Ireland at the time, the *Irish Federation of Musicians*. Band managers also owned many of the bands they represented and booked - they owned the name, hired the musicians and paid them. In a move so puzzling as to be unexplainable, these band managers, and the dance hall owners, were both members of the only union, the two sides that were doing business with each other, often in dispute, were in the same union.

The long neglected dance halls, whose owners enjoyed significant success for years, yet didn't update the dance halls with more modern conveniences and comforts, or even a coat of paint, were now paying the price for their parsimony. Broken glass, lack of heat and things like poor seating were the norm. The dance hall owners got the full brunt of a change in direction, as Ireland's entertainment dollars shifted away from the dance halls to a new wave sweeping Ireland, the cabaret. The dance halls had run their course and although the owners blamed the bands, their lack of any progress in a stagnated union and most importantly, the lack of even general upkeep and improvement of their halls, speeded their own demise.

Life in a country band can be like a bad country song, filled with loneliness, and for Johnny, the recurrence of the debilitating blackness that at times filled him completely when he was not on stage, returned. He was lost; missing his wife, Odette, and home, struggling with depression and fame, the unhappiness of performing in a way he did not like, and missing the day to day joys of seeing his children grow and develop. So this change from Country to Irish Country, and Johnny's refusal to accept it, turned out to be a blessing in disguise.

The dance halls often finished at two in the morning, while the cabarets were usually done by eleven thirty. The cabaret also offered more plush accommodations; from the front door to the bathroom, and from offering better food and drink to having warm and comfortable halls.

Performing less often, in a style much more to his liking and much better suited to his style of music, Johnny returned to his first love; ballads, and it opened new doors for Johnny. It also brought him more time with Odette and his two children.

The story of how Johnny met Odette goes back to 1967. Johnny met his future wife accidentally. "I was picking up my sister (Emily) at a hair dressing salon in Dublin. She was going to her first dinner dance and I was picking her up in the car. It was shortly after Boston Burglar was #1 and I was sort of celebrating. Odette was working in the reception, in the hair dressing salon. All I saw were her legs. I saw these long, golden legs. I said, 'Would you meet me for a drink after you finish work?' and she said 'No.' She turned me down straight away.

"My sister came out and I asked her to go back in and ask again. I said, 'If you go back in and ask her to come for a drink, and if she meets me for a drink, I'll pay for your hairdo.' So she went back in and asked her and she did agree to meet me then. We met in the Russell Hotel and we had a couple of drinks and we've been together ever since.

"Odette's an artist and she's going back to college. She paints in oils; impressionist, and she's a sculpturer too. She's got one of her works on exhibition at the Botanical Gardens at the moment. She's at that stage of her life where the family is all grown up and moved away. It's great. I have to listen to her talk about it all day long. It's a change for her having to listen to me talk about me all day long!

"Family life I find very important. I wouldn't survive in this business without my family. I am grateful. I've been married for thirty-five years. My brother Tom sings and plays the accordion. My daughter Alice is a great singer, but is not interested in doing it professionally. I recorded a song with her, on the album, *Going to California*, called, *When You Say Nothing At All*. She's an excellent singer but not interested in entertainment, performing, things like that. I am very pleased with that. I wouldn't like any of them to come into the business now. It's too difficult. So the family life is very important and I needed it. It keeps me sane; it's great to have the support of your family when things do go wrong.

"A major regret is when I had the band in the '70's. The group lasted for about ten years. I was away from home, family; six, seven nights a week for fifty weeks of the year. My manager at the time was a workaholic, and thought I was too.

"I was away for a lot of the time my children were growing up. My wife had to look after them. I missed a lot of good times with them. I deeply regret that. I should have paced myself better. I should have got less work, and more time at home. I regret, musically, forming that band [as well].

"I often wonder how it would have gone if I had just stayed on my own. Maybe I would have had more success, or maybe I would have gone to America, like Danny Doyle did. Who knows, I might have done that. I wasn't happy with the band in those ten years. I was singing material I wasn't happy with. I was performing in a way that I didn't like to perform. It was almost like a pop performance. I even stopped playing the guitar for a while, introduced a girl singer. It wasn't the image that I wanted. I didn't want to be one of many, being grouped among hundreds of other bands. But it gave me great security, at a time when my children were young, growing up.

"It was a lot of work and I was away a lot from home, for the best part of ten years. It was very stressful. I missed the growing up of my children. I regretted it musically as well. I wanted to be a ballad singer. I wasn't singing the music that I quite liked. So, eventually, at the end of that, I started doing ballads again."

"If I ruled the world, I would make everyone love ballads. I would make everybody love the folk music and the ballads, particularly the songs. I probably wouldn't be very popular. But that's the way it would have to be!" Johnny recounts with a smile.

"I don't like the way music is going. I'm not saying that as an older person but as a person who is in the business. I make my living in the business, in show business. I'm a performer and a singer and a musician and I know what's happening, I know what's going on. I don't like the changes; I don't think they're good. I think the last really good thing to happen was U2. There's no one come since to produce good lyrical music and good melodies. I like the Irish Celtic rock groups, its good music. They still tell stories. They are just ballads that are rocked up. It keeps young people interested in it. Later, Riverdance revitalized Irish dance, it had become very staid in some ways. Riverdance made it all come alive again.

"Ballads will never die out. People have been singing ballads since the beginning of time; ballads of the American Civil War, ballads of Irish Rebellion, going back hundreds and hundreds of years. The ancient man sang about hunting, and slaying animals. He told stories about the old people that lived before them and the happy hunting grounds and where they would go when they died. They sang of the battles and wars with the enemy. They sang and they told their stories in their tents and around their campfires. Ballads were there since time began, and will go on forever."

The ballad tradition has fallen steadily since the heyday of a balladeer singing in every bar, in the Ballad Boom era. From the days of over six hundred balladeers in Dublin alone, in the 1960's, there are now fewer than eight or ten successful ones in Ireland now and their primary platform for performing is in the U.S., with some touring in Australia, New Zealand and in smaller tours throughout Europe. There would be far less without the thriving festivals that generate new interest and followings for the performers.

This heartbreaking diminishing has roots in mistaking the passion for the music, and the stories, as a passion for rebellion. Johnny is equally passionate, and a little frustrated, in his review of the old ballad tradition. "Many start out with rebel songs. God Almighty, can we not get past it? Can we not do something besides rebel songs and hate and hate Britain and hate everyone else around it? Get on with it. They thought all they had to do was rock and be loud and rebellious all the time and sing rebel songs a lot. They soured it, turned people off to it. I'm convinced of that. You didn't have any feeling in the song. The good ones survived. Because it has thinned out, the standard is better.

"Good ones are Dublin City Ramblers, The Fureys, New Barleycorn. The New Barleycorn has worked hard at what they are doing. They rehearse the songs, the presentation; they are professionals. I have worked with them recently, on Phil Coulter's show [*Coulter & Company*, the annual ten-week summer replacement for the RTE's *Late Late Show*], they were excellent. We sang all the old songs, the traditional ballads, that we sang for years. They work hard at what they do and their hard work shows in great successes. Barleycorn is a prime example of a group, that when they dropped performing only rebel songs, to then performing the ballad, they took off again; they're a prime example of that."

"Love of the ballad, love of folk songs, got me into it. The Clancy Brothers coming onto the scene, and the Dubliners. A lot of the ballad tradition died out or became less popular because there were so many bad ballad groups playing. The fact that there are not a lot out there probably helps to keep me in it, to carry on the legacy.

"Besides that, there are two main reasons why I stay in it; one is, it's my living, my profession, and the other, is that I love it. They are both equal. I love the singing. I get a great kick out of it. I always feel a hundred percent better when I finish singing. I love the physical act of it. The physical act of standing up on stage and just performing; of just singing out, and getting something out of the system, it's great. An added bonus is if it's a song I've written myself. That is what keeps me in the business.

"There are very few writing in the style of Pete St. John, or Tommy Makem, or myself. There are very few writing in that style; the story song, the ballad song, simple ballad songs, power ballads. They're writing contemporary songs (that do not tell a story, and do not last). Tommy Makem has written songs, that if you didn't know he wrote them, you'd think that they were about a hundred years old, some of mine as well [The songs touch deep, they're timeless].

"I know it is a minority music, but it is very important, very powerful. It is the word. The word is handed down in song. Certainly our history of Ireland, we would have no history without the songs. And the same goes for America as well. The sad songs and stories of the Wild West, and songs and stories the gold rush, and the Civil War and such. No, they'll be around forever.

"If I wasn't a performer, I'd probably curl up and die, I would. The day will come where I'm going to have to. As long as my voice holds out and my health is still good, I don't see why I can't perform for a long time to come. It helps me a lot with the depression. If I wasn't performing I think I would be much more depressive. It's a great outlet. It doesn't cure it, it doesn't drive it away - it makes it a bit easier, for a few hours anyway. Makes me forget about it."

Johnny easily and almost matter-of-factly discusses his own struggles, especially in dealing with depression, with his usual disarming frankness and open honesty. This calm acceptance, combined with a steely will to stand tall and work to overcome it, as well as his active support of organizations and fund raising efforts to combat this illness, have earned him recognition and admiration from health professionals, colleagues and fans alike. Johnny has fought bipolar depression since he was a young boy.

It is not at all unusual to find people who are very successful in their fields struggling with depression. But the numbers jump significantly when the profession is one that is outside the normal, nine-to-five realm, especially in the performing and visual arts.

Johnny talked candidly about his daily, often debilitating battle with depression with Joe Jackson, in a 2003 *Sunday Independent* interview:

"Johnny's wife, Odette, often jokes about how she's 'married to two men.' She's actually referring to the huge, even cavernous, disparity between her husband's public image and his private self. On one hand there is the 'legendary' Johnny McEvoy who gets up on stage and sings, and on the other hand there is the man who recently spent three years deep in the blackest of shadows, surfacing only long enough to sing in public. Indeed, at one point Johnny's depressions nearly ended his marriage. And those tendencies were evident, in embryonic form, when he was a boy.

"'Kids suffer from depression, but that's ignored,' McEvoy recounted. 'I remember coming home from school and I'd sit on my father's armchair by the fire on a winter's evening and cry. My mother would ask, 'What's wrong?' and I'd tell her, 'I don't know, I just feel so sad.' And she'd say, 'It's only growing pains.' Or my dad would say, 'Do something, get off your arse and go out and play.' But that's all they'd say. Yet I believe that was the start of my depression, though I didn't know it at the time.

"'I absolutely loved music,' McEvoy enthuses. 'I used to listen to a Radio Luxembourg show called *Pete Seeger and the Weavers* and I'd be singing Burl Ives songs, folk stuff, from the start. But from the age of twelve my ambition was to be an artist, in advertising. Yet if I was drawing in the bedroom, my father would say, 'That's a waste of time.' And when I'd tell him I wanted to be an artist he'd say, 'Over my dead body. You're going to get a trade.'" [1]

Johnny's struggles with getting acceptance from his father continued well into his adult years.

Continuing on, Johnny talked about depression and the lowest point of all in his life. "The saddest day was the day I was diagnosed with Bipolar Depression. It was kind of a shock because I didn't know I had it. I knew something was wrong but I didn't know what it was. I thought I was different. I thought I was a bad person, intolerant, or I was becoming a bad person, with a bad temper, certainly very sad. I couldn't understand why I was feeling so sad all the time, I couldn't understand it. I was only seeing the negative in everything. I couldn't see the beauty in anything. There was just a terrible feeling of gloom, doom and utter, utter sadness, that I couldn't put my finger on, on what would make me so sad? And yet I could walk onto stage and perform. The only way it affected me on stage was that it would make me very nervous. But I didn't realize something was causing it."

Johnny's father was suffering from cancer at the time and passed away. Johnny attributed some of the way he was feeling to this. But his boyhood sadness, which he seemed to have gotten past, for a while, now was back and Johnny knew that something deeper was gone wrong, within his mind.

Odette was leaving, with the children, on a vacation to see her sister, and to get some time away from "the shadow" as she called her husband. She told Johnny that he that he had to get help, now. The stark ultimatum, of get help - or else, got Johnny to phone a doctor and the words of the doctor got Johnny to go in to see him. The doctor immediately saw patterns in Johnny's behavior and warned him of the combined effects of drink and depression, as well as the after effects, that matched Johnny's own experiences.

"When I was told what it was, I got very sad, mainly because I was very depressed at the time, feeling sad anyway [and then this was added]. I was feeling overwhelmed. There was certain relief when he told me what it was. There was a certain relief when he told me that there was something wrong. There was a certain relief in knowing that I wasn't a bad person, that I was ill, that I had an illness and that although it couldn't be cured (because it was bipolar depression not reactive), it could be controlled by medication. I remember being told I could never drink again.

"I was working that night and I had to drive down to Tramore, in County Waterford, with the knowledge that I would never have another drink again in my life. I was probably drinking a bit too much for my own good at that point anyway. I was certainly drinking too much for the depression. It didn't help that, that's for sure. The hangovers were pretty bad and the depression the next day was horrendous. I knew that I couldn't have a drink again and I knew that my life was going to change again.

"There was only one thing to do and that was to get on with it. It changed my life, changed my outlook. It changed my very way of life. I lost a lot of friends, so called friends, they were drinking mates really. I still go into pubs for the company and the craic, but I don't go into pubs, just to drink anymore.

"But after the depression [was diagnosed], and learning how to deal with all of it, my life changed again. When I knew what was wrong, it was a weight off my shoulders, and I knew that, with medication, I could put it as right as possible. It takes an awful long time. It's been an awful long road.

"My mother had great willpower; I think I got that from her. I just made up my mind and said, 'It's not going to beat me. It's not going to beat me! I'm going to carry on. I'm going to work. I'm going to continue to work. I'm going to continue to have a family. I'm not going to lose my family. I'm not going to lose my job. I'm going to continue on. I'm going to continue on! It's going to be hard' - it was very hard.

"Sometimes it didn't feel like it was worth doing and sometimes I was so low that I didn't feel like I could go any farther. Something always happened to give me the strength to carry on. The highs were as bad as the lows. You think you are on top of the world and you think that you can do no wrong. You do stupid things and then you crash back down.

"That was the saddest day of my life. I was sad when my parents died, but that is a part of life and time heals that," Johnny spoke, with resignation. "Time doesn't heal depression. It doesn't go away. It stays with you. It's always a monkey on your back. There are times when you want to be feeling your best; you've got a performance or you've got somebody's wedding to go to or you've got Christmas Day to celebrate and everybody's happy and cheerful and you're not feeling that good. It's hard. You can't make it right. You have to wait until it passes over.

"I've had lots of lessons. I've learned you just can't, you can't win all the time. My business is a great leveler - you can go on. I had three nights last weekend where I had a standing ovation after each performance. And after forty-two years in the business, it's just not that bad! And that brings you up and you feel great and you feel like, 'I've won tonight.' And then last night I had a bomb. It was the worst night I've had for a long time. It brings you back down to earth again. So I've learned to accept the failures with the successes."

In talking to Johnny, the love and commitment that Johnny and Odette share comes up over and over again. He quite obviously has a deep and profound love for Odette and treasures her, professing to be abundantly blessed to have her in his life. He also expressed the desire to tell her of his love more often, how she has always lifted him up, kept him going, and he has only to think of her, and his love for her, to know that she always will.

"The happiest moment of my life was the day I got married. I have to be honest with you and say that. It was a great day. It was an important event in my life, a big step, a very profound effect on me. I never regretted it, never for one moment."

Besides Odette, who Johnny credits with keeping him grounded and from wallowing in depressions dark void, Johnny sees his children as giving him reason to keep on, no matter the emotions that try to control his life.

"When the two kids were born, that woke me up! Those two days, I can't choose one over the other; I had really done something that was worthwhile. I had given life to someone. They were days that changed my life, and made me into a better person, more responsible, more caring.

"I am proudest of my children, to be happy is the most important, to be happy and healthy. For them to have a family, I'd like that. I'd like to be a grandfather. I look forward to that. I think I'd be a good one because, despite being away for so long, I was a good father. I always loved them and when I had my time with them, I spent it with them. I didn't cut them out of my life and I think I would be a good grandfather. I look forward to it anyway."

In looking back for Johnny, life has a way of banging, bruising and pushing you down the correct path, where you are meant to go. "With the onset of depression, I certainly wouldn't have been able to hold a job. I certainly would not have been able to survive in advertising, due to all the stress in it. I'm lucky that I'm in a job that I can hide it. I can make it work for me. Some of the best songs that I have written have been when I was depressed.

"It wouldn't have worked out in the job. That dream wouldn't have come true, I'm convinced of that. I'm very lucky to go on the road I chose. I've worked for myself for the best part of forty-two years. I'm not going to change that now. If anybody is going to fire me, it's going to be me! I have that right."

"I don't have any other regrets - I don't think they are productive. The one with my children would be the one that gets me the most, when

I see them grown up now, a man and a woman. They talk about things when they were kids and I realize that I wasn't there. But that was my fault and I have to accept that. But at least they grew up well and we talk to each other and we have great times together now.

"I am terribly proud of the children, that I was part of bringing them up as decent human beings. Normal, well balanced people. My wife had most of it, to do with that, but I was proud I had something to do with it. I look at them now and say, 'I'm proud of you,' and carrying on from where I left off."

Johnny prefers to play his own compositions and signature songs, but his response to what is his favorite song was unique, in that Johnny won't play it. "My favorite Irish song is Paddy Kavanagh's *Raglan Road*, particularly Luke Kelly's version of it. Luke Kelly, in the early days, I used to see him in the folk clubs. He wasn't singing Raglan Road then but he sang it later on. It is one of those songs that I will never sing, because I figured I could never do it the justice that Luke Kelly could. It's one that moves me greatly when I hear that song. That was Paddy [Kavanagh] at his greatest. Paddy wrote it and it was adapted to song. Luke sang it to the air of *The Dawning of the Day*, which was an older song. I don't know who set it [to that tune], Patrick could have done that himself, but I don't know.

"Also *The Coolin*, a version that was sung by Dominic Behan many years ago. A song that I have recorded, but never released, I like Dominic's version so much. The older ones, *Carrickfergus* would be a favorite of mine as well. The nostalgia of the song reminds me of all those great days when I was young and everything was happening."

A defining moment occurred for Johnny in one of the Mecca's of the performing world. "It was in Carnegie Hall, it was very fleeting. I played at a Carmel Quinn concert, in 1968. It stands out in my memory because I was in America on a seven week tour through Boston, Philadelphia, New York, Chicago, San Francisco and Canada and I was asked to appear on Mecca. It was St. Patrick's Day week. Bill Fuller, who was married to Carmel Quinn at the time, was part of the tour and used to bring over bands and artists from Ireland, asked me to do it. I only sang three songs but it made such an impression on me.

"I remember the size of the stage, walking out and seeing the vast stage and singing the three songs and the first three rows filled with all my aunts and uncles and cousins from America, that I had just met for the first time. It was a great feeling, just to stand on the stage of Carnegie Hall, that I'd heard so much about down though the years, and say, "Well, I made it. I got there and no matter what happens, or where I go in the world, I can always say I sang in Carnegie Hall.

"I did some concerts in the Royal Albert Hall, in London and they were big events. I was on my own, standing on stage with just a guitar and looking out at this vast auditorium, full to the doors with people, and not a worry in the world, not a nerve in my body. I loved that. I played it four or five time. It was just great.

"I did several quite extensive folk festivals in Germany. I also did American bases in Germany. *The Gateway to Europe* in Frankfurt, bases in Stuttgart, Heidelberg and Berlin. They were tough going. Playing to Officers early in the evening, playing the second show to NCOs, and then the third show would be for enlisted men. It was the time of the Vietnam War, very tense. I felt sorry for the men because most of them were going to Vietnam, maybe the next day or the next week. I often wonder what happened to them. Did they make it? Did they come back?

"That made a big impression on me, meeting these young guys. They were all about seventeen or eighteen years of age. I wasn't much older myself. I did quite a few tours of Germany like that, as well as around Europe. I kept wondering myself what I would feel like if I was going off. And I was just a singer, trying to entertain them and get their minds off their problems."

Johnny turned to writing in earnest around 1975. "That was when I wrote *Long Before Your Time*. It was important for me because I didn't think I could write a song. I found a small disused graveyard outside of Mullingar, in County Westmeath. In the graveyard, I found a headstone and it contained twelve names that were an entire family that had died, been wiped out, all within a year of each other. It was around 1900, 1901, at the turn of the century. The headstone inspired the song. I was recording an album. I was one song short and thought I'd write one to finish it off.

"I didn't tell anybody that I wrote it. We did the backing track first. Nobody knew what the song was. Then I sang the song and the producer said, 'Ahh, that's a good song, you should release that [as a single].' The powers that be heard it and they said they'd release it and it went to #1. So that encouraged me to write and I realized I could write the songs. That's how the writing started. And all the other songs followed that."

These original compositions reveal Johnny's wide range of influences and abilities, often pulling from personal stories and experiences (such as *The Sailor*, and *Matthew*). Like all great writers, his songs are inspired by his own life. *Matthew* is written about a person with Alzheimer's - Johnny's own mother suffered from this disease. He changed the gender for the song, as singing his own mother's name was too painful for him. She suffered from Alzheimer's for more than ten years, before passing away in 1988. *Old Fashioned Tune* was a story that was running around in Johnny's head, after the Boer War, in Africa, and he thought of a young soldier, coming back to Dublin and going to the dances.

McEvoy has a great love of history that comes across in his heartfelt and often timeless songs. Filled with poetry and stories, the music teaches and broadens the knowledge of the Irish and Irish perspectives, almost without awareness. Learning, while being entertained, provides a much more satisfying experience.

So many of Johnny's songs have earned great recognition and success, scoring big, on the charts and among his legions of fans, including; *Michael, The Ballad of John Williams, Matthew, Going to California, Long Before Your Time, Old Fashioned Tune*, and *You Never Learned to Dance*. These are just a few among the many signature original Johnny McEvoy songs.

As imitation is the sincerest form of flattery, Johnny's work has not gone unnoticed by his fellow balladeers either. Foster & Allen, Dublin City Ramblers, Dermot O'Brien, Barleycorn, Paddy Reilly, Brendan Grace, Brendan Shine, Andy Cooney, Derek McCormack and Ann Breen, among many, many well known performers, have recorded Johnny McEvoy compositions.

"Johnny is my hero when it comes to traditional Irish ballads. No one will ever touch him in that department." - Andy Cooney

On the personal side, Johnny talks of his love for history and historical leaders. "I was always interested in history. Historically, people who would have had an impact on me; people like De Valera. I grew up in a part of his era, the end of his life. Padraic Pearse - his dream of a free and independent Ireland. His dream was strong enough, and he believed in his dream strongly enough, that he would give his life for it. I think that takes some courage. Michael Collins was the same. He believed in a free Ireland and a Democratic Ireland. He gave his life for the same thing. I admire them. They were a part of my upbringing and I admired their courage."

"Johnny had a huge hit when he was in his late teens here," says Tom Sweeney, "Huge success as a very young man. Johnny has been treading the boards here and in the States very, very successfully and always of a very high standard. I admire the man so much. He is writing songs which are a very high quality. Songs like the Ballad of Anne Frank, John Williams, Staten Island, that lovely song of his about Michael Collins. I think great songs. He is where he should be, right up there, because he works so hard and you don't stay up there without great effort."

Michael, Johnny's popular composition, was inspired by a life long admiration for *The Big Fellow*, as Collins was called. "I've been an admirer of Michael Collins since I was a kid. In school in the 60's in Dublin you learned nothing about Michael Collins. Irish history seemed to end in 1921. There were no songs about the civil war, no songs about Michael Collins.

"During my teen years I became aware of someone called *The Big Fellow*. I started to look him up and I read a book called *The Big Fellow*, written by Frank O'Connor. That got me fascinated in him. I read all that I could about him down through the years. I felt very bad that he had been ignored by our historians here in Ireland, felt very strongly about that, as a matter of fact. We talk about Pearse, Connolly, and about De Valera, and everybody else that took part in the 1916 Rising, and there was no mention of Michael Collins. A young man, he led the War of Independence, from 1919 up 'til 1921. Then he was Commander in Chief of the Free State Forces, from 1921 up until the time he was killed, on August 22, 1922, killed by Republican Forces. He was killed by his old friends.

"About 1991, there was sort of a revival, he started to come back into the public conscience and everybody started to talk about Michael Collins. You could, read everything about him. This was long before the movie was made [*Michael Collins*, starring Liam Neeson, 1996]. It was like people had discovered him again and people were not afraid to talk about him. A lot of books were written about him, biographies and such. There was one book in particular that inspired me to write the song and that was a book called *The Day Michael Collins Was Shot* [by Meda C. Ryan, Poolbeg Pr Ltd, 1989]. It was an account of the ambush that he was killed in, in Beal na Mblath [*pron.* Bale nah Blah, *The Pass of the Flowers*]. I wrote the song based on the ambush, really, and on Collin's ideal, he seemed to be the only one who had an idea of what to do about Ireland, if we got our freedom.

"He was young and he was vibrant and he was full of vitality. He had a girlfriend and he was romantic - the whole thing about him. He was on the run for so long, and nobody ever caught him and he got away with it. Just the tragedy of it, being killed by his own people, after doing all that, that's why I wrote the song, after reading that book.

𝔐𝔦𝔠𝔥𝔞𝔢𝔩

by Johnny McEvoy

Spoken:
 The curlew stood silent and unseen, in the long damp grass, and he
  looked down on the road below him that wound its way through
 Beal na mBlath, and he heard, the young men, shouting and cursing,
  running backwards and forwards, dodging and weaving and ducking
 the bullets that rained down on them from the hillside opposite, Just
 as quickly as it started the firing stopped, and a terrible silence hung
  over the valley. A lone figure lay on the roadside, in the drizzling
 August rain, dressed in green great-coat, leggings and brown hob-
 nailed boots, that would never again set the sparks flying from the
 kitchen flagstones, as he danced his way through a half-set, a hurried
  whispered act of contrition, and the firing breaks out again, The
 curlew takes to flight, and as he flies out over the empty sad fields of
 west Cork, with his lonesome call, he must tell the world that the big
   fellow has fallen, and that Michael, is gone.

Sing:

On a far off August day, Cold young men in ambush lay
On a roadside by a hill where flowers grow
So much hate for one so young, who was right and who was wrong
Though a thousand years may pass we'll never know

Chorus:
Candles dripping blood they placed beside your shoulders
Rosary beads like teardrops on your fingers
Friends and comrades standing by in their grief they wonder why
Michael, in their hour of need you had to go

And when evening twilight came gently fell the autumn rain
Oh but you lay still and silent on the ground
As we hung our heads in prayer in our sorrow and despair
We wondered was it friend or foe who shot you down

Chorus

Now the flame that you held high when you called out to the sky
To end this senseless killing and this shame
Has now passed to other hands and is carried through the land
By some not fit to even speak your name

Chorus
Michael, in their hour of need why did you go

"In America, it would have been Abraham Lincoln and Eisenhower and people like that, who impressed me. I did a lot of reading about them. I read about Eisenhower's career in the Second World War I remember when he was President, and Kennedy as well. I often wonder what ever would have happened if Kennedy had lived, would he have changed things in Ireland? The American Presidents have done awful lot for Irish peace. Kennedy was a great lover of Ireland. He was greatly admired here and I think he was a great President.

"I admire Mary Black; I love her voice and her songs, so fresh and original. I admire, love, U2. They've been great ambassadors for Ireland, for America as well, because they are more Irish-American than Irish, because of the music they sing - but they are Irish.

"The first Bob Dylan concert I saw, in 1966 in Dublin, in the Adelphi Cinema, a cinema being used as a concert hall. That stands out in my memory. He was just going electric at the time. The concert was magnificent. He did an acoustic set in the first half, which was out of this world. He did an electric set with the band in the second half, which most people booed and jeered. But I was quite impressed by it.

Johnny Cash was one of the ones I admired. I saw him in several shows. He was a folk/country *artist*. Again, another storyteller, and a big man. You always knew who he was. It was very sad that he died. I had the pleasure of meeting him once and found he was a complete gentleman. Not like the big stars at all. Johnny Cash would stand out as the top folk/country performer that I've ever seen."

"We're in a bit of a slump here. There's a gap at the moment. There is nobody coming up to fill the space left by us. We all served our time, served our apprenticeship and learned something as we went along. But people come along, as in *You're A Star* [the European, and original, version of American Idol] and their hopes are built up and then their hopes are dashed. In three months, they are forgotten.

"People like to see people make fools of themselves. The poor kids who don't win are shattered. Their confidence is gone and they'll never make anything for themselves [in music] again. [They won't put in the time, the apprenticeship, and won't develop to become stars with staying power - this is the gap now clearly seen in the Balladeer ranks]. I'm glad I'm not starting out in the business at this time."

"I love the movies, especially American movies. Well, most of the movies made are American anyway. We go out to eat, my wife Odette and myself, and go to the movies. We go as a family as well, the four of us, especially at Christmas. We make a tradition of it, to take in a movie. Its good entertainment, good escapism. Christmas is very important in our family. We all get together, the extended family, and have a party.

"I read a lot; novels, history, biographies. I've always been a reader, ever since I was a child. Reading is my favorite pastime."

Even though he professes he is pulling back, Johnny is as busy as ever. "The main goal would be that I could keep going for as long as I like, for as long as I want to. The day will come when I will say, 'Ok, that's it. I've had enough.' I'm trying to cut back, do the best ones. At the moment now, I continue to tour Ireland, do concerts and things, going around the country up until the week before Christmas. In 2005, I went on tour with Brendan Grace, from the 29th of December through the end of January, this year. Then I did a documentary on Auschwitz, which my son, Jonathan, produced. He is a video producer for safety and health, such as informative videos on Alzheimer's and such, for use in hospitals."

Jonathon also produced *The Original Johnny McEvoy* record, released in the United States in 1995, and is a fantastic guitar player, even better than his father, Johnny proudly proclaims. Johnny's daughter, Alice, followed her Dad's pre-performing profession and is a graphic artist with Arnotts, in Dublin.

Johnny continued, "Then I'm doing concerts for the radio, going on tours with Brendan Grace, or go for a short tour of my own. In between, I do one night stands around here. I did a few concerts in Spain in May, Cleveland's Irish Cultural Festival is set for July, a tour of Newfoundland in October and a Mediterranean Cruise in September. That'll keep me busy and that's just the ones I know right now.

"I love playing Cleveland and I'm not saying that because I'm talking to you. I'd like to tour America, a bit more than I have been doing. I like to play in America, I think it is exciting. People listen! They listen to the songs and they want to listen to the stories. When I am singing my songs, I introduce them by telling stories of the songs. People appreciate that; they listen to them [in America].

"I love playing Newfoundland. Newfoundland is a new audience for me. They know me because *Michael* was a radio hit there, as was *Going to California.*

"I have never been to Australia. I would like to go to Australia and perform there. I don't see it happening at the moment. I'd like to do another album of my own songs. I did one already [*The Original Johnny McEvoy*]. I'd like to do that again, given the chance. I've been working on songs with that in mind, with the album in mind. I have several new songs set aside for that. But you have to please record companies. You have to please the men with the suits.

"I'd love to fly an airplane. I'd like to have been an actor, a straight actor (not comedy or musical), in a drama on TV or in the movies. I get jealous when I see those that are good at what they do. If the road had gone a different way, that might be something I would have done.

Johnny's choice of trade has blessed the world with songs sung the world over, inspiration, celebrations and yes, more than a few tears, when he sings. But being remembered is not a goal for this Festival Legend, a man who is recognized for his long-lasting impact on the Irish music world. "I don't think that that is important. I don't think I'm going to be remembered. I will be remembered by my family for a short time and then time will take over and heal all the wounds. I'll be forgotten in time and a generation will go by and no one will know that I was ever here.

"Greater men than I have lived, and lived their lives and achieved greater things than I have achieved. And they have gone on, and passed on. They are memories. Who talks of some of the great men of history anymore? Most young people would be bored if you talked of John F. Kennedy now. So for me, it's not important to be remembered. I've managed to live my life the way I chose.

"I haven't worked a nine-to-five job since 1965. I travel the roads of Ireland. I stop outside a garage if I'm down in the country in the early hours of the morning. I buy a coke and a bar of chocolate and I eat that on my way home and I read my book. There's where I get my kick. I sing songs to the people. If I've made people happy along the way, that's enough for me."

The timeless and eloquent songwriter, the classic voice, the legendary songs he has written, recorded and passed on to fans and other singers alike, all are the streetlamps that have illuminated the path and the past of this wonderful performer. Irish music, and the culture it represents, is so deeply and permanently enriched by the songs and contributions of Johnny McEvoy.

Johnny McEvoy Signature Songs: Muirsheen Durkin

Traditional, tune originally "Cailini Deas Mhuigheo"
(The Beautiful Girls of Mayo). Arrangement by Johnny McEvoy

In the days when I was courtin',
I was seldom done resortin'
In the ale house and the playhouse,
And many's the house beside
I told me brother Seamus,
I'll go off and get right famous,
And when I return again,
I will have roamed the world wide

Chorus:
And it's goodbye, Muirshin Durkin,
I'm sick and tired of workin'
I'll no more dig the praties,
I'll no longer be a fool
As sure as me name is Carney,
I'll go off to California
And instead of digging praties,
I'll be digging lumps of gold

Farewell to all the boys at home,
I'm sailing far across the foam
to try and make my fortune
In far Amerikay
There's gold and money plenty,
For the poor and for the gentry
And when I come back home again,
I never more will say,

Chorus

I courted girls in Blarney

169

In Kanturk and in Killarney
In Passage and in Queenstown
That is the Cobh of Cork
Goodbye to all the pleasure
I'm going to take my measure
And the next time you will hear from me
Will be a letter from New York

Chorus
Chorus

Long Before Your Time

by Johnny McEvoy

You ask me why I look so sad
On this bright summer's day
Or why the tears are in my eyes
And I seem so far away
Well sit yourself beside me love
And put your hand in mine
And I'll tell of someone I loved long
Long Long before your time

I'm sitting here and thinking
Of those days so long ago
When I was just a child like you
And a girl I used to know
Through fields of green we laughed and played
And sang our merry rhymes
Oh summer days were warmer then
Long Long before your time

Through childhood years our love did bloom
Till our hearts were just as one
And we promised each eternal love
In the church below the town
We settled in this little house
I was proud to call her mine
Oh we were young and happy then
Long Long before your time

One lovely year was all we had
Until the sickness came
And stole the roses from her cheeks
My tears they fell like rain
For nine long months she carried you
But in the end she died

She chose to go so you might live
Long Long before your time

So you ask me why I look so sad
On this bright summer's day
Or why the tears are in my eyes
And I seem so far away
It's just you seem a lot like her
When your eyes look into mine
And you smile so much like she did
Long Long before your time

Michael

by Johnny McEvoy

Spoken:

The curlew stood silent and unseen, in the long damp grass, and he looked down on the road below him that wound its way through Beal na mBlath, and he heard, the young men, shouting and cursing, running backwards and forwards, dodging and weaving and ducking the bullets that rained down on them from the hillside opposite, Just as quickly as it started the firing stopped, and a terrible silence hung over the valley. A lone figure lay on the roadside, in the drizzling August rain, dressed in green great-coat, leggings and brown hob-nailed boots, that would never again set the sparks flying from the kitchen flagstones, as he danced his way through a half-set, a hurried whispered act of contrition, and the firing breaks out again, The curlew takes to flight, and as he flies out over the empty sad fields of west Cork, with his lonesome call, he must tell the world that the big fellow has fallen, and that Michael, is gone.

Sing:

On a far off August day, Cold young men in ambush lay
On a roadside by a hill where flowers grow
So much hate for one so young, who was right and who was wrong
Though a thousand years may pass we'll never know

Chorus:
Candles dripping blood they placed beside your shoulders
Rosary beads like teardrops on your fingers
Friends and comrades standing by in their grief they wonder why
Michael, in their hour of need you had to go

And when evening twilight came gently fell the autumn rain
Oh but you lay still and silent on the ground
As we hung our heads in prayer in our sorrow and despair
We wondered was it friend or foe who shot you down

Chorus

Now the flame that you held high when you called out to the sky
To end this senseless killing and this shame
Has now passed to other hands and is carried through the land
By some not fit to even speak your name

Chorus
Michael, in their hour of need why did you go

Ballad of John Williams

by Johnny McEvoy

When last I saw John Williams, a young man full of pride
His lovely bride of just four days was standing by his side
He smiled and took me by the hand, saying "Boyo can't you see
I've seen the last of windswept bogs and bogs the last of me!
And the peelers and the landlords and the risings of the moon
And if ever I return again, 'twill be too bloody soon"

Chorus:
Rich man , poor man, beggar man, wife
Sailed away into the night
Where they'll end up no-one knows
Round and round the story goes

He said "I'll go and take my chance in far off New York Town
For they say there's lots of work there and
a good man won't stay down
And with my lassie by my side we'll build a better home
And when the sea trip's over lads we never more will roam"
So we said farewell upon the quay, there was nothing left to do
But to pray for John and his lovely bride, that their dreams
might all come true

Chorus

How I envied you, John Williams, and your lovely fair haired bride
To be sailing on that mighty ship across the ocean wide
For she's the finest liner, that was ever built by man
And they say there's naught can sink her,
no not even God's own hand
Man's pride can be his own downfall,
that great ship sailed from home
And I thought I heard the banshee cry, and it chilled me to the bone

Chorus

Going to California

by Johnny McEvoy

He was never there when needed
and oh how much she pleaded
saying "Darling, wont you stay home just one time"
He'd just smile and say "I'm sorry, but there's no need to worry
just going to meet some army buddies,
drink some beer and fight the war.

In the kitchen making wishes as she tidies up the dishes,
on another lonely weekend and the wine she drank alone
and the nights they hold no pit, in the cold of New York City,
as she waits there in the darkness to hear his key turn in the door.

Chorus:
She said "I'm going to California to taste the sunshine and the wine,
sit beside the rolling ocean and slowly pass the time,
reading books and old love stories and forget about my worries,
and maybe who knows maybe, we'll meet again.

Then one night he came home sober, with a longing just to hold her.
When he found the note she'd written waiting by the telephone,
and she said "I'll always love you. and never will forget you,
but I just can't take this lonely feeling any more".

Now the nights are cold and lonely as he sits and watches TV.
Drinking beer and chasing whiskey,
wondering where it all went wrong,
and his eyes are tired and burning from the dreams that keep returning,
and all his yesterdays wont leave him alone

Chorus

Chorus

Old Fashioned Tune

by Johnny McEvoy

Her eyes are as bright
As they were the first night
When we danced to an old fashioned tune
In a dusty old schoolhouse on Saturday nights
How we laughed as we waltzed round the room
You came from the valleys
To the dark city alleys
To care for the young and the poor
And me a young soldier
With medals galore,
That I won in the African war

Chorus:
How my heart filled with joy
As the others passed by
By the look in their eyes I well knew
That never before
As we swept round the floor
Had they seen someone lovely as you.

Your hair shone like gold, a joy to behold
Your beauty was known far and wide
There was many a young lad who'd lay down his life
For one moment to be by your side
But you gave then no glances, you gave them no dances
As you gracefully stepped on the floor
With me a young soldier with medals galore
That I won in the African war

Chorus

When the morning had come, and the dancing all done
We would walk in the dawn of the day.

I would tell you tall stories, of battles and glories
And comrades who fell in the fray
Now the years come and go
Still the love that you show
Is as sweet and as warm as before
When I, a young soldier, with medals galore,
came home from the African war.

Chorus

Johnny McEvoy Discography:

- For the Poor & the Gentry   (1967)
- With an Eye to Your Ear   (1968)
- All Our Wars Are Merry & All Our Songs Are Sad   (1969)
- Johnny McEvoy   (1972)
- Where My Eileen is Waiting For Me   (1973)
- Sounds Like McEvoy   (1974)
- Long Before Your Time   (1975)
- 20 Greatest Hits   (1976)
- Sings Hank Williams   (1976)
- Sings Country   (1977)
- Christmas Dreams   (1977)
- The Golden Hour of Johnny McEvoy   (1978)
- Collections   (1979)
- Live in Concert   (1981)
- Since Maggie Went Away   (1984)
- Songs of Ireland   (1986)
- The Singer   (1987)
- Celebration   (1988)
- The Original (Same as The Singer - but only released in America)   (1995)
- Portrait   (1996)
- Going to California   (2003)
- The Essential Collection   (2004)

Compilations:

These are records put out by record companies, with no knowledge, or consideration, given to the performer recorded. The list in NOT all inclusive:

- Celebrating 30 Years
- 20 Collected Irish Ballads
- Favourites
- Greatest Hits
- Greatest Hits - Live

- 20 Best Loved Songs
- Classic Irish Folk (Vol. I)
- Classic Irish Folk (Vol. II)
- Classic Irish Love Songs (Vol. I)
- Classic Irish Love Songs (Vol. II)
- Raised on Songs and Stories
- A Bit of Blarney - 20 Irish Favorites
- A Celebration of Dublin - 21 Street Ballads

DVD's & Videos:

- In Concert   (1981)
- The Singer   (1987)

Some of the Johnny McEvoy Original Compositions:

A Long Way From the Sun
As Soon As I Can
Ballad of Amy Johnson
Ballad of Anne Frank
Ballad of Jack Riley
Ballad of John Williams
Bound for Botany Bay
Dublin Fusiliers
Famine Song
Going to California
I Can't Believe
I'll Spend Time With You
Leaves in the Wind
Lincoln's Army
Long Before Your Time
Long Way From the Sun
Matthew
Michael
My Old Boat
No Other Love I'll Know
Old Fashioned Tune
Play the Game

Rich Man's Garden
Riverside
Rosaleen, Sweet Rosaleen
Sing Me A Song
Soldier of the Hill
Staten Island
The Band Played Red River Valley
The Old Man and the Donkey
The Sailor
The Town I Left Behind
The Wheels Round
Tonight You're With Another
You Never Learned to Dance
You Seldom Come to See Me Anymore
You're So Far Away

Hits:

- Muirsheen Durkin #1   (1966)
- Those Brown Eyes   (1966)
- Boston Burglar #1   (1967)
- Nora#1   (1968)
- Three Score and Ten #5   (1970)
- Eileen Is Waiting For Me #2   (1972)
- Long Before Your Time #1   (1975)
- Old Fashioned Tune   (1987)

The Godfather's Mother - Sarah Makem.

Tommy celebrates 50 years in music with a proclamation from Cleveland's Irish Cultural Festival

Tommy, Liam Tiernan & the Immortal Luke Kelly

Tommy and brother Jack (kneeling)

Where it all Began - Liam, Tommy, Paddy and Tom

John Delaney, Tommy Makem, Alec DeGabriele and Eddie and George Furey joined with The Makem Brothers and Danny Doyle at Cleveland's Irish Cultural Festival in a stirring song tribute and memorial to Derek McCormack. The tribute CD, A Lifetime of Memories, featuring Derek singing his favorite songs, was released at the same time

Rory usually accompanies Tommy when he is performing, providing backup as well as singing a few favorites himself

In Concert at Carnegie Hall, 1974

Danny Doyle, Bill Martin and Phil Coulter

Danny Doyle - in the midst of the journey, 1969

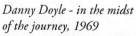

In Concert, at Sidney Opera House

Phil Coulter, Al Bart, Henry Mancini, Danny Doyle, Bill Martin and Noel Pearson

*Whether performing in a
pub or a palace, Danny's
ability to bring the songs
and stories of the past into
bright and memorable
performances set him apart*

*Danny Doyle,
Elmer Bernstein,
Sir Stanley Baker
and author James
Clavell*

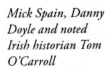

*Mick Spain, Danny
Doyle and noted
Irish historian Tom
O'Carroll*

Mr. Liam Clancy - A master at transporting his audience to the time and scene of his songs and recognized as one of the greatest balladeers to ever sing a song

Cherish the Ladies' Joanie Madden had toured with The Clancy Brothers. Here, with Liam and Paddy (behind Liam) and Robbie O'Connell (behind Paddy)

The Legendary Singer, Songwriter
and Storyteller, Johnny McEvoy

In the Beginning
- Johnny started as a
duo, called Ramblers
Two, with future
Dublin City Rambler
Mick Crotty

Johnny meets Mary McAleese, President of Ireland, in 2004.

Johnny plays
Carnegie Hall,
1968

Country Hey-days

Close up of the introspective and talented singer/songwriter

Sean's got Gold

I got this banjo, lets start a group

It started with two brothers:
Sean (l) and brother Matt

Dublin City Ramblers, Luke
Crowley, Sean McGuinness
and Pierce McAllorum
surround Tommy Makem at
Cleveland's Irish Cultural
Festival

The Dublin
City Ramblers
today, still
wowing
audiences the
world over

The DeGabriele Clan - Alec's father (in black, in front of mic), joins his brothers and sisters, pre The Shannon Players.

The New Barleycorn today

Liam & Paddy (f), Brian & John. Barleycorn in America, 1975

Cruising with Phil Coulter

John, Paddy (f) Derek, Denis (1985)

John, Brian & Liam (1971)

John, Paddy, Denis and Derek surround famed soccer goalie Pat Jennings, at a tribute dinner given in his honor

Team Ireland joins Team Barleycorn

Irish physio, Mick Byrne, leads the team on a sing-song after the Ireland-Malta game in Valetta last night.
Picture by Joe St. Leger.

The Makems and Tom Sweeney share songs and stories in another sessión

Brilliant singer and historian Tom Sweeney

March 17th, 1998, Tom performs for President Bill Clinton and the Irish peace delegation, just before the Good Friday Agreement was reached.

irish
storytelling

Seanachie extraordinaire Batt Burns

Batt is known for his stories, written work and ability to teach, transport, and enthrall audiences, the world over. Using songs, poetry and stories, that go back generations, Batt is one of the last of the tradition-steeped seanchies.

The Promo Shot -
The Makem &
Spain Brothers

The Next Generation
- Joanie Madden with
Conor Makem

Mick Spain, Robbie O'Connell,
Aiofe Clancy and Rory Makem

The Makem
& Spain
Brothers
on their
annual tour
in Ireland
- here in
Carlingford

Harpist, Bard, historian, educator, singer and presenter, Dennis Doyle

Annually, Dennis performs at the outdoor mass at Cleveland's Irish Cultural Festival, Here he plays with the Irish Sopranos as they sing Ave Maria during mass

A noted authority on the greatest harpist, Turlough O'Carolan, who provided Dennis with so wonderful material and inspiration, Dennis stands in front of the memorial to him, located in Mohill, County Lietrim.

The Brendan Shine Band today

The gifted and brilliant singer Emily Shine continues the Shine legacy while performing with her father.

Brendan receives a Gold Record, for Abbeyshrule.

Ballad, Ceili, Country, Cabaret - Brendan and the band are huge hits in any genre.

Legends on a fence - Paddy Reilly, Noel Ginnity (seated), Jim & Phyl McCann, Danny Doyle, Johnny McEvoy and Andy Irvine

The Paddys - Paddy Reilly, Paddy Sweeney, Paddy Clancy, w/ Sean McGuinness.

Can you imagine the stories? Paddy Reilly, Johnny McEvoy and Danny Doyle.

Mr. Derek McCormack

Derek and his father, during their traveling "Fit-up" days

The Three Amigos

John and Derek

Young Derek, next to his mother on drums, part of the 'Fit-up' tradition, spent his youth traveling and performing all over Ireland, until he left to join Dermot O'Brien & His Clubmen, in his late teens, before joining Barleycorn twelve years later (1983).

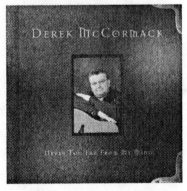

Never Too Far From My Mind - Derek's last CD

V.

Sean McGuinness
Dublin City Ramblers

*"Since the beginning of man, the hours between the coming
of night and the coming of sleep have belonged to the
tellers of tales and the makers of music." -Anon.*

The founding member, leader, and driving force behind one of the most successful bands in Irish music history is a gifted *"teller of tales and maker of music,"* and a friendly, honorable and engaging man. Through band changes, unprecedented successes, fortuitous timing and a lot of hard work, the leader of the Dublin City Ramblers has stayed true to the upbringing provided by his family and the song tradition. Being true to this is part of what makes him tick.

Sean Anthony McGuinness, born the 16th of September, 1948, in James Street, Dublin and living most of his life in Inchicore, Dublin, came from a very traditional Irish background. His mother, Mary Tyson McGuinness won *the Cap and Gown*, the highest awards granted in piano playing, at the London College of Music. Matthew, Sean's father, was All-Ireland Champion Dancer three years in a row, winning the *Cilteann Belts* in dancing, as well.   Sean has two brothers, Patrick and Matthew, and one sister, Maura, who is a great Irish dancer and singer herself.

"We always sang. Ahh, there were always parties. The door was always open and there was always a party in the house, especially around Christmas time. Even as a kid, my father was having us sing Irish songs and ballads. Then around fourteen or fifteen, I got my first banjo. Two of the first albums would have been the *Clancy Brothers & Tommy Makem* and *the Dubliners*. It had an immediate impact on me. I went out and got a small banjo. Never had any lessons or anything, just picked it up and started playing it. That's when I started, around fourteen or fifteen years of age.

"When we were kids, we didn't have much, but we had each other. My mother and father were both musicians, both musical. My uncle was a great mandolin & fiddle player. My mother's uncle, Harry Tyson was a great portrait and still-life artist. I think that's where the influence came from for one of my favorite hobbies, painting. If I wasn't a performer, I would dearly love to be a professional artist or golfer."

Sean is an accomplished painter. "Van Gogh, the Dutch Artist, for his determination under exceptionally difficult circumstances, was a big influence on me." Sean's paintings of Irish landscapes and scenery bring to life the magnificent views of the greenery, water and landscapes of Ireland. After years of using watercolors, he took up oil painting in 2003 and his work is both stunning and a tribute to the rich scenery of his homeland [You can see Sean's work on the web; www.dublincityramblers.com/pastime, "Go to Sean's paintings"].

"My parents taught us the songs about Ireland's history, and were both very Republican and Nationalistic. I think my favorite Irish song of all time is *Dublin in the Rare Ould' Times*, because it epitomizes Dublin in the days when I was growing up. It's all changed now, and *not* for the better, thanks to all the plastic pubs, foreign restaurants etc.

"Another favorite song is *Down by the Glenside*. We were born near a place called *The Liberties* on James Street in Dublin.* The song

---

* The Liberties, originally an area of what is now Dublin city, was a neighborhood of religious houses with manors. They had privileges, or tax exemptions and controls, almost independent of the royal courts and administrators. These privileged holdings became known as liberties, eventually giving way to the whole area being called *the Liberties*

always reminds me of my father. My earliest memory, would have been, I suppose, of my father coming home and bringing some friends, on a Saturday night. I was probably only five or six years old and I always remember him singing his favorite song, *Boulavogue*. A song he was once arrested for singing outside Nugent's Pub in James's Street. It always stuck with me. At the time, I didn't realize the impact [Irish music] was going to have on me. There was always Irish music in the house. I also have great memories of my father taking me to Croke Park as a kid to see the Dublin Footballers and Hurlers playing."

Sean attended Basin Lane Christian Brothers School in James's Street from 1952 to 1961. Classmates included next door neighbors Terry Woods (of *The Pogues*) and Jim Lockhart (of *Horslips*).

"In 1963 I got a Tenor Banjo and at the suggestion of Pat's [Cummins] brother-in-law, Bob Aylsworth, who played in a country band called *The Cowboys,* decided to form a Ballad group with my brother Matt, and my best friend, Pat Cummins. The Cowboys used to sing a song called The Jolly Tinker on stage.

"Our very first gig as *The Jolly Tinkers*, consisted of me playing the Banjo, Matt playing the tin whistle, and Pat playing guitar & singing. Before this, we had a Pop group, for a bit of fun, called *The Young Savages,* with two other guys; Alan McCann (RIP) & John Preston, now a prolific songwriter. I always had music in my blood, and that hasn't changed.

"Our first gig with the Ramblers was in 1970. We had heard of a place called *The Embankment,* in Tallaght, Dublin, and the three of us decided to hitch a lift to it one Saturday night in 1963. We got as far as a place called Jobstown and we saw a horse in a field. We caught the horse and rode it to the Embankment. The session was in full swing when we approached the bar door. The horse proceeded to shove his head in thru the door of the packed house. The owner, Mick McCarthy, was standing just inside the door, and we frightened the life out of him. He just said, 'Can you sing?' (to us , not the horse), and we said yes. The rest is history."

Various sessions held at the famous Embankment, in Dublin, with the legendary Mick McCarthy (RIP) are some of Sean's favorite memories of being a performer:

"One time Mick left the establishment at about 4 a.m., a few days before Christmas 1987, left the rest of us singing & playing, and proceeded to return at about 8 a.m. on the back of a Police motorbike. He said his car was stuck. He rejoined us for the session until about 10a.m., when we all left to find his car. It wasn't stuck, we found it nose down in a ditch."

Returning to his family, Sean continues, "The music, history and songs were always in my blood. Regrets are too negative, but one thing I do wish is that my father had lived to enjoy the success of the Ramblers. My father passed away in 1975 and my mother in 1991. We were a very close family. After my father passed away, I became even closer to my mother. She was not only my best drinking buddy; she was my best friend as well. I couldn't play for at least a month after she passed. I couldn't sing, couldn't play an instrument. But she's there with us all the time."

"One of the happiest moments would have been meeting my wife Breda." Breda, Sean's wife of almost thirty years, and Sean met in 1977. "She's a very easy-going person. We were playing in Galway, in the west of Ireland. She was down for the weekend with a friend and we just got to talking. She'd never really been into ballads and she came down to hear the Ramblers with her friend. She knew one of the lads in the band from earlier; she was a neighbor of his. She came to hear us and we met up [after the gig] and stopped for a session in *The Roseland Bar*, in Moate, County Westmeath. We gave her a lift back to Dublin. She didn't think I'd remember her phone number, but I did and called her a week later." Sean's deep love and connection with his wife of almost thirty years is very apparent in his voice and his expressions. There are soul mates in this world.

One of the proudest moments for Sean was meeting actress Maureen O'Hara, who starred in many big-hit movies, one of her most famous being, *The Quiet Man*, with John Wayne. Hollywood Actor's Organizations were honoring one person a year, for their contributions and Maureen O'Hara was selected for 1988. Her husband, Charles Blair, an airlines captain (a pilot), had a museum honoring him located in Foynes, County Limerick, called *Foynes Flying Boat Museum*.

The Dublin City Ramblers had recorded the theme song of The Quiet Man, *The Lake of the Isle of Innisfree*. A good friend of O'Hara's, Margaret O'Shaughnessy, who oversaw the museum, heard the recording and gave it to Maureen. She liked it and asked if the band could play for the honoring dinner.

"In 1988, in the Marriott Inn in LaGuardia Airport, Maureen O'Hara, a Republican [supporter of a united, free Ireland], asked us to sing the song for her. It was a very proud moment. She was a lovely lady. There was a big reception for her. Robert Wagner, Robert Redford, lots of [famous] people. We sang the Lake Isle of Innisfree, *Rare Ould Times*, three or four songs and she came down, shook hands. She was a very down to earth lady.

"This is most important. Always be kind to people. There is an old saying, 'Be kind to people on the way up because you'll meet them on the way back down.' I say be kind to people, whether they're on the way up or down. I don't believe in egos. Be humble. I come from humble beginnings and that's where I'm at. Life is too short. I enjoyed a bit of fun. Be kind to people. If you can't do a good turn, don't do a bad one. Everybody differs in who they admire, but people should follow their own conscience and do what they think is right. They should know about the people in the world who are always there for others."

The Dublin City Ramblers acknowledging and honoring others for what they do is heard throughout this brief biography. An example of the Dublin City Ramblers working (and paying) to offer tribute to those already gone can be found in Glasnevin Cemetery, in Glasnevin, on the north side of Dublin. The Dublin City Ramblers, at the suggestion of then band mate Kevin Molloy, made up for the egregious omission of any monument to Michael Moran, otherwise known as *Zozimus*, an 18th Century poet and street storyteller who is buried in a pauper's grave there, by erecting a statue in his honor. The honoring was a big event at the time and drew numerous TV cameras and brought the true story of Zozimus to a whole new audience.

St. Patrick Was A Gentleman

by Zozimus

"Saint Patrick was a gintleman, he came of decent people,
In Dublin town he built a Church, and on it put a steeple;
His father was a Callaghan, his mother was a Brady,
His aunt was an O'Shaughnessy, and his uncle was a Grady.
Then success to bold St. Patrick's fist, He was a saint so clever,
He gave the snakes and toads a twist, And banished them for ever."

"Once described by P.J. McCall as the last Gleeman of the Pale, *Zozimus* was born Michael Moran in 1794 in the Blackpits area of the Liberties, one of the oldest parts of Dublin, just south of the River Liffey. His family, typical of many in Ireland during the late 18th century, was desperately poor, and this, coupled with an illness suffered very early in his life, caused *Zozimus* to lose the sight of both eyes when he was only two weeks old. During those poverty-stricken days in Dublin, a blind person would have had a very difficult time indeed surviving on the streets of Dublin, but *Zozimus* was able to earn a healthy living due to the fact that he possessed an exceptional memory for old poems, songs and stories, as well as an enormous talent for composing and reciting his own. It is from this that he received his unusual nickname, for Zozimus was the name of the priest who administered the Holy Sacraments to St. Mary of Egypt in the 5th century AD. Michael Moran was fond of reciting the verses composed by Bishop Coyle regarding this incident, and so came to be called by the same name as the priest."[1]

Zozimus was buried in a grave unmarked, until the Ramblers stepped in and attended to the erecting of the monument, near the resting place of Daniel O'Connell. Because of Zozimus' financial straights, he is buried in what is known as the "Poor Ground." So many of Zozimus' poems have been adapted to song by admirers the world over. The monument still stands, still looked after today.

Sean himself particularly has great admiration for Sean O'Riada, of Ceoltoiri Cualann; the precursor to The Chieftains, The Clancy Brothers & Tommy Makem, Riverdance and the explosion of Irish

Festivals across the U.S., all for the defining influence and impact that each has had on Irish music.

"The defining moment for me in Irish music would have to be the Clancy Brothers & Tommy Makem; they started the whole thing off. They set the plan for everybody else.

"Riverdance was definitely a major turning point for Irish music, on the world stage. Before that, you had Irish music in Ireland and America and possibly Australia, but I think Riverdance put it on the world stage. Riverdance was great for the Trad music. It was also great for our end of it. It just took all of, the whole of, Irish music to a different plane. It was good for us too. It opened doors to an awful lot of people who would never have even heard of Irish music. The incredible association of Riverdance, it put us in the picture. People ask for *Dublin in the Rare Ould Times* [because of the broadening of Irish music awareness]. It put us, ballads and traditional, all under one umbrella. It opened doors for us all.

"So I would say opening doors for people coming along new is absolutely very important, very, very important. I get tapes in the post everyday. I listen to everything. If I think a song doesn't work, I contact them and offer advice. If you take the time to write it, we should listen to it. I always return the call and say if the song doesn't suit us. But maybe it might be for *Foster & Allen* or *The Wolftones* or it might be for somebody else. At least you give them a chance. It's a springboard for them to get the music heard. You can tell they are grateful that you at least rang them back [and gave them advice. It keeps them going and they don't get frustrated and quit the business for lack of progress or affirmation]. You hope to get a whole new generation that wants to do this. They certainly aren't there back home.

"One of the problems is airplay. I'm not going to promise these young kids anything because I can't even get our songs played on the radio stations back home. They're all pop, disco and country. It is very hard to get a ballad played back home. The radio stations are killing us. The government is killing us. There are no grants for us. There's nothing. They've incorporated what they call the arts - the traditional music, but they very seldom incorporate the ballads. This is what tells the story and the history of Ireland but they very seldom think of that.

They consider all of Irish music [to be] Trad music. There is a lot of tunnel vision."

Ballads are our heritage and our history, and are responsible for putting Ireland on the map worldwide. Sean went on to say that by the time it is recognized, we will have lost the guidance, stories, experience and most importantly, the teaching ability of the Sean McGuinness', Danny Doyle's, Johnny McEvoy's, Liam Clancy's, Tommy Makem's, Tom Sweeney's, Mick Foster's and Tony Allen's. Time vanishes quickly and recognizing living art comes too slowly. Under current practices, by the time recognition comes, and leads to action, it may be too late and an immeasurable wealth of knowledge, passion and experience will be lost, forever.

"I think it was 1968, a fella called Shay Healy [prominent producer, songwriter and Dublin radio personality] did a survey on the balladeer groups at home. And, in Dublin alone, in 1968, there was something like six hundred and sixty ballad groups. We weren't even heard of at that time, we were in the Quare Fellas. Now there are five or ten.

"The festivals reintroduce the music to a lot of people [often hearing the songs sung by their original artists, drawing recognition of the song's voice from when their parents played it when they were young. Then making the association to the name of the band will hopefully inspires further interest, then, and after the festival is over]. That is one of the reasons I want to keep it alive, do as many gigs as possible. So that more young people will come to hear us and then maybe form their own bands.

"There is a group of young lads, from Offaly back home. Anytime we play within fifty miles, they come to hear us. I think there are four of them in a local band, just playing for fun at local sessions. They ask us if we would mind if they copy our songs, things we say on stage. I love when young kids come up and say, 'We've got our own band and we do all of your stuff.' It's great. There isn't enough of it. The only ones in that age group doing it [on a national scale], are The Makem & Spain Brothers. I keep up with those lads. Unfortunately, they're the only ones I see anywhere; at the festivals, on the internet.

"The whole festivals, I never realized, until I came over here, how big Irish music was in America. I think all of those who took the step, as far as festivals [in doing all the work to put on and carry on the festivals]; it was a major step for Irish music. If that hadn't happened, if nobody had bothered to get the Irish festivals going, we wouldn't even be over there today [in the U.S.]. I think the whole festival explosion is a defining moment in Irish music."

"I think it is very important to keep it going because of the great, great lack of bands coming behind us," Sean continued. "Your dad [John O'Brien, Sr.] said it to me a couple of years ago, as we were at the Cleveland Festival. I remember walking down the grounds with him and he said to me, 'Sean, just a question, what's going to happen when the Dublin City Ramblers, the Wolftones, The Fureys, everybody, either dies or retires,' he said. 'I'm not wishing anything on anybody, but what's going to happen?'

"'I really don't know, that's a good question,' was all I could answer. Because back home, there's a lot of pop groups, and rock groups, all over the place and they last for a very short time. But in our field, the ballad field, there really, really is nobody coming up behind us. It's kind of scary.

"I think there is a huge credit to be paid to the festivals all over America, who have kept the Irish music on. If it wasn't for them, Irish music would be dead a long time ago. You can play pubs and halls and such, but you wouldn't be doing that if these festivals didn't keep it going. You wouldn't make a living at it, if these festivals didn't keep the whole music alive."

"One thing I saw changing, I always thought there was always a great relationship between the trads and the ballads. Riverdance lifted it to a different plane. I never saw major changes; I just saw it getting a lot more commercialized. Not the music itself, but ...[long pause here]. When I started back in the 60's, it was kind of everybody for himself. You got a manager and you got a gig and one manager would have twenty bands. [They were not working exclusively for the best interests of The Dublin City Ramblers, but for their own benefit, and enrichment]. They might have ourselves, the Fureys, Brendan Grace. And record companies are the same way.

"The big change I see is that it is every man for himself [in being the primary representative in all matters for the band], because a lot of the bands have had bad experiences [financially with band promoters and record companies] over the years. They've gotten frustrated with it, and have taken control themselves. A lot of the bands went independent. I would never hand over control to anyone again. That's the way Irish music has changed, and that's good."*

"Two roads diverged in a wood, and I - I took the one less traveled by. And that has made all the difference." - Robert Frost

"I took a chance, back in 1970, when I was told to leave the job and go professional, or leave the band. We were asked to go to America. A friend, Brian Molloy, asked us could he get some gigs for us. We agreed. He contacted a friend in the U.S.A., who set up six weeks work for us there, and it took off from there. We'd never been to America before. And people said, 'Ahh God, you're letting the good pension, or the job, go.' But it was a great honor and a great adventure kind of thing. I was indebted; it was the whole axis of where I was going to go. I headed for the music instead of the job. That was a major turn of the road and if I hadn't taken that road, I may never have met my wife.

"Especially in the early days before I met Breda, my own family encouraging me in what I was going to do was unwavering. They never said [anything negative or] you're taking a chance. They just encouraged me all my life. They always said whatever you do; we're behind you all the way. You'll never be stuck. I was always very proud of my family, myself and my wife's families. They never had any qualms about what I did or where I went or traveling and such. Whatever I decided to do was my choice. The two families I would be very proud of.

"I've seen the world and kindly got paid for it. When I was a kid I worked for the telephone company here. Even when I was in vocational

---

* Today, you still see many promoters advertising that they represent many different bands. A group like Dublin City Ramblers might have six or eight promoters who claim to "represent" them. In fact, none of the promoters are the actual representative, they are just looking to get a gig for the band and take their percentage for doing so. The bands will usually take these gigs, if they are not already booked, but primarily tend to do their own bookings.

school, I had dreams of seeing the world, traveling quite a bit, but I never really thought I'd have an opportunity to do it. I think if I hadn't taken up the music, I would probably still be repairing phones - retired now with a pension [with a laughing emphasis on the pension vs. no formal retirement programs in performing].

"But I would have been repairing, indoors all the time, repairing switchboards, telephones and stuff. I would have been drifting along, not really seeing much of the world. It turned out much different because I have seen lots of places in the world and met some great people. We tell all the people over here [in Ireland], the reason we come to America so often is because it just like family. We could arrive in America and find somebody; we could go for a drink, to help us out if we needed it, or whatever. I always think of America as a second home because it always is like family over here."

"I have no regrets but I think I would be a lot more careful management wise. We were kind of young and we got managers who saw that we were young and enthusiastic [and vulnerable] and led us down one road, which was a great road because we're still seeing the benefits from it today, as far as music goes. But I would have been more careful. I wouldn't change one bit of it in regards to the band and the friends we've made. I've had a good time. I've enjoyed every second of it and thank God I'm here today to enjoy it and hopefully for a long time to come. We've gotten good benefits from it, because we're still coming over here. We got to travel the world playing music. But, at the end of the day, we could have been a lot better off [with artistic control, financially]. I don't have any regrets. I try to look forward and see what the hell [is next].

"I continue because I love it, and the day I stop loving it, I will pack it in. Hopefully, that day will never come. I would like to live and work in the U.S.A. for maybe six to eight months of the year and the rest in Ireland and elsewhere. I would like to keep going for as long as possible, make as many more CDs, DVDs of all our favorite songs as possible. Recording a Christmas album is on the cards. I would like to get together with all the major acts, do a show and a CD/DVD from it, and donate the lot to charity.

"[I had many influences] musically; The Clancy Brothers, Dubliners, and Judy Collins. Being completely self taught, I was able to use different types of music to enhance my own style."

In addition to singing, Sean plays the banjo and mandolin and enjoys reading, the GAA (Gaelic Athletic Association - Gaelic Football and Hurling) and is a fan of Mohammed Ali, the Dublin Gaelic Football team, Irish golfer Padraig Harrington and the Irish soccer team. Favorite views include "my home on my return from a tour."

"My favorite memories are of our first group, the Jolly Tinkers. We traveled the country and had to sleep in sheds, hay barns etcetera. I remember, mostly, coming in from gigs in Galway, Kerry ..., at 5 a.m. and having to be in work at 8 a.m. I also remember the huge encouragement I got from my mother and father, and indeed, all my family Also, sitting by the fire in my parent's house with my sister Maura, singing *Eileen Aroon*, going to hear my brother Patrick playing with his band *The Blue Caps*. He played guitar when we worked in The Post & Telegraphs (Our phone company, now known as Eircom), in the 1960's."

The early predecessor to the Dublin City Ramblers, the Jolly Tinkers played their first gig in a pub called *The Kingsway Lounge* in Dublin's Capel St. in 1963, for a few pints. Sean played tenor banjo & mandolin, brother Matt played tin whistle & fiddle, and neighbor Pat Cummins played guitar and did most of the singing. Their first paying gig was in *The Parkside,* a hotel on the Nth Circular Road in Dublin. They received the princely sum of a half-crown each for their night's work, a total equal to fifteen cents today. The group recruited Patsy Watchorn in 1964. The Jolly Tinkers carried on until, at the suggestion of good friend and Irish comedian, Noel V. Ginnity, they changed the name from the Jolly Tinkers to the *Quare Fellas*, after Brendan Behan's play.

Quare Fellas recorded two albums in 1967- 1968; *The Quare Fellas At Home* and *The Quare Fellas, A Fond Tale*. Their first TV appearance came in 1969, on *Ballad Sheet*, hosted by Shay Healy. Christy Moore and various other artists were on the same episode.

The Quare Fellas disbanded at the end of 1969, and Sean went on to become a founding member of the *Dublin City Ramblers,* in 1970. Besides Sean, original band members were Kevin Geraghty, Mick Crotty and Patsy Watchorn. Mick, already known for the group *Ramblers 2* with another Festival Legend, Johnny McEvoy, came up with the name Dublin City Ramblers. The Dublin City Ramblers turned professional in 1972 and were a fixture at the ballad/folk scene in the early 1970's. They were featured every week at Mick McCarthy's famous *The Embankment*, in Tallaght (Jobstown), County Dublin The Embankment was where most of the now famous Irish acts like Barleycorn, Paddy Reilly and many others first performed and learned the ropes of the business, before going on to successful careers.

Then, in 1976, they got a call from good friend Pete St. John, regarding a song he had written, called *The Rare Ould Times*. The song was to become a huge hit for the group and marked their "arrival" throughout the international Ballad/Folk scene. Sean recalls, "We were booked to play in Waterville, in County Kerry, when Pete called us and said he wanted to meet us in the car park of Goff's in Kill, County Kildare, as he had a song for us that he was sure would be a big hit. Little did we know that it would go on to become an anthem worldwide, Everybody tries to claim it, even groups and solo artists who would be supporting us, but it was written for us specifically. It was not written for any one person, as some egoists would have you believe. It was written for the Dublin City Ramblers as a group, so it will remain forever ours."[1]

Another big hit for the group was *The Ferrymen*. "We recorded The Ferrymen in 1983, and even today, the second we start playing the first few lines of that song, people start singing and clapping their hands. The author of The Ferryman, was their old friend Pete St. John (a prolific songwriter, whose works include: *Rare Ould Times, Fields of Athenry, Spirit of the Gael, The Shamrock and the Rose* and over 100 other great songs). Pete said that the Dublin City Ramblers sound was so distinctive, for the fact that Sean tuned his banjo a little differently than most. The resulting sound had given the Ramblers such a distinctive trademark sound, unequaled before or since.

The Ramblers have been major successes through the 70's, 80's, 90's and right on through today. Among their many recordings, they have eight Gold Albums; *The Guinness Record Of Irish Ballads - Vol. 1, 2, 3 & 4, the Rare Ould Times, The Ferryman, The Flight Of Earls* and *Home And Away.*

Their achievements include; headlining at *The Royal Albert Hall* in England, supporting Ray Charles in Paris in front of 300,000 people in 1981, receiving the Keys to the Cities of Fort Lauderdale and Hollywood in Florida, Little Rock, Arkansas and Moorhead, Kentucky, and having had the honor of playing for actress Maureen O'Hara. They are in the Hall of Fame in the *Helen Stairs Theatre* in Florida. They have played in Dublin's *National Stadium, Carnegie Hall* in New York, Cork's *Opera House* and *National Concert Hall.*

As Sean puts it, "I would be very proud of The Ramblers. They've come a very long way from very humble beginnings, our folk beginnings, and we're still very humble, in our own way. We've had a great 'ould way from the music."

"We are very proud of our Gold Albums, Awards, and Keys to Cities. They are a measure of our work throughout our careers."[1]

The Dublin City Ramblers have also played for many of the Irish soccer teams and Dublin GAA teams down the years. January usually finds them in the Caribbean with all the other major Irish acts, performing for Irish Festival Cruises. The Dublin City Ramblers have headlined most major Irish festivals worldwide, including the largest Irish festival in the world, Milwaukee Irish Fest. They continue to tour across the U.S., and the world, with the help of manager John Ryan.

From the original four members, the Dublin City Ramblers have evolved over the years: Mick Crotty and Kevin Geraghty both left in 1974, replaced by Phil (The Horse) McCaffrey and Kevin Molloy. They both left in 1989, replaced by Paddy Sweeney (1988) and eventually, Shay Kavanagh (1992). Patsy left to go solo in 1995. Paddy was replaced by Pierce McAllorum in 2002 and Shay Kavanagh was replaced by Martin

Paul Conway (2002). Keyboard players Luke Crowley, Eddie Lynch or Martin Corcoran alternately play with the band as well.

There have been many changes in the Dublin City Ramblers over the last thirty plus years, says Sean. "I'll keep it going for as long as possible, as long as I want, as long as I have to, because I really enjoy it. I keep it going and I make sure that anybody who comes into the band knows where they're at, to our standards, standards we've had all these years. We will keep going on as long as we can."

When asked what the secret was, Sean replied, "Firstly, treat every show and every audience with the same respect and enthusiasm as the last one, and once you're enjoying it, keep doing it. Secondly, make no room whatsoever for egos and you'll go on forever, PG. [Please God]"

Dublin City Ramblers Discography:

Records/CD's:

- At Home   (1969)
- A Fond Tale   (1969)
- A Nation Once Again   (1972, 1975, 1980)
- Boys of the Old Brigade   (1973)
- An End to It Someday   (1974)
- The Guinness Record of Irish Ballads Vol. I   (1974)
- The Guinness Record of Irish Ballads Vol. II   (1977)
- The Guinness Record of Irish Ballads Vol. III   (1978)
- Irish Republican Jail Songs   (1978)
- The Guinness Record of Irish Ballads Vol. IV   (1979)
- Rare Ould Times   (1980)
- The Ferryman   (1983)
- In Concert   (1985)
- Radio 2 Marathon Song / The Titanic   (1987)
- Flight of the Earls   (1987, 1992)
- Millennium   (1988)
- Luke Kelly's Land   (1988)
- Best of the Dublin City Ramblers   (1988)
- Home and Away   (1989)
- Live @ Johnny Fox's Pub   (1992)
- The Craic & Porter Black   (1995)
- The Crack Was 90   (1997)
- Raise the Roof   (1998)
- On Holy Ground   (2000)
- Ireland My Ireland   (2003)

Quare Fellas:

- The Quare Fellas At Home   (1967)
- The Quare Fellas, A Fond Tale   (1968)

Videos:

- Dublin City Ramblers Live @ Johnny Fox's   (1995)

www.dublincityramblers.com

VI.

The New Barleycorn
John Delaney and Alec DeGabriel

*"When you hear the New Barleycorn, you'll know that
Irish music is alive and well." -Tommy Makem*

For more than thirty years, Barleycorn, and now, The New Barleycorn, has been delighting, entertaining and inspiring audiences all over the world. They have performed in Ireland, the U.S., Canada, Germany, France, Scotland, Wales, Australia, Malta, England, New Zealand, Virgin Islands and the Dominican Republic. Their signature songs, *Men Behind the Wire, Cavan Girl, Portland Town, This Land is Your Land, Song for Ireland, Roisin, We the People, Boys of the Old Brigade* and *On the One Road,* among many, are sung in those countries and anywhere else the Irish and Irish music lovers gather.

Most recently, The New Barleycorn were invited by Phil Coulter to appear on his show, *Coulter & Company,* the annual ten-week summer replacement for the RTE's *Late Late Show.* It was filmed at the Grand Hotel, in Kilarney, in front of a live audience, and will be seen by more than a million and half people on RTE television. From these performances, Phil picks one show to be the Christmas Special. The episode with New Barleycorn was chosen to be the Christmas Special for 2005. The shows include well-known groups from all over the world, including Dermot O'Brien, Johnny McEvoy, Songwriter Ron McTell, Banjo player Gerry O'Connor and many more.

As this book goes to print, New Barleycorn are working in the studio to produce their next CD, as yet untitled, due out in spring, 2006.

John Delaney

"My father had a guitar when I was about five years old and one day, when there was nobody in the room, I set it too close to an electric fire. After a few minutes, the guitar started 'twanging' by itself and after a while, the back fell off, when the glue melted. I think that was the first music I made (accidentally), but I always have music in my head."

John Delaney grew up in and around the countryside in County Down, moving around the Downpatrick and Newcastle area. As a young man, He was interested in the local history, noting that Saint Patrick was buried in Downpatrick and, in 1798, there was much rebel activity in County Down connected to the '1798 uprising', which was centered between Down and County Wexford.

John's father played the piano and liked to sing songs from the stage 'shows' for his own amusement. He enjoyed listening to singers like Paul Robeson and Mario Lanza and many other popular singers of the time before TV was widespread and listening to the radio was the main way to hear music.

As a child, John listened to Burl Ives on the radio. He didn't know who he was, but liked the music, and his mother singing along to it, "She swallowed the spider to catch the fly....." There were plenty of folk type songs introduced on radio in Ireland from the U.S., even though at that age he had no idea where the songs came from or who was singing. Some of the lyrics were usually picked up along the way.

"The sounds and the feelings in the music got to me and when I was not much older, I pestered my mother and father to get me this 'Melodica' (wind instrument) for my birthday, it had a little keyboard and you blew 'till you were blue in the face."

When he was a little older, John picked up an old John Grey tenor (four string) banjo that was sitting around after one of his older brothers had attempted to play it but gave it up. After listening to other musicians who would frequent their house; having sessions, singing and playing together with his brothers, he started to get a few reels and jigs together.

"*Comhaltas Ceoltoiri Eireann*, an Irish organization for the promotion of Irish music and culture, hosted a local Irish music gathering (*sessiùn*)

217

which was a great place to meet friends on a Sunday afternoon in the winter, in front of a big fire, and a good place to learn and play tunes and sing a few songs. There was something special about listening to old songs that (at that time) had possibly never been recorded but handed down verbally from one generation to the next."

The music and methods of the time is wonderfully explained by world renowned fiddler and former *Planxty* and *Patrick Street* member James Kelly, in an interview with *Fiddler Magazine.* In the pe-1930's, people in Ireland "would get together in the rural parts of the country at the crossroads and the house dances and have their own social activities, dances, stories and songs. A family in the locality might have an old gramophone player, and when some of the 78 records would come from the States, it was like going to Disneyland! People would get together at whoever's house it would be and they'd listen to this record over and over and over again. It was a great time for excitement, you know.

"So that was going on when the early recordings were coming into Ireland from the States and the musicians who were making those recordings were becoming influential because they were making recordings no one had made before. Then in the '30s, there was a bit of a switch and the clergy in Ireland at the time played a role in that. They started to discourage the crossroad dances and the country dances and encourage people to go to the bigger towns and villages [and] into these halls.

"In a sense it kind of put a stop to all that stuff, you know. The music itself went through a period in the '40s and '50s where there wasn't much going on at all. In a lot of cases people just played in their own homes – – you might invite people in, get together and play. It wasn't as if you'd go for a festival like you would these days.

"In Dublin in the late '50s, there were two plays going on. One of them was called *The Song of the Anvil,* and there were two groups of musicians together for those plays. One was a man called Sean O'Riada, and some of the other musicians were [John Kelly], Paddy Moloney, Michael Tubridy, Martin Fahey, Ronnie McShane, Sonny Brogan and Eamon DeBuitleir. Out of all that came the idea to form a group, which wasn't done before.

"Technically speaking, the idea of actually arranging folk music, or dance music, had been done on at least one or two 78 recordings, but they were folk tunes done in a classical way, highly orchestrated. And I presume they were classical musicians. But in this case, they were all traditional musicians who called themselves Ceoltoiri Culainn. Ceoltoiri is the Gaelic word for musicians, and Culainn is a place name, just outside Dublin. The idea of the band was to present traditional songs with accompaniment and traditional dance tunes and slow airs, arranged with instruments: harpsichord, bodhran, piano, fiddle, flute, pipes, whistles. Sean O'Riada himself started to dig up the music of Turlough O'Carolan, and Ceoltoiri Culainn introduced the music of O'Carolan for the first time.

"When it started off, a lot of the traditional musicians in Dublin were absolutely confused, they couldn't figure it out at all. Particularly when they got the first bit of air play on the radio, because at that time the idea of doing a radio broadcast was something unusual, something very special. Some people liked it from the first, and others thought it was modern, they didn't like the ideas. Sean O'Riada himself probably was criticized because he was a musician with a jazz and classical background. In 1963, out of Ceoltoiri Culainn came the Chieftains, under the leadership of Paddy Moloney."[1]

"One of the great offshoots of playing music is that there was always plenty of fun and laughter," John says, "and occasionally when there was a local Ceili dance, a bunch of us would get together as *The Harbour Lights Ceili Band* and play for the night until we could play no more and the dancers were satisfied with *The Siege of Ennis* and reels and jigs galore."

"I heard much of the music when I was young in Ireland. The sounds got to me and the feelings in the music, so I picked up an old guitar, the banjo when I was seven. After several years of playing for the family, I started playing out with various line-ups when I was twelve."[2]

As John was growing up and in his early professional career, he was heavily impacted by a variety of influences; "The Dubliners; all great characters, singers and musicians, especially banjo player Barney McKenna, who was a major influence in promoting the tenor banjo as an Irish thing. The Clancy Brothers & Tommy Makem, The Kingston Trio, The Weavers, The Limelighters, Lead Belly, Woodie Gutherie, Pete Seeger, Ewan MacColl and the whole folk revival of the 60's and 70's in the U.S."

John became interested in this folk style of music but concentrated on learning tunes and collecting old songs as a hobby. Some of the songs he collected have rarely seen the light of day.

Delaney spent time in the three-year music program at the Dublin College of Music but had to leave as "it was an expense I didn't need at the time." Behind the music were the bands, and the mix. This is what caught John's attention. He also enjoys performers like Eric Bogle, Stan Rogers, John Williamson, Ewan MacColl, Christy Moore, Ralph McTell, Joan Baez and Tommy Makem, who have all made significant social commentary in their songs, while also being highly entertaining.

"Irish music for me is much more than just playing notes that create tunes," John said, "there is a feeling in the music that can be heard, but not written. It can evoke a feeling in time and create emotions that seem to transcend time and sometimes illuminate our history.

"[Musical] influence had a major impact [on society] by the civil rights way of 'play fair,'" recalls Delaney. "[The] music I was hearing was very outspoken about the things that were wrong. Music was a platform about the things that can be corrected. I don't like to see a whole night of music that doesn't say something. Some of the songs, *Green Fields of France* [for example], are such powerful songs. People had the right to say their piece; I just wish they could have done it without drawing a gun. Songs carry a strong message – very much part and parcel of what we do. It is much more a civil rights feeling than anything else.

"From day one, I was interested in civil rights songs; from Joan Baez to you name it. That's the sort of thing that floats my boat, with the situation in Ireland. With music, it has nothing if it doesn't have heart. ...A song is good as long as it is sung. If it isn't, then it doesn't have any life."[2]

John moved to Belfast around 1970 and started playing in sessions there and soon got together with friend Liam Tiernan, a fantastic singer from Belfast. Together, they started *Barleycorn*, a name synonymous with whiskey making. Barleycorn started to make a local impact on the ballad scene in 1971, and then added Paddy McGuigan, to broaden the songs and sound. Brian McCormack was added within a few months [no relation to Derek McCormack].

"There were many social and political injustices taking place at that time and songs were a good way of highlighting them and focusing attention on them, which we helped to do when we recorded Paddy McGuigan's song, *Men Behind the Wire*, a song written about the injustices of internment without trial at a time when civil rights were being abused and manipulated," John recalled, "the song helped focus the attention of a much bigger audience, nationally, and even internationally, on the problem."

Barleycorn's very first public gig was with *The Chieftains* and *Horselips* at the Cork City Opera House. With laughter, John remembers when they were first asked to play, he thought, "Why do they want us?" But then he found out that the groups 'single', The Men Behind the Wire, was in the Irish Record Charts, unknown to them, where it remained for forty-eight weeks, eight weeks at #1. It became the biggest selling Irish record at that time. The B-side was *Freedom Walk*.

The Men Behind the Wire is a song about Internment. Internment was a British policy giving police and Army free hand to do as they wished to solve "the Irish problem." On Monday, August 9th, 1971, at 4:00 a.m., British soldiers stormed Irish homes in Belfast without warning. 342 men and boys, one of them blind, as well as one dog, were grabbed up, often beaten, and taken to Long Kesh Prison (which would later become *The Maze*), and held, without trial, for months. Denied sustainable food and any medical treatment, some were forced to run gauntlets in which they were beaten, while a helicopter hovered, to drown out the sounds. Soon after Internment started, Paddy wrote The Men Behind the Wire, a song calling for solidarity with the men behind the wire in Long Kesh. In a typical political irony of that time, Paddy was interred for writing a song about internment. The boys carried on the song, and the message, while Paddy languished in Magilligan Prison for more than four months.

The Men Behind the Wire

by Paddy McGuigan

Chorus:
Armoured cars and tanks and guns
Came to take away our sons
But every man must stand behind
The men behind the wire

Through the little streets of Belfast
In the dark of early morn
British soldiers came marauding
Wrecking little homes with scorn.
Heedless of the crying children
Dragging fathers from their beds
Beating sons while helpless mothers
Watched the blood flow from their heads

Chorus

Not for them a judge or jury
Or indeed a crime at all
Being Irish means they're guilty
So we're guilty one and all
Round the world the truth will echo
Cromwell's men are here again
England's name again is sullied
In the eyes of honest men

Chorus.

Proudly march behind our banners
Firmly stand behind our men
We will have them free to help us
Build a Nation once again
On the people stand together

Proudly firmly on your way
Never fear, and never falter
Till the boys are home to stay.

Chorus

Liam Tiernan, former band mate and founding member of Barleycorn, recalls the band's start, and the tumultuous time around Men Behind the Wire:

""John and I started together, and we had a girl singer with us, called Christy (Christine) McCallister. We played a couple of the bars up North there [in Northern Ireland]. It was for something to do, for a bit of fun. Then later, the Civil Resistance Committee for Andersonstown, which is in west Belfast, they were organizing what was called the *Rents & Rates Strikes*, non-violent civil disobedience, to draw attention [to the problems]. So The Men Behind the Wire came about because they asked us to write a song and the idea was to get the single made and have volunteers go around the area, to houses, and sell it door to door. The proceeds were used to buy food for the families of those interned, and pay for buses so families could visit them. And the song went through the roof.

"It was the largest selling pop record in the history of Ireland, until U2 came along. The presses were going full bore and couldn't keep up with it [produce enough copies]. After that, every single thing we recorded was banned, both by the Irish and the English government. It couldn't be played on the radio. We did very little television. The proceeds were donated to the PDF [Prisoners Defendants Fund] and helped to create the *Andersonstown News*, which is now the second largest distributed newspaper in the north of Ireland.

"We weren't of the folk set. We were doing our own thing. We weren't like the traditional style folk trios or anything. We were more on the stronger Bardic tradition of things. You see what you see in one town and you write a song about it and you sing it in the next town, so that they know [what's going on]. It was like the early news, centuries ago. We weren't able to be put in any category.

"I remember, Paddy was put in Magilligan, the concentration camp they had up in the north, near Derry. Of course, the newspapers down south, he was in it every day, a bit of a hero, interred for writing a song. Right after he got out, we were down playing in Cork, and the following night at a place near Bandon. The groups criteria of how to rate the hotel was *How late did they let us drink and how early did they run the Hoover?* We'd never drink before a gig, because we wanted to be as good as we could be.

"We were staying at the Munster Arms, I think, was the name of the hotel. So we pulled up to the hotel, and I had my bag on my lap. There was a night porter there, a big fella, an older guy, about 6'4", who was a farmer by day. But he always asked how Paddy was. The boys were getting their stuff out of the trunk and I was in the door with the big guy and I said,

'You'll never guess who's with us?'

"He says, 'Ah, he's not.'

"And I says, 'He is, yeah.'

"'Is he all right?' he says.

"'Ah, he got a terrible beating and the torture,' (which wasn't true, I was messing with him), 'with all the torture, he got his hearing about gone. You have to shout at him.'

"He says, 'No problem, no problem. Thanks, thanks for letting me know that. I'm looking forward to seeing him.'

"So I go back out to make sure the boys are all set, to give them a hand at the car and Paddy says to me, 'Is your man all right?'

"I said, 'Yeah, he's a nice big fella. The only thing you have to remember about him, Paddy, he's a bit hard of hearing. You have to shout at him a bit.'

"'Ah, no problem,' says Paddy.

"So the two of them are shouting at each other all night. Brian McCormack had to go to bed, he couldn't keep a straight face for any longer."

The Men Behind the Wire stayed in the Top Ten Irish record charts for forty-eight weeks and went on to sell over *three million* copies worldwide. Barleycorn was presented with a Gold Record for the recording in 1973.

The Men Behind the Wire was followed by *Sing Irishmen Sing* and *This Land is Your Land*, which were all top ten hits.

John plays 5 string and tenor banjos*, mandolin, guitar, whistle and bodhran. He also has played banjo on many other Irish artists' recordings. Paddy played the guitar and harmonica (he entered a competition in London where one of the judges, World-class harmonica player Larry Addler said that Paddy was one of the best he had ever heard). Paddy also wrote *Irish Soldier Laddie* (recorded with great success by another Festival Legend, Danny Doyle), *Boys of the Old Brigade* and the words to the Irish version of *This Land is Your Land*, among many others.

John played the banjo, Liam played guitar and Brian played base. Along with guitarist Paddy McGuigan, the foursome now formed the distinctive sound and style that would become known the world over as Barleycorn.

The original founder of Barleycorn also enjoys classical guitar. He didn't get far in learning it though. Instead, he picked tenor banjo up after his brother, Dermot, tried to play the instrument and gave up. John started playing at local sessions of Comhaltas Ceoltoiri [traditional sessions] on tenor banjo. One day at a Barleycorn rehearsal an idea was put forward that a "5 string banjo" would be a good sound to have in the group. As nobody else took up the challenge, John volunteered to try and master the instrument and still continues to play it today.

Paddy McGuigan left the band in 1976 and now lives in North County Dublin, near Dobabate. Paul Anderson, a fiddle player, joined with Barleycorn in 1977, adding a wonderful voice, the tin whistle and good humor but then Liam Tierney left the band:

---

* A tenor banjo is a 4-string banjo tuned an octave lower than the violin, for the purposes of Irish music. A 5-string banjo is a standard bluegrass banjo developed in the U.S. Irish-Scottish songs came here, which eventually became bluegrass music, then went back to Ireland. Earl Scruggs played this style.]

"I left at the end of August, 1981," says Liam. "It was very amicable. I wanted to explore America and I'm delighted that I did. I enjoyed the time and I enjoyed playing with the boys and we never had a bad word. We all got along very well. The boys carried on. We all got something out of it. "I'm still dabbling in the music and I've got some recordings coming out in 2006."

Liam also released *Straight From the Heart*, an album of love songs that received great reviews, which was recorded with Bonnie Raitt's band. He owns *Tiernan's*, a music pub and restaurant in Boston's Lincoln Wharf, and in October, 2005, Liam opened his second restaurant and music bar, also called Tiernan's, at the corners of Beach and Hyde Streets, in San Francisco's Fisherman's Wharf. He lives nearby.

The foursome now became a trio, with John, Paul and Brian. Later in 1981, Paddy Sweeney became part of the world famous band, where he stayed for almost six years, before joining another historic group, and Festival Legend, the Dublin City Ramblers. Barleycorn continued to record high selling albums, including *My Last Farewell*. Brian and Paul left to pursue other interests. "I had fun, fond memories and great times with the guys that played together over the years," recalled Delaney. "It was a great experience."

The fantastically gifted singer, Derek McCormack joined The Barleycorn in 1983. Derek started his musical career almost at birth, as part of his family troupe of touring Fit-ups, then joined *Dermot O'Brien and the Clubmen* at the age of eighteen. He performed with Dermot for twelve years before joining Barleycorn and John, Paddy Sweeney and fiddler Denis O'Rourke. Barleycorn collectively decided to refocus their music to folk and ballad, rather than strictly rebel songs, a move that has proven to both show foresight and yield great success for the group. They continued to record top selling albums/CD's such as *Song For Ireland* and *My Last Farewell*.

Barleycorn became the first group to record Phil Colclough's, *Song for Ireland* as well as the original version of Pete St. John's, *The Fields of Athenry*, which had entered the charts for a few weeks in the late 1970's. Some of the other Barleycorn recordings to list in the Top Ten Irish Charts include; *Sing Irishmen Sing, This Land is Your Land,* and Thom Moore's *Cavan Girl* (which won the Emmets Cavan International

Song Contest and became the unofficial theme song for that contest thereafter), *Portland Town, We The People* and *Fields of Athenry.* Paddy Reilly recorded the Fields of Athenry again, two years later and had huge successes with it around the world.

Paddy Sweeney left the Barleycorn in 1986, playing on his own, then with the Dublin City Ramblers, and now on his own again. The Barleycorn then performed as a three member group with John Delaney, Derek McCormack and Denis O'Rourke, which including the first of many gigs at Milwaukee Irish Fest in Milwaukee, Wisconsin, in 1987 and 1988.

1988 brought the group a new challenge. Invited to play at the World Expo in Brisbane, in Queensland, Australia for two months, the group left not knowing what to expect. The World Expo goes on for six months, with many countries of the world represented. 16.2 million people went through the World Expo that year – very near the total population of all of Australia at that time. Barleycorn played daily through the months of May and June, six nights a week. Great weather led to the Barleycorn playing outside the *Young at Heart Restaurant.*

On their first night in Brisbane, they ran into six members of the Australian Army's bomb squad. There was no designated "Irish" stage at the World Expo so, after a few nights, and a few jokes about the band taking the area over, members of the Army, guys who are still friends with the band members today, climbed up the massive geometric pixie stix overhang on the stage and erected a sign saying "World Expo Irish Pavilion."

The Barleycorn were asked to stay on for the rest of the Expo. Prior commitments to Cleveland's Irish Cultural Festival and Milwaukee's Irish Fest would not allow them to do so. But then they were made an offer that they could not refuse, to return for the final two months of the World Expo, after meeting their obligations back in the States. Barleycorn went back to Ireland, the States, and then back to Australia.

Another highlight for Barleycorn occurred in the midst of their brief time in the States, before returning to Australia. The host of *Macca*, a four time zone radio program, called John while Barleycorn were playing in Milwaukee. He had heard their recording of *Roisin* and wanted to know if he could play it and include it in an annual compilation album that was widely distributed throughout Australia. Roisin got a lot of airplay and other stations picked it up. The group also got a lot of radio pre-event publicity because of the compilation album and the playing of Roisin on Macca, as well as appearing on most of the national morning shows.

In a fateful meeting in 1989, that wouldn't bear fruit for another five years, John met Alec DeGabriele, then playing with *Alec & Darby's Folk*, in Cleveland, Ohio while John was playing with Barleycorn. Barleycorn regularly played gigs at Alec's music bar, Darby O'Toole's, when on tour in the U.S. and when playing Cleveland's Irish Cultural Festival. Fortunately, their future would become interlocked.

The experience at World Expo was such a profile raising series of performances for the Barleycorn that they went on eight extended national tours of Australia and New Zealand, playing to huge crowds, from 1988 until 1994. During this time, Barleycorn also headlined the *Australian National Folk Festival*. In 1990, in the midst of this incredible run, Denis O'Rourke informed John and Derek that he loved Australia so much that he was "not going home" and left the band. He still lives in Australia today and is still in touch with his band mates.

So the group said goodbye to Denis O'Rourke and hello to fiddler Maurice McCarthy. John had met Maurice in Dublin a few years earlier and tracked him down. John, Derek and Maurice continued playing throughout the early '90's, recording more CD's and spent much of their time abroad, touring. Maurice left to pursue other interests in 1993 and Liam Tierney kindly obliged and stood in with his old band mates part-time when his schedule allowed.

In 1993 John and Derek got their 'Green Cards' and considered moving to the U.S. By 1994, Barleycorn was spending 75% of their time outside Ireland on tour, as the entertainment business in Ireland had declined for everyone. They agreed that if business in Ireland didn't improve by the end of 1995, they would break up the group, ending their incredible twenty-five year run as Barleycorn.

Alec told John and Derek that if it happened [the break up of the band], they were always welcome in Cleveland, maybe they could do something together.

During this time, the entertainment business was dropping year by year. From the late 1980's through the early 1990's, folk music and musicians were taking a beating. Specialists were getting hammered. As John recalls, "It was a soul-destroying time. Media had such a change around. Before, if we recorded, it would be played on RTE and then the local radio stations would get it. But then trying to get a song played became next to impossible. They were importing songs from everywhere. That's what was getting played.

"I think that 'Music Marketing' as opposed to 'music' is currently winning in Ireland. Commercial music marketing is steering the air waves in Ireland like everywhere else and unfortunately limiting the scope of what the minority listening audience may like to hear.

"Considering that this music and style was once regularly listened to in Ireland by the majority, it is a great pity that the powers that be have been allowed to make sweeping decisions that have affected everyone's choice and those decisions may in turn relegate this style of music (and part of our culture) to the History Channel. I would like to give a fair amount of air time to all the national music and arts in Ireland; it should not be just about commerce where the Arts are concerned and more especially when it was an interwoven part of our modern culture. [Folk/ballads] … that once held a respected and unbiased place on the Irish air waves have no place any longer. I don't believe people should be presented with tunnel audio but that's what is presented in the air waves, then that is all they'll know.

"I've seen a lot of change but I'm not easily daunted, I'm the eternal optimist. A good environment and being surrounded by good people helps you to be creative."

September of 1995 signaled the end of Barleycorn in Ireland. The group played out the rest of their contracts, with the last gig being on the Caribbean Irish Festival Cruise in January, 1996. In the midst of winding down Barleycorn, John emigrated to the U.S.A., in September of 1995, and came to Cleveland, Ohio, where he joined forces with Alec. Soon after, *The New Barleycorn* was born. The long legacy of Barleycorn would not be lost, with a breakup, but continued to evolve, in another form. Five CD's and ten years later, it's still going strong from Vancouver to the Caribbean.

Derek went on to play with *The Fureys* and also formed a band called *Nickelodeon*, with Ronnie Kennedy and Billy Condon, who were also touring with Daniel O'Donnell. Somehow they found time in all this touring with two different bands to release a four track CD and an album, entitled *Together As One*, before the time constraints with their other commitments forced them to break up Nickelodeon. After Nickelodeon, Derek did occasional solo performances and set the goal of doing much more of that. He released *Never Too Far From My Mind* in 2000.

Derek passed away, unexpectedly, while on the Irish Festival Cruise on January 30th, 2004. He was fifty-one years old. Alec, John and Derek's old friend and band mate, Gerry Simpson, released a tribute CD, featuring Derek's recordings of his favorite songs, in memoriam to him. *A Lifetime of Music* was released at Cleveland's Irish Cultural Festival in July, 2004, in the midst of a special tribute featuring stirring performances by Alec, John, Danny Doyle, the Fureys, Tommy Makem and the Makem Brothers. The special release CD sold out amidst many tears and all proceeds went to Derek's wife, Bernadette, who was brought in for the tribute.

For Derek

By Isabelle Murphy, written for A Lifetime of Music

Your guitar lies silent
Now that you've gone,
But you are still with us
In memories and song.

In your songs are memories
Of where we should be,
A small piece of home
You always brought me.

And when I hear your voice
I know where I'll be,
I'm back in Ireland,
And you've taken me.

You brought your sweet music
To all you met,
Your voice now an angel's,
We'll never forget.

In losing Derek, we lost one of the giants of Irish music, maybe before his enduring legacy was fully written. Derek had set a goal of doing more touring on his own. We can still hear his music on the recording gifts he left us, and in our memories - we hear an illustrious performance each time we play one of his CD's.

The New Barleycorn … John Delaney's vision for the future of The New Barleycorn is rooted in the personal philosophy he has already talked about, "In a general sense, I'd like to see the music at least maintained as part of Irish culture. You don't travel around the world for so many years and then say that it was meaningless. Irish performers/balladeers were and are a modern version of the bards, always an ear for a good song. It is a way of addressing social or religious issues, it's a good platform. I hope it is not forgotten. I've seen the wheels turn – seen a lot of changes, but even now, cream comes to the top. All forms of music should have their day.

"I would like to play more concerts nationally and internationally. I'd love to create an interesting or fresh approach or dynamic to what we do without changing our style. We have progressed and now include original material in our shows and recordings and hopefully we can continue on that path. It would be nice to do a CD or album of our own music, as well as having a chart hit in the U.S., a good target to aim for. That is a part of our legacy that someone will pick up when we're gone and be inspired the same way. The nicest compliment is when someone says, 'I was influenced by you.' This music was so much a part of our culture that I hope it continues to create new interest and enjoyment for generations to come.

"I started playing and, with a bit of luck, was reasonably successful quite quickly and although I had no particular intention of making it a life time career, I found that I enjoyed it and I believe that you should enjoy what you do if possible, so I just kept playing.

"I love music. I enjoy playing and I get a buzz from performing and I've never done anything else. So it still seems like a good idea. There's no high like you get from an enthusiastic audience reaction and it is often very touching to hear how your music has evoked feelings and memories and passions in other people's lives. I hope when I am much older I can continue and still enjoy playing. It is a labor of love as well as anything else. If I didn't play anymore I would probably be involved in some other aspect of music, maybe recording. I've never done anything else, so why would I change now? It's what I like doing."

John has influenced so many listeners, performers and fans. But those that influenced him? "The Clancy Brothers initially, when I started playing, theirs was one of the first song books I got and I was impressed by their music. They were musical gods in Ireland and now I feel privileged to have known some of them. Now they're friends of mine, which is a nice way to have gone. [I was also influenced by] Earle Scruggs on banjo."

Other influences on both John and in Irish music include Corkman Sean O'Riada, who formed *Ceoltoiri Eireann* – the predecessor to

The Chieftains. "He orchestrated some traditional music *(Crossroads Ceili* kind of thing) into something that was nationally staged. He also composed and arranged music for *Mise Eire,* taken from *Roisin Dubh."*

Michael O'Sullibhean, Arty McGlynn, Donal Lunny and U2, their successes in very different fields, and the invention of CD's, round out the other influences.

But for John Delaney, the success of Men Behind the Wire was probably the biggest of his personal impact moments, for both him and for Barleycorn. Another such moment occurred when John and Derek McCormack got together, and with Denis O'Rourke and Paddy Sweeney, then reestablished the focus of the group, showing them as a group with staying power. It proved that the group was not a drop in the ocean of the Irish music scene. He also has great respect for his current partner and friend, Alec DeGabriele, "For his enthusiasm, professionalism and musical ability not only as a great guitarist and as a singer, but also as a song writer and comic. We have fun and laugh a lot!"

If not performing, John would be working on the water, on a boat. He knows that if it weren't for the water in Cleveland, he probably would not have stayed there, maybe ending up in Boston or New York. John also enjoys traveling and enjoys working in the sound recording area as an engineer/producer.

"I've had the good fortune to travel quite a bit and music has been my passport to a lot of places that I might not otherwise have seen. Cleveland has been a kind of a passport [as well] to allow me to do what I enjoy doing most, playing music. It is more down to earth, with more decent people than anywhere else. Cleveland has an edge - We're on the same wavelength. Living in a good environment and being surrounded by good people helps you to be creative.

"I love Cleveland and the longer I'm here, the more I like it. The people here are great and there's a very comfortable feeling of home and belonging. I've been here for ten years now and I think I've grown roots at this stage. Cleveland is home now. It is hard to get away from calling Ireland home. [But] now when I am in Ireland, I look at 'going home' as going to Cleveland."

The ballad tradition, performed so memorably and with such historic impact, from the very first days of Barleycorn, continues to evolve, expand, and be proudly performed from Lake Erie to the Isle of Eire, thanks to the continued dedication, vision and hard work of John Delaney.

Alec DeGabriele

One of the last of the *"Fit-ups"* or *Traveling People*, still performing for a living, Alec (Alexander) Patrick DeGabriele brightened this world immensely when he entered it on November 27th, 1953. The brightness has only grown since that day.

Born in Sandymon, outside Dublin, Ireland, Alec followed an older brother Michael and sister Christine and in turn, was followed by younger brother Patrick. Alec's father, Alexander (also called Alec), a fine actor and violinist, traveled the length and breadth of Ireland, performing, for over forty years. Alec's mother, Molly Kelley DeGabriel, was an actress, a former student at the famous Abbey School of Acting and played the accordion.

The DeGabriele family has an amazing musical history as well. Alec's great grandfather, Alexander DeGabriele, was a student at the Conservatory of Music in Naples, Italy and was a student of Guiseppe Verdi. He conducted the Royal Italian Opera but left the opera in Scotland, while on a European tour, to accept an appointment as resident pianist for the Duke of Edinburgh. His responsibility was to arrange and write music and arrange performances.

Alec's grandfather, Joseph Gabriele (it is not known why he dropped the "De"), played piano in the orchestra with *The Mummers*, a show starring Charley Chaplin and Stan Laurel (pre-Oliver Hardy), which featured comedy, slapstick and sketches done in complete silence. Joseph, Alec's father, and uncles and aunts were all in the orchestra that went from town to town playing for the silent movies. In the early days, in Scotland, Alec's aunt played the Cello, his uncle the drums and his grandfather the piano. When 'Talkies" [movies] came to Scotland, Alec Sr., moved the family to Ireland. He was told the country was so far behind that it would take ten years for the talkies to get there. So he took a job in an orchestra. Six months later, the talkies arrived.

Alec Sr. changed direction to get ahead of the times and joined the *Andrew McMasters Traveling Show*, where he met Molly Kelley, his future wife, while she was a student at the Abbey School of Acting. They married in 1948.

Since the day young Alec was born, he was part of the renowned *Shannon Players*. Started by his father, the touring group of "Fit-ups" entertained throughout Ireland until after Alec left the group at seventeen years old. The Shannon Players were *Fit-ups*, or *travelling folk* as they were then called, theirs a troupe of around a dozen people who put on full-length productions in theatres, church and city halls, for the local towns folk. While the Shannon Players performed in halls and theatres, many of the travelling folk performed in tents or "booths" which were wooden walled constructions (often looking like tall picket fences) with canvas tops.

Starting at 8:00 or 8:30 p.m., the shows were divided into two parts, drama and then a variety show. First the troupe performed a famous play, such as the *The Pal O' My Cradle Days, The Big Sweep, Lady Audley's Secret, Colleen Bawn* or *Peg O' My Heart*, among many others. The play would last two to two and a half hours. These productions included professional costumes, lighting and sets, no matter where they performed. The play was followed by an intermission (to allow for set changing), which included a raffle. The second part of the show would include comedy, sketches, dancing and singing. Talent shows would be a big part of this half of the show - everything building up to the big finale on Sunday nights. Of course, every contestant, no matter how bad, "made the finals," thereby insuring a large crowd at the Sunday night shows.

The week's schedule was clearly defined in posters (made narrow and long to exactly fit telephone poles), detailing the play to be shown each night, and the times and the place for the week Alec Sr. would take part of a day and go to the town that the Shannon Players were going to perform in the following week, and put up the posters.

Traveling day for the DeGabriele family was Monday. Alec Sr. would talk to the parish priest to reserve the hall but often had to contend with other events already scheduled. On Tuesday, Alec Sr. would take the children to the local National School. Knocking on the door, he would wait for the Headmaster to answer. "Good Morning to you, I have new recruits for you and don't spare the whip," were his opening words to each Head Master he met. Since the three children were only in that school for four days, until Friday, before moving on to the next town, not a lot of attention was given to them, they managed as best they could. Week after week, all during the school year, until young Alec left school for good at twelve or thirteen years old.

While the elder Alec was getting the performance hall set up with the rest of the troupe, Molly was searching for new "digs" for the week as soon as they arrived in the new town. She would go door to door, knock and introduce herself. "Hello Ma'am, I am Molly DeGabriele of the Shannon Players. We are performing in this wonderful town all week and I was wondering if you had digs for me and my family?" The person at the door might not but would say that so-and-so, just down the street, had room.

Travelling folk looking for overnight or week-long accommodations was not unusual in Ireland at that time. These traveling troupes were an integral part of Ireland and towns would see one to three shows, and troupes, per year. Molly would search until she found appropriate lodging and she did all the cooking for the family, working around the landlady. On returning to the town or parish hall, Alec Sr. would greet her with: "Did you fix us?" Molly would respond "Yes, it's a lovely place..." and set construction would continue.

Of course, the town or parish hall did not have a theatre set-up. Any size place at the side of the road would be transformed into a magnificent theatre by the sets the family carried. Constructed of large walls with holes pre-drilled into them, the walls could slide in or out to exactly fit the stage. This fit-any-size stage set up is where the name Fit-ups originated. The bolts were then inserted into the lined-up holes on the boards. They were anchored to the back wall and then the side-walls, set at an angle, and then tied down. Four poles, two at each end of the back wall and one at each end of the side-walls kept everything in place. Using hooks, long black curtains were hung on a rope stretching across the back wall. A small curtain, also black, hung across the top and hid the ropes and hooks. Red or green curtains were hung down the side-walls the same way, giving a staggered effect, adding depth as well as exits and entrances, to the stage. The pre-drilled holes, bolted at the right place, allowed the set to slide perfectly, "fit" into the space available, thus called 'Fit-ups." The name eventually transferred to the performers as well.

Chairs were found the same way digs were. The family would go door-to-door with a piece of chalk, introduce themselves and request any chairs. They would write the lender's name on the bottom of the chairs or "forms" (think picnic table benches) and take the chairs to the hall. After the grand finale on Sunday nights, you would see folks get up, applaud, pick up their chairs or forms and head on home.

A different play was shown each night of the seven nights that the Shannon Players would be in that town and hall. Alec, Derek McCormack (who grew up in his own family's travelling troupe as well) and most young Travellers played *Little Willie* from the play *Pal O' My Cradle Days*, multiple times. Other appearances included child roles in many other plays.

Alec, Sr. always planned the troupe's travels to insure they were at the holiday places, by the ocean, during the summer. Places like Bundorin, in County Donegal. He called these *the summer sessions*. Ending up the year somewhere in County Offaly, the Shannon Players only took one week off per year, centered around Christmas, which they would spend with their grandmother in Dublin.

Until television hit Ireland in the 1960's, the Fit-ups and the Travelling Shows were huge events, well attended and looked forward to. The dawning of the television age was the end of the Fit-ups era. The Shannon Players eventually developed into a four-person group when Alec's sister, Christine, married and left the group. Michael had left around 1961, to join *The Archers*, who were based in Cork. He then joined the *Jim Farley Showband*, who were very popular in Dublin.

The family traveled by caravan now, as they only had Alec Sr., Molly, Alec and Patrick. They changed with the times, doing just variety shows, and eventually they added bingo, after the conclusion of the show, too.

The impact of the Fit-ups cannot be overstated. Many successful Irish performers today earned their stripes in that time, including Alec, Derek McCormack, Hal Roach, and Noel V. Ginnity. Another Festival Legend, Tom Sweeney often performed in Fit-up shows as well.

"Alec DeGabriele, another man whose family is absolutely steeped in the traditions of Ireland. Alec's family were actors, in the old Fit-ups, the people who went around Ireland putting on plays and concerts. Just a great night's fun, a lovely man, decent and honest and I think the poem he wrote when Derek McCormack died was beautiful, really beautiful." - Tom Sweeney

Tom is referencing *Just A Thought Away*, a song Alec wrote for friend Mike Jones, who had passed away. Derek really liked the song and wrote the words down on a piece of paper, intending to add it to his repertoire. He placed the paper in his wallet and it was found by band mate Gerry Simpson. Not realizing it was a song, he read it as a poem, at the service held for Derek on the cruise ship in the days immediately following Derek's passing.

𝔍𝔲𝔰𝔱 𝔄 𝔗𝔥𝔬𝔲𝔤𝔥𝔱 𝔄𝔴𝔞𝔶

by Alec DeGabriele

So now I have to say goodbye, to the best friend I've ever known
The years have sadly passed him by, now God has called him home
The times we shared together, as we laughed and sang and played
And just remember my old friend you're just a thought away

When I think back on, how we met so many years ago
And all the good times that we had, and how the beer did flow
And telling stories at the bar of Ireland, far away
So just remember my old friend, you're just a thought away

Chorus:
You're just a thought away from me, you're just a thought away
And I just thought I'd like to say you're just a thought away

I see you struggle now my friend, so tired and so afraid
I wish that I could ease your pain and make it all go away
You've been a special friend to me and I can only say
That just remember my old friend, you're just a thought away

So now your journey has begun, a new road just ahead
You know that I will think of you each night before my bed
And I will travel down that road, to meet you there someday
And just remember my old friend, you're just a thought away

Chorus

1970 brought the end of Alec's Fit-ups career. He came in one day to find his mother reading the paper. She told him about an advertisement for auditions for a base guitar player being held in Ballinagh.

Alec nicely said, "So?"

His mother asked didn't he want to try out for it?

He asked "Why?"

"It would be a good thing," she replied.

After some convincing from his father and mother, Alec hitched a ride to Ballinagh and went to the audition. There were four other men there, trying out for the open spot. The first was doing a fair impression of Jimi Hendricks and Alec thought he was out of his league. Just as he was getting up to leave, Tom Kelly, the leader of the *Tom Kelly Sound*, called to him said the first auditioner was just finishing up and to go up on stage and give it a try. Alec auditioned, and then returned to his family, but told his folks he didn't think he got it. Alec Sr. wasn't buying it.

In those days, since the traveling folk had no permanent address, the DeGabriele's would stop at the post office of where they were leaving and tell them where they were going, mail or most often, telegrams, would be sent to the post office of the new town. In Tulsk, a week later, Alec got a telegram from Tom Kelly asking him to join the band.

Alec was deeply conflicted. He loved the only life he knew and didn't want to leave his family. But without saying it, his parents knew their way of life was ending and encouraged Alec to take the job. He did. Moving to Ballinagh, Alec joined the Tom Kelly Sound. The seven-piece band was very popular in the Mayo and Roscommon areas. He then joined the *Gary Streets and the Fairways Band*, out of the Ballinagh, County Mayo area, three years later. They were also a seven-piece band, that did one-night stands everywhere, in dance halls, playing Top 40 and dance tunes.

Soon after, life threw its usual curveball when Alec met American Mary Kay O'Toole, getting her a job as a singer with the band. Gary Streets even changed Mary's stage name to Karen King, as O'Toole was "too Irish and not enough American." To attract audiences, they advertised Mary as "the great American singer who sang with the tremendously popular [actually fictional] U.S. band, the *Celtic Stompers.*" There was no such band. Then in 1974, Mary Kay and Alec left the band and moved to Cleveland.

Alec expected that the performing scene in Cleveland would reflect that in Ireland but found it did not. He also noticed that there were no bands playing the showband or "come all ya's" [sing-alongs] Irish music of his home at that time. Cleveland's own *Sean Moore and Gusty* were the only thing similar. He saw the opportunity staring him in the face, got out his old books of songs he used to sing as a child and refreshed all the old favorites. Instead of singing with another band, Alec decided to go out on his own with Mary. *Alec & Mary* was born.

For fifteen years, Alec & Mary were mainstays throughout the Irish Music scene, calling *Fagan's*, in downtown Cleveland, a second home. Alec purchased *the Brass Rail*, on the west side of Cleveland for a few years and then opened *Darby O'Toole's* (in North Olmsted, Ohio), in 1989. Alec & Mary ended and Alec went solo for a while, then started *Alec & Darby's Folk*, in 1991.

Alec met Clara Marie Monk in 1985, when she used to watch Alec's band perform at Fagan's. They started dating in 1992 and married in 1995. Alec was asked who the most beautiful woman in the world is: "You mean besides Jessica Simpson?" he laughingly responded, then quickly added, "My wife Clara, of course. I am so blessed, she is my support, my love, the reason I am where I am today. I couldn't possibly have made it without her, I would be nothing." They have been married ten years and live very happily in Fairview Park, Ohio.

Darby's Folk members included the very young, very shy, but very talented, Pat Quinn and Mary Agnes Kennedy, as well as Dermot Summerville, for a short time. Shifting the band around a little, Alec added Peggy Goonin, to the line up. Paul Baker, who was then playing with a band called *Triad*, asked Alec to teach him some Irish songs. Alec didn't play the fiddle, Paul didn't play the guitar. Paul, a classically trained fiddler who played rock, blues, jazz and county music, also played with the world renowned *Cleveland Orchestra* at seven years old.

So Alec played a tune slowly; Paul sounded it out on the fiddle. Paul's Irish heritage and love for music had finally met. Alec then added Paul Baker to Darby's Folk, around 1994. The trio was a huge hit at Darby's and all around Cleveland.

Darby O'Toole's also gave Alec the opportunity to feature other bands coming through Cleveland and became the after-hours gathering place for all the entertainers from around the world that were performing at Cleveland's Irish Cultural Festival and performing at Darby O'Tooles during the year. A grand *sessiùn* would be held each night -- and well into the morning. Very conveniently located across the street from Darby's was the Day's Inn, where bands often stayed when playing in town.

In 1994, while The Barleycorn were again performing at the festival, John Delaney mentioned to Alec that the band was probably going to break up and that he was thinking of coming to America. Alec told him if he ever wanted a place to start, Cleveland, and Darby's Folk, had a place for him. John responded "That might be a possibility."

Approximately one week after returning from his honeymoon with Clara, Alec got a call from John asking if the offer was still open. It was, and John immigrated to Cleveland. John joining Darby's Folk instantly gave the band international recognition. In 1996, Paul Baker and Peggy Goonin left Darby's Folk and formed *Brigid's Cross*, adding another feather to the cap of the many successful and talented groups that call Cleveland home. Brigid's Cross' first festival gig was at Cleveland's Irish Cultural Festival, where they have appeared every year since.

Alec and John continued on as a duo, changing the name to The New Barleycorn, "and we haven't looked back since," said Alec. Curt Wright and Ed Canor often joined in, playing base and fiddle respectively, with the New Barleycorn. Fiddler Janice Fields joined the band in 1999 and plays many of their gigs throughout the year.

The New Barleycorn, an international band based in Cleveland, Ohio, are at the pinnacle of Irish Music. Second, and third, "homes," with large and devoted followers, are in the Virgin Islands, St. Thomas and the Dominican Republic (can't beat the winters either). From Festival season to cruise season, to the Islands, to the bashes around St. Patrick's Day, back to festival season again, the New Barleycorn tour relentlessly, playing over 225 dates a year, as well as on several cruises, including the *Super Bowl Cruise* and *Phil Coulter's Tranquility Cruise*.

When asked about the difficulties of such a schedule,* DeGabriele says, "Sometimes it gets old, for a minute, then you get up on stage, see the people there ready for a good time, and it all seems to disappear.

---

* Booking a band is an integral part of music events. Booking a band to play an hour at a wedding or other event is not really an hour. The bands have to get there before the event starts to set up, do sound checks, change etc... Then they play an hour and sit there until the other stage events are completed so that they can get their equipment off the stage. Then they load it all up and head out. A one hour gig from 8:00 p.m. to 9:00 p.m. is actually 5:00 p.m. to 12:30 a.m. or even 2:00 a.m.

On stage is the one place I can be completely happy, leave all the outside things behind, for a while. You look down at the crowd in *Sullivan's, Brendan O'Neills, Flannery's, The Rockcliff* or any of the other places we regularly play and you see you are doing the same thing for those listening. They are here to forget their troubles, have a good time. They are cheering, clapping, dancing, singing along. As soon as you start singing, the 'same thing, another day,' feeling goes away. This is what I love to do. This is what makes me happy.

"My father always said, 'It's not so important, what you do, those people out there, they are here for a night of entertainment; this is their weekend. They work hard all week and come here for entertainment. What about the doctor working on the heart – he's a lot more important than you burying your three cords on your guitar.'"

Alec continued, "It is my job to say, C'mon folks, meet me half way and I guarantee you'll have a great time. An audience is automatically nervous, especially if they don't know you, just as a performer is. That nervousness is contagious; it can spread through a crowd very quickly, just like happiness can."

The New Barleycorn played at the Atlanta Olympics in 1996 for Team Ireland, were invited to play at the White House for President Bill Clinton and spent a fantastic week with Ronan Tynan (on his annual cruise) which led to Alec and Ronan becoming fast friends. Besides their touring schedule, The New Barleycorn continues to play at many special events and weddings. Alec has also sung at many prominent Clevelander's funerals, usually singing his version of Phil Coulter's *The Old Man*. Alec teases Phil that Phil has not gotten as much value from that song as Alec has.

Alec is striking and emotional when talking about the funerals. He knows how hard it is to lose someone close. His father passed in 1981 and Molly DeGabriel passed away in 2003, at eighty-five years old. Alec was absolutely awed at the number of people who came to the service for her in Cleveland. "I try to pass on that emotional support to those families who ask me to sing at their loved ones funerals. It is emotionally very difficult and I am deeply honored to be asked to be a part of something so meaningful."

Excerpt from The Old Man

by Phil Coulter

The tears have all been shed now,
We've said our last good byes
And his souls been blessed
And he's laid to rest
And it's now I see the light
He was more than just a father
A teacher, my best friend
And his words are heard
in the songs we shared
As we played them on our own

Chorus:
No, I never will forget him
For he made me what I am
Though he may be gone,
memories linger on
And I miss him, The Old Man

One of Alec's favorite people is John Delaney. "Of all the people I have worked with over the many years I have been in music, John is a true professional, the best, in every sense of the word. In ten-plus years of playing together, we have never had words, not once. That is highly unusual when you see bands breaking up or replacing members almost every year."

When asked about his memories related to being a performer, he is hesitant at first. "I wouldn't know where to start," he says. "Defining moments seem to come by every few years or maybe a decade. The lifestyle of the theatrical existence that we had, it molded me from the cradle. Coming to America, I don't think I could have gone anywhere else in the world and done as well. Then, meeting my wife, Clara, she used to come down to Fagan's. She is a huge part of my life in every way."

"As far as my influences in Irish music are concerned, Makem & Clancy, back in the 60's. They opened up so many doors for Irish singers. Also, the Dubliners, Dublin City Ramblers.

"River Dance – huge influence internationally, not just in dance. And I guess the amount of work that opened up at festivals due to their explosion in America. There used to be a very few, now they are everywhere.

"I'd like to see Traditional music encouraged as much as possible. The traditional format can be scary when it is taken out of context – will those tunes be lost? Friends come up and tell us 'Geez, there was nothing like you guys over there,' [back in Ireland] after visits back home. I'd like to see the ballad tradition not lost. We used to pick up two or three songs every time we went over there off the charts. Now the young people are more interested in discos and such. In the day, any event that happened, whether it was men fighting or two dogs fighting, there would be a song about it and it would be sung all over the county."

Alec talks of other interests, "Outside of music, I love travel and to play golf. I love Cleveland, San Francisco, Newport, Rhode Island, U.S. Virgin Islands, St. Thomas – looking down on Megan's Bay and the Virgin Islands as the sun is going down. Of course, I love Dublin, where my aunts, uncles, cousins still live. I love giving the bus tours that we do now [Alec and John lead a group tour to Ireland each year]. There isn't a town that we visit that I can't give a story or anecdote about.

"There is something very rewarding, after leaving [Ireland] with $150.00 in my pocket, thirty years later, sitting on a bus, staying in the very best luxury hotels, hearing myself on the radio or hotel music system, taking one hundred and fifty people on tours around where I grew up performing.

"I saw Paul McCartney at a concert here in Cleveland a couple of years ago. He is the biggest hero of my life. He played for more than three hours and then had a bunch of curtain calls. After the show, when most are long gone, he was sitting on the end of the stage, signing autographs, and talking to people. He still took the time to do that. I hate when entertainers are not sensitive to that, they let it go to their heads. There are other things more important.

"I guess Tiger Woods would be my favorite sports figure. If I wasn't a musician, I would probably work with animals, I love animals. I really admire doctors and those that work in research, in the health business. I hate people in this business who think that what they do is the world, and they just ignore people. What about the guy who is working to stop cancer or a surgeon, healing hearts. That's important!

"I admire Tommy Makem as well; because of his legendary existence in Irish music. The influence he has on people, even today. He still belts the songs out with great conviction and heart – among the great ballad singers; he still stands out above all the others. He still has time for others, doesn't just disappear after the show.

"I remember as kids in Ireland, in Sneem [County Kerry, where Festival Legend, Batt Burns is from], someone brought out an album cover – *Makem and Clancy's* – the one with the white sweaters. I remember *the Jug of Punch* [starts to sing the words] and thinking that sounded awfully good. It opened up the doors of the imagination for a lot of people. I love the Dubliners, Val Dunegin, who sings humorous songs like *Mrs. McGinty's Goat*. I remember when The Furey's hit several years later, I very impressed with the uniqueness of their songs; the way they blended their music - the sadness and the heart of their songs."

Developing an engaging stage presence, so naturally part of the great performers, like Alec DeGabriele, takes a lot of practice, time, experience and good humor. Alec has it, and he learned it very early. He learned how to read a crowd, to select not only the tunes but the order in which they are played, for fine tuning marks the professional and it doesn't happen automatically. Alec has fine-tuned his performances over nearly fifty years - and does so masterfully.

Alec professes he is lucky to have as many good friends as he does, especially in Cleveland. Because he is always on the road, it is hard to set down roots, get involved in the community or the Irish Clubs. He has prospered anyway.

Having played with almost every big time performer, musician and singer, Alec expresses a feeling of being honored to be considered as belonging in their presence. He particularly enjoys festivals where he can see other bands and catch up with performers that are old friends, meet new ones and hear all the news related to the business. He loves to catch the newest talent. "Phil Coulter introduced me to Zoe Conway, she is a favorite of mine. I would like people to hear how talented she is," he says. "A very good friend, Patrick O'Sullivan, a singer and accordion player, he too deserves recognition.

"I remember sitting at the back of the ship [Phil Coulter's Cruise], where a bunch of us, in the middle of the Caribbean Ocean, sat looking up at the stars, with some of the finest musicians in the world. [I thought] It doesn't get any better than this."

To both the question of regrets, and of what he would do differently in his life, Alec answers, "Bless me, father, for I have sinned," and laughs. But then he softly whispers, "I regret I won't see my friend [Derek McCormack] until God calls me home."

As for his future, Alec hopes to feature some of the groups own material in a new CD or DVD. He has been doing a lot of writing [songs] and tries to live by the advice Phil Coulter gave him three years ago: "When you start something, finish it. Don't review it in the middle, good or bad. Finish it. Otherwise it [the rhythm of it] will be lost."

The passion, stories, good humor and memorable voice that is Alec DeGabriele has awed and entertained audiences the world over. Alec's versions of *Patriot Games* and *Grace*, among many others, capture the songs and the emotions completely, seemingly, these songs were written just for him. The unique voice, timely and often deadly humor, life-long accomplishments, abundant sincerity and deep passion for the music of

Ireland puts Alec solidly in the ranks of the best that Irish music has to offer, and easily earns the mantle of Festival Legend.

Of course, the New Barleycorn will continue to play all over the world, on cruises, tours and at the festivals. They have just begun to have fun. Like all Festival Legends, they exemplify the passion, the experiences and the love and respect for Irish music that has secured their place in the amazing legacy of legendary Irish music performers.

𝔇𝔦𝔡 𝔶𝔬𝔲 𝔨𝔫𝔬𝔴 – 𝔅𝔞𝔯𝔩𝔢𝔶𝔠𝔬𝔯𝔫 𝔥𝔦𝔤𝔥𝔩𝔦𝔤𝔥𝔱𝔰:

- Were presented with a Gold Record for
  The Men Behind the Wire, 1971.
- Were given the Freedom of the City of Los Angeles,
  by then mayor, Sam Yorty in March 1974.
- Appeared on BBC Wales radio with John
  Inman (Are you being Served TV show.)
- Performed a live televised show with RTE Concert
  Orchestra in Cork City Hall on New Year's Eve, 1985.
- Performed at the World Expo, 1988 in Brisbane, Australia.
- Performed on the field after the World Cup qualifying
  soccer match between Ireland and Malta in Malta in1999.
- Performed on the Irish Festival Cruise in the Caribbean 1996.
- Perform regularly on Phil Coulter's
  Tranquility Cruise in the Caribbean.
- Perform regularly on the Super Cruise [Superbowl Cruise].
- Performed at the pre- Summer Olympics, Atlanta, 1988.
- Performed on Andy Cooney's Irish All-
  Stars Caribbean Cruise, 2004
- Guest on Coulter & Company, Top rated
  Television show in Ireland, 2005.
- Played at an Irish Festival in Great Barrington [Western
  MA.], put on by former Barleycorn band member, Liam
  Tierney. They shared the stage with The Dubliners
  (including legendary Luke Kelly). Makem & Clancy
  and many more – all on stage for a memorable finale.
- Played a concert with the Chieftains at the International
  Celtic Festival in Lorient, Brittany, France, 1975
- Played on the Guinness Celebration of Irish Music
  tour in Australia and New Zealand with; Christy
  Moore, Donal Lunny, Davy Spillane, Stockton's
  wing, Nollaig Casey, Frances Black, Kieran
  Goss and Brendan Grace in March 1993.
- Alec and John shared the bill with and Nancy Griffith
  and Tommy Makem at a concert in Atlanta GA.

- Barleycorn have performed in: Ireland, U.S.A., Canada, Germany, France, Scotland, Wales, Australia, Malta, England, New Zealand, Virgin Islands, Dominican Republic.

www.thenewbarleycorn.com

𝔅𝔞𝔯𝔩𝔢𝔶𝔠𝔬𝔯𝔫/𝔑𝔢𝔴 𝔅𝔞𝔯𝔩𝔢𝔶𝔠𝔬𝔯𝔫 𝔇𝔦𝔰𝔠𝔬𝔤𝔯𝔞𝔭𝔥𝔶:

Some albums may be Out of Print

𝔅𝔞𝔯𝔩𝔢𝔶𝔠𝔬𝔯𝔫:

- Live at the Embankment   (1972)
  John, Brian, Paddy Mc & Liam
- The Winds Are Singing Freedom   (1974)
  John, Brian, Paddy Mc & Liam
- Barleycorn in America   (1975)
  John, Brian, Paddy Mc & Liam
- For Folk Sake   (1977)   John, Brian, Paul & Liam
- Live in New York   (1979)   John, Brian, Paul & Liam
- The Fields of Athenry   (1982)   John, Brian, Paddy S
- A Song for Ireland   (1985)   John, Paddy S, Derek, Denis
- My Last Farewell   (1987)   John, Derek, Denis
- The International Barleycorn   (1988)   John, Derek, Denis
- Green & Gold   (1990)   John, Derek, Maurice
  (briefly originally released as *New Decade*
  only in Australia, then re-released)
- Spectrum   (1991)   John, Derek, Maurice
- Waltzing's for Dreamers   (1993)   John, Derek, Maurice
  (Released as Hearts on Fire, then picked up
  by Dolphin Records and re-released)

𝔗𝔬𝔭 𝔗𝔢𝔫 𝔥𝔦𝔱𝔰: 𝔜𝔢𝔞𝔯𝔰 𝔞𝔯𝔢 𝔞𝔭𝔭𝔯𝔬𝔵𝔦𝔪𝔞𝔱𝔢

- The Men Behind the Wire   (1971)
  B-Side Freedom's Walk (Eight weeks at #1)
- Sing Irishmen Sing   (1973)
- This Land is Your Land   (1975)
- A Song for Ireland   (1985)
- Portland Town   (1986)
  (Seven Weeks at #1)
- Cavan Girl   (1986)
- Roisin   (1987)

The New Barleycorn:

- Ireland's Celtic Heartbeat   (1996)
- Live at Flannery's   (1997)
- Sing Irishmen Sing   (1998)
- Music in the Woods   (2000)
- Live at the Public House   (2001)
- Bring Our Freedom   (2002)   (September 11th tribute CD with the Cleveland Fire and Cleveland Police Pipe bands).

Alec & Darby's Folk:

- From Eire to Erie   (1991)   (*featuring Alec, Pat and Peggy*)
- Scared Stiff of Work   (1995)   (*featuring Alec, Peggy & Paul*)

Alec & Mary:

- Ireland is Ireland   (1981)   45 single

VII.

Tom Sweeney

"The greatest time of my life is to stand on the stage and share the songs and the stories that I do with people. To me, the whole thing is not me entertaining them, the whole thing is the sharing of these songs. They don't belong to me, they belong to the people of Ireland and the Irish Diaspora abroad. We all own these songs and to share them, to make people aware of them, I can't think of a better thing to do. I love teaching people the history of the songs. I think the song means more when you put it in its proper context, historical or social or whatever. I don't just sing a song; I would never sing a song unless I knew as much as I could about it. I would just never sing a song because I like it. That's not enough for me. I have to know all about the song, or as much as I can and then impart that to the audience." - Tom Sweeney

Tom Sweeney has been playing music to audiences since he was eight years old. From solo gigs to gigs with his brother Jimmy, *Fiddler's Elbow* to *Chaff,* from the internationally renowned *Barley Bree* to coming back full-circle, back to outstanding and memorable performances as a solo singer and storyteller, Tom has continued to bring the history, passion, and poetry of Ireland to his audience, no matter the time, place or year.

Outside of his solo career, the most famous of these groups is Barley Bree. Formed in Derry around 1974, by Donegal fiddler P.V. O'Donnell, Derryman Nicky Bryson (on guitar, whistle and vocals) and Scotland's Davy Steele (on vocals and guitar), the internationally renowned Barley Bree earned high praise and honors for more than twenty years.

Barley Bree went through a few changes, before Tom's arrival to the group, but got stronger with each new addition. Austin Rouse, from Strabane, County Tyrone, replaced Davy, who would go on to form and lead the seminal *Battlefield Band* until his untimely death of a brain tumor at age fifty-two, on April 17, 2001. In late 1975, Barley Bree were joined by Jimmy Sweeney, on vocals, guitar, banjo and mandolin. Seamus O'Hagan, from Cookstown, County Tyrone, on banjo, mandolin and bodhran joined the group almost two years later, fresh off winning the All-Ireland Tenor Banjo Championship, replacing Austin.

In 1977, Barley Bree were invited to tour Canada by an agency in Ontario, who set up a tour around Ontario. The band members; Nicky Bryson, P.V. O'Donnell, Seamus O'Hagan and Jimmy Sweeney, tagged on a couple of gigs in the Maritimes, eastern Canada, towards the end of the tour.

Barley Bree returned to Canada in the spring of 1978, on another tour. By that time, Nicky Bryson had left the band and Tom Sweeney joined. The band toured Canada twice in 1978, in the spring and in the fall, and then all four moved permanently to Canada's Halifax, Nova Scotia, in March of 1979.

Touring for months and months at a time all over the States and Canada was too much for Seamus and he called it a day in the mid 1980's. Steven Wainwright then joined in the late 1980's. The Barley Bree's short tour had turned into a twenty year stay.

P.V. O'Donnell left Barley Bree in 1987, due to the hectic traveling schedule and made a home in Manchester, Connecticut, just outside Hartford. He is still very involved in Irish music, teaching fiddle and hosting a weekly session at the *City Steam Brewery* in downtown Harford.

In 1995, anxious to not become stagnant, the group officially ended. All felt they needed new challenges and both Tom and Jimmy had young families. They didn't want to be away so much. Jimmy Sweeney still lives in Halifax, touring and performing, mainly within the Maritime Provinces. Tom's solo career boomed but lately he has turned to another love; writing and performing songs and stories for children. His own story starts here.

Tom is one of eight children. His father, Frank Sweeney, came to Omagh, County Tyrone, from Derry City as a young boy. Tom's grandfather had lived and worked in Derry City, as an engine driver for the Great Northern Railway, before moving to Omagh. He was also very musically inclined, playing the French horn and cornet in a brass orchestra. In the evenings he would play in the orchestras all across the north of Ireland for the Gilbert & Sullivan Operettas.

Tom's mother, Monica Makem Sweeney's family legacy has been well documented, as the daughter of source singer Sarah Makem. "My grandmother, was a very well known singer of Irish songs," said Tom. "Very famous, maybe even more famous now than she was when was living. She was the repository of literally hundreds upon hundreds of songs. There probably isn't an act today in the field of Irish music that hasn't recorded at least one of her songs. My mother, Sarah's daughter, being reared around these songs, all of her life, knew an awful lot of songs as well and would have sung them all around the house as I was growing up. And I was very fortunate to learn many of these songs from her. So I suppose I learned an awful lot of songs from my grandmother, through my mother, by osmosis, and for that I am eternally grateful."

"Learning those songs, for me, was as natural as breathing or walking. They are going to be with me forever and I am honored to be telling them to a whole new generation," he says.[1]

Thomas Peter Sweeney was born in Omagh on the 28th of December, 1953. As he points out, "You will note that December 28th is *The Feast of the Holy Innocent*. How apt for me. I was actually due Christmas Day and I came late and I've been late for everything since."

"My grandmother, obviously, and my mother, had a big impact on me. My father as well because he was very into classical music, so on one side, I had my mother singing all the old ballads of Ireland, she also played the fiddle, jigs and reels. And on the other side I had my father listening to Mozart, Haydn, Bach and Beethoven.

"I recall we got our first record player, maybe when I was ten years of age, and my father bought one record. Being a French horn player himself, he bought an album of the four Mozart horn concertos and he played that record over and over and over again and by the time I was about twelve years of age I could whistle the four Mozart horn concertos back to front, and still can. So that was a good thing to do.

"My father had a big impact, my mother had a big impact, my grandparents. And then there were local people, like Paddy Tunney from Fermanagh. When I was young I would have learned so many songs from Paddy Tunney, Geordie Hanna, from County Tyrone, wonderful singer. Old Felix Kearney from Omagh here, from Drumquinn, who would be a grandfather of the famous guitar player, Arty McGlynn. Felix Kearney would have written so many songs about local places and local things.

"I think the local writers of every parish and every town land in Ireland are very important because it is the local songs that make up the great canon or the great body of Irish songs, not the big hits, but a man writing about his parish, about his local river, about the people of his neighborhood, that's what makes Irish music what it is."

It is at the local level that Irish music goes past the inspired, often short term stage, to the committed-for-life love of Irish music. But often, it is at the nationally relevant and successful level that a person first takes notice of a connection between what is on stage and what is in their heart. They become inspired, tweaked, to get involved in and learn more about the music of their ancestors. Three events stand out in Tom's mind as history altering - bringing new awareness and acceptance to and for the music, in the field of Irish music.

"When they began to record a lot of the fiddle players who had gone from Ireland to New York in the earlier part of the century, like James Morrison and Michael Coleman, that was pivotal because all of the sudden these recordings began to make their way back home here. I think that spawned a great revival in the fiddle playing here. So these recordings back in New York, back in the 20's and 30's were very important in the progression of Irish music.

"Maybe a second defining moment was the advent of the folk boom in America and the fact that the Clancys and Tommy Makem were there at the time and they took Irish songs that had been sung in kitchens, and I suppose pubs, for centuries, and suddenly they put them on the world platform. What a nice thing. Irish people then had a certain sense of pride in seeing that the rest of the world were accepting these songs and it gave impetus to younger Irish singers and musicians to sing the same songs. So that I think was a crucial moment in the history of Irish music when the Clancy Brothers & Tommy Makem did the Ed Sullivan Show and began to tour the world singing these songs. One great movement in the development of Irish music today, I think.

"More recently, the advent of Riverdance, the whole world knows it appeared for fifteen minutes initially, as sort of a break, during Eurovision Song Contest, where people made up their minds who to vote for, and it absolutely blew everyone away and it became an absolute phenomenon world wide. And it spawned a total revolution in Irish dance and Irish music worldwide. The advent of Planxty, Sean O'Riada and Ceoltiori Culann, when they played that concert at The Gaiety [was also vital. This was a seminal concert, recorded live and called *Ceoltiori Culann Live at The Gaiety*]."

Steeped in Irish music from birth, whether in the voices, music and songs that lived in his home daily as a child, from the deep roots of his parents, his grandmother, his Uncle Tommy Makem or the now famous neighbors like Paddy Tunney, Tom began his professional career before most kids his age were even in second grade. Although he had found his passion, his calling, and knew what he wanted to do with his life at such an early age, Tom found knowledge, inspiration, and a mentor, in school.

[In Ireland], "You go to school at age five, you are taught for your first two years by the Loreto Nuns at the convent there. I have very vivid memories of the lovely nuns there, who were a good influence on me for the rest of my life. Like Mother Frances Paul, Mother Oliver, who had a band in the elementary or primary school. And then when you left the nuns at the age of seven, you went to the Christian Brothers Primary School.

"Now the Christian Brothers were very tough. Man, they had a very tough regime and you knew from day one, that there was no messin' in those schools. Most of the brothers gave you a sense of order, a good sense of manners. You knew your place and I think only for them, the Christian brothers, in the north of Ireland especially, we wouldn't have learned so much about our Irish culture. Had it been left to the government here, we would have learned nothing. But going to the Brothers, you learned a great, great sense of Irish history, Irish music, you learned the fundamentals of the Irish language, about the great legends of Ireland, CuChulain (*Coo Hull in*), the Red Branch Knights, you learned the great Nationalistic songs, songs of '98; *Kelly the Boy from Killane, O'Donnell Abu, the Croppy Boy*, you learned all those songs.

"I began performing locally when I was eight years of age, along with my brother Jimmy, who was four years older. In those days over here in the North of Ireland, there were parochial concerts in all the little parochial parish halls, generally on a Sunday evening. There were various touring parties, people would put together five or six acts, and then go around the various halls with them. Myself and Jimmy joined a touring company ran by a local singer and comic called Paddy Mossy, God be good to him, he passed away a number of years ago. We would travel around, singing at parochial concerts, and amazingly enough for two Catholic boys, we also played a lot of Orange Halls at concert there in the North of Ireland. That's how it began and we were very lucky in one way, because at the time we began singing, Tommy and the Clancy's were becoming very big in America and throughout the world, and we just could not understand how these songs that we had been singing all our lives, my mother and my grandmother and all my cousins, suddenly became very well known all over the world. We were puzzled and delighted, and very proud of Tommy as well.

"My first [solo] gig was a very strange gig because in this town where I live, the town of Omagh, we have the asylum for the two counties. When I was a young lad I went to play there with some of these concert parties. And a man called Paddy Gormley said to me, before the concert, we were playing for the patients, he said 'Now Tom, I know you are only ten years of age, but tonight we're going to make you top of the bill, we're going to put you on last.' So I was all over the moon, I was delighted by this until I realized half way thru my first song that the top of the bill went on at about ten minutes to nine and was supposed to play until ten minutes past nine. But they didn't tell me that at nine o'clock, all the patients were programmed to get up and leave and go for their supper. So in the middle of my second song, the entire audience got up, and left."

"When I left the Christian Brothers, I went to St. Patrick's High School, where I met the principal of that school, who became a lifelong friend of mine and a very big influence in my life. He was a man called Anthony Shannon, and Anthony Shannon had taught my father and when I got to that school, he realized, even when I was the age of eleven, that I was interested in poetry and music and literature and songs and stories and verse. And he was very interested in the same things. So he and I became very, very close and he became a big influence on me when it came to reciting verse and taught me a great deal about verse speaking and diction and projection and pronunciation. I owe a great, great debt to him.

"He would correct me on my diction, my pronunciation, my projection, my pace. I hated it at the time [but] I suppose it stood me in good stead because a lot of the reviewers today would comment on things like that. [when they review Tom's performance]"

As Tom passed into his teens, he was, "… heavily influenced, by a lot of American folk singers, because at the time, Tommy was involved, right in the hub of the great folk revival of the 1960's and he was rubbing shoulders with people like *Pete Seeger, Sisco Houston, the Kingston Trio, Peter, Paul & Mary, Leon Bibb, Odetta* and all these wonderful singers and he would send my brother and I records of these people and these records you simply could not get over here. So when we were in our teens, Jimmy and I, our repertoire was unreal. We were singing Old American spirituals and Appalachian love songs and work songs of the Negro slaves and just Irish ballads as well. So a big influence as well, all those American people I mentioned, also *Burl Ives*, I'm a big, big fan of his."

After completing his secondary education, in 1970, Tom left for America, to take a summer job performing in and around the Boston area. Every summer, Tom, Jimmy and one of Tom's school mates, John Daugherty, a fiddle and mandolin player from Gortin, would get together and perform, as Fiddler's Elbow. At the request of Tommy Makem, *The Harp & Bard* hosted the group at the string of clubs they owned. When the owners decided to open a similar club the following year, called *The Tara*, on Broadway in newly growing Nashville, Tennessee, Fiddler's Elbow played there too, serving as the house band at Tara Club, for the summer.

The Tara Club was co-managed by the legendary Shay Healy, * "Shay would do his set and then Fiddler's Elbow would do their set, so many nights a week," recalls Jimmy Sweeney, "Shay did more of an esoterical comedy, but from an Irish slant, along with Country & Western songs and things like that. Mick Moloney came in shortly after we had left. We got to know a lot of the TV people there, local and national, that used to come in at night and drink there, at Tara Club. So we were on a couple of talk shows and stuff like that."

Returning home after the holidays, Tom began training as a Librarian. He played in Barley Bree part time with brother Jimmy and P.V. O'Donnell. While Jimmy continued to play full time with Barley Bree, Tom also played with a group called Chaff, with Roy Arbuckle and Joe McDermott. P.V. O'Donnell also played with the group occasionally, until being replaced by John Daugherty.

The explosion of Irish music begun by his Uncle Tommy met with Tom's love of the song, its history and its presentation. The opportunity for Barley Bree came along in Canada and the group became based in Nova Scotia (which means *New Scotland*).

They decided they need to add a base player, so they brought out Brian Daugherty [of *Evans & Daugherty* fame] from Ireland. Jimmy and Tom had grown up with Brian and he had done a little bit of playing

---

* Shay Healy, mentioned throughout this book, was a well known singer, songwriter, producer and presenter of television programs on RTE Television as well as a well known radio personality. He also wrote the musical *The Wire Men*. His influence is felt throughout Irish music.

with the Sweeney's back in Ireland. So Brian became the permanent base player for Barley Bree, which was now a five piece group, made up of Jimmy Sweeney, P.V. O'Donnell, Seamus O'Hagan, Tom Sweeney and Brian Daugherty.

"With my brother, P.V. O'Donnell, Seamus O'Hagan and Brian Doherty, we went to Canada on a tour in 1979," said Tom. "While we were there we were offered a residency in a very well known folk club in Halifax, Nova Scotia, called the *Black Knight Lounge*. The Black Knight was very famous for folk song performers and Irish performers and Scottish performers, which is very strange when you consider that the Black Knight was owned by four brothers from Sparta, in Greece, named Panopolis, but they were brilliant.

"While we were the house band there, a national television company called CTV [Canadian Television] came to hear us play and they offered us a television show, a thirteen part series, called *Barley Bree in Concert* which was filmed in lovely theaters all across the Maritimes of Canada." Barley Bree in Concert was then re shown, for another thirteen weeks. The following year the show was renewed, again for thirteen weeks, and was again repeated. The second year's series was called *Live at Dick Turkin's*, which was a pub in downtown Halifax. Dick Turkin was an infamous highwayman, much like the famous Brennan, in *Brennan on the Moor*. "My memories of those days are fantastic," Tom said.

Jimmy Sweeney also has great memories of the Barley Bree days and the Black Knight Lounge, "We got noticed when we were doing that residency, in the Black Knight Lounge. A couple of the local TV people came in and saw us. That led to the two series. After we did that year and a half residency, from that point, we started touring all around the Maritimes, and further a field in Canada. Eventually we started moving into the States. We were still based in Halifax, but we were doing a lot of touring in the States. We went out and toured all the festival in the States and Tommy Makem's place [*Tommy Makem's Irish Pavilion*] in New York and cruises. We played all over the United States, wherever the Irish gathered, we played.

"We had a wonderful time. It was a lot of hard work and we did an awful lot of hard slogging, touring wise; driving back and forth across the country. But it was a wonderful time. It was really, really wonderfully enjoyable. We got to meet an awful lot of really good folk and saw a lot of lovely places. Things that I would never have gotten a chance to do, had I stayed in my teaching profession, which is what I did in Ireland. There were so many good things happening all at once. You just took it in stride.

"Tom and I have been singing for over thirty years, maybe not always together, but always singing. It is a long, long time. I love it. It goes so quickly. As Yeats said, 'From your best day, until you die, is but the blink of an eye.'"

Tom has appeared regularly on television, both at home and in the U.S. as well as in Canada, including CBS, The Nashville Network, CTV in Canada, BBC and UTV in Ireland and often on the PBS Network across the U.S. He starred in, *Off To Philadelphia,* a one man show of songs, stories and verse relating to the Irish in that city, which aired on PBS in 2000. Tom has acted numerous times in live theater and appeared in *Windows,* the Canadian television drama series. He has also periodically hosted his own radio show on Irish independent radio.

"They say every man's got a place and his river and his mountain range. Well where I was born and raised and came back to after twenty years in North America, is the town of Omagh," says Tom. "I love the town of Omagh, it means a great deal to me. It means more to me now then it did when I left. When you get away and see things from a distance, you get a whole different perspective of things. The beauty of the mountains, it is a spiritual home to me. I like to walk there.

"I've always loved the Midwest. I always said to people in Ireland, the real America was to be found, not in New York City or San Francisco, the real heart of America was to be found in the Midwest. Both as a solo performer and with Barley Bree, I spent an immeasurable amount of time traveling in the Midwest, normally by road, I'm glad to say. It was one of the few places in America that I did explore greatly, almost all the states there; Wisconsin, Iowa, Minnesota, all lovely places, Illinois, everywhere where we traveled by road. You got to meet the real people of America, the people in the Midwest. They are wonderful, wonderful, kind people; patriotic, decent, honest, hard working people there.

"I love Montana, just the pure sense of space. George Bernard Shaw once said about Ireland, "great hatred, little room." Well I'll tell ya, when you saw Montana, the room! I know now why they call it the Big Sky. It was incredible.

"We went to play in Butte, Montana, perhaps the most Irish town in America. People are surprised to hear that but, per capita, the most Irish town in the U.S. A man called Marcus Dailey, originally from County Cavan, discovered copper there in 1898. And he opened a copper mine called the *Anaconda Mine* in Butte, Montana. Well that very same year he opened the copper mine, a copper mine called *Hungary Hill*, closed in West Cork. He came back. He brought all the West Cork miners out there and Butte became a real big Irish town."

When looking for workers, Dailey advertised in the local papers in Gaelic, insuring the Irish would be the ones to respond. The largest mine, called *Dublin Gulch*, is a tribute, and reminder, of Dailey's Irish roots.

"A man called David Emmons, a friend of mine, Professor of History at the University of Montana, has written a wonderful book called *The Butte Irish*. In Butte, when the Irish were raising money for the 1916 Rising, they raised more money per capita in Butte, Montana, then in New York or Boston or all these other so-called Irish cities. Now the Irish Christian Brothers had a school there, built in the 1950's, and to this day, there is great pride in the Irish in Butte.

"My memories of the fall in New England are as vivid today as the first time I went there. We used to always try and get a tour set up, around New England, for the autumn. We would drive down from the Maritime Provinces in through New Brunswick, down into Maine, New Hampshire, Vermont. We played Boston and all those lovely places in the month of October. That was stunning and still remains very stunning to me. And even now I try to get to New England at least for a day or two in the autumn.

"Both my parents lived in New Hampshire for a while in the 1950's and all my uncles and aunts on my mother's side lived there as well, including my Uncle Tommy Makem. You see my mother's uncles and aunts, every one of them went to the States, except my grandmother. So we have a great affinity with Dover, New Hampshire, because in the early 20's, the big textile mills would be set up in New Hampshire and those places and they came to places like County Armagh where there had been linen and weaving mills, to recruit people, and so many of the people from there went to New Hampshire, including my own family. So there's a big connection between myself and my family and New Hampshire. So the fall there is always beautiful, not only for the scenery but my good friends, Eugene Byrne and Steven Wainwright, and Tommy and all his family, all the good friends - I love going there.

"I love playing the Irish festivals during the summer, Cleveland Irish Cultural Festival, Milwaukee Irish Fest, Gaelic Park, and it's not just because of the festivals themselves. It is the only time all the performers, all the guys and girls you've known for years in the business but you never meet, because you're always in your separate tours and separate roads. But at these festivals you at least get the opportunity for three or four days, to stay in the same hotel and to catch up on the news nighttime at the bar and to talk to the people that you love talking to and hear all the news from the last year or so."

In 2005, Tom was playing in Cleveland, heading to Florida the next day, and he suddenly realized that Milwaukee Irish Festival would soon be celebrating its 25th Anniversary. A tune and lyrics came to his head and Tom called Ed Ward, founder and President of the Board of Milwaukee Irish Fest, from the airport. He told Ed he had a song to celebrate the 25th Anniversary and ended up singing it to him over the phone, from the airport. Ed loved it and told Tom to record it and send it to him. *Milwaukee 25* became the theme song for the 25th Anniversary and was performed throughout the weekend.

Milwaukee then called Tom with a request of their own; would he consider reuniting Barley Bree to perform at the 25th Anniversary? Tom said yes and Barley Bree reunited for the first time in ten years, performing their old hits and favorites, to huge crowds at the festival. Milwaukee Irish Fest, the largest Irish festival in the world, draws almost 140,000 people each year.

Tom is definitely a man who treasures and cares deeply about personal relationships, whether it be his colleagues in music, his friends, or his family. He met his wife Frances around 1968. "We'd been going out together since I was fifteen and she was fourteen. We got married

July 14th, 1977. We've been together ever since, very happily. So that was a defining moment for me [meeting Frances]. And I think, the birth of my children, it changes everything. You realize that there are more important people than you, that there are more important things than Irish music." Tom and Frances are as close as the day they married. Each feeds off the other. They have two sons and a daughter.

"My youngest, Fionnuala, just graduated from Queens University in Belfast in July of 2005. Brendan, my eldest, works in a book shop in Belfast. My second son, Kevin, works for me in the house here, running the business part with me and the publishing company and so forth. He's a very fine musician himself, and a great artist. He also illustrates the books that I put out for children." Tom runs his own publishing company, *Gallows Hill Music*, named after the town in which he was born, where he remembers the hangings that occurred from Gallows Hill town jail.

"There is a big reward for this business. It is not money. The big reward is performing. That is the reward for all of the things you do. The road, generally, can be rough when you are on tour. Traveling all day, making connections, and if you are on a one night tour, when all you ever see is the gigs you play, airports and hotel rooms [it can be rough]. There are some very, very early mornings and sound checks in the afternoon and even when your off the road, when I'm at home here; [it goes] seven days a week. I record. I prepare things; I'm preparing books, I'm preparing records. I'm talking to promoters, agents, trying to do gigs, learning, learning new songs. I'm a very avid reader, always trying to brush up on new books, rereading some of our folklore, trying to reread some of the classic books. Sometimes it is a bit of a nightmare when you consider that most of us guys have a wife and family as well. I suppose it is important to understand that, the only part they see is the tip of the iceberg, the lovely part.

"Doing what I do makes me happy and I realize that what I do is something that I love and an awful lot of people don't like what they do. It may have been G. B. Shaw who said, again, that most people live their lives in quiet desperation. Well I'm glad to say I don't. I'm a fairly happy camper. I've got a great family life; a great wife and a great family. I've got a great career and I've made a decent living doing it. And the fact that I left my job as a librarian at the right time and turned professional at the right time, it just seemed that the God's were with me. All the cards fell face up. I just seemed to make the right decisions at the right time. I'm very happy and my family is happy, which makes me even happier.

"I've had a very, very good life. I wouldn't do too much different. I think I would have begun playing the States a lot earlier. We spent the first four or five years principally in Canada, and then it took a while for us to break into the American market. If we had gone to the States and began touring in the States a few years earlier, that definitely would have made it easier.

"I would have not signed with any major recorded companies like Schanachie or anybody else. When you sign with a major record company, you are one of a million performers and there is no real promotion of your work. I have now found that most of the performers I know are now on their own independent labels, where you have control. You have artistic control as well. So that's something I would do and would tell other people as well to do. To don't sign with a major record company until you are absolutely sure they're going to promote you because you have no control over anything, once they sign you."

"I would like to write more and better songs. Some day I'm going to get the courage to put out an album of all of my own songs that I have written. I'm not to sure who would buy it but ... When you write a song at two o'clock in the morning it seems good but when you sing it the next day it mightn't seem quite so good. It takes other people's reactions to let you know whether it is good or not.

"If I could divide myself in four, I would like that because everything I want to do I could do. I'd like to spend more time seeing places in America, I've been everywhere by airplane. I've driven a million miles in America but never really stopped to see things, like the Grand Canyon or I've drive over Donner Pass,* in the Rockies. I'd love to spend time exploring those places and seeing more about them.

---

* Donner Pass was named after the Donner and Breen families, who left Missouri on May 12, 1846, bound for California. In all, the party was thirty-one people, from Springfield, Illinois, mainly Irish emigrants. They met up with other Irish emigrants, forming a party of eighty-seven people. On July 19th, 1846, they spilt off from the main party and tried a short cut, which cost them three weeks. They

"I've been to Alaska four or five different times but you always just flew in, did the gigs and flew out. I'd go there again, if I had the chance. I realized that I have played every state in the Union, except Hawaii. I've played every single state. I suppose to play Hawaii would be the cap to the whole thing. Then I could say that I've played every state in America and every State and Province in Canada, and that would be nice to say. So who knows, I might go and busk on a street corner sometime in Hawaii just to say that I did that."

"I have about 10,000 ideas rolling around in my head at any one time for albums. I have recorded five or six albums of children's songs. I have another four or five albums already planned in my head and the songs chosen, and it's getting around to recording them. I've also written a lot of songs for kids which I haven't recorded yet."

Introducing kids to the rich cultural heritage of Ireland through song is a never ending passion, and quest, for Tom. "I'm very pleased that in October of 2005, I had a brand new book come out. It's called the *Ninepenny Fiddle, Irish Songs for Children*. It is a beautifully illustrated book with sixteen children's songs, music, lyrics, and illustrations and accompanied by a CD with all the songs on it." Eventually the series will contain ten books and CD's and Tom is well into the production of the series.

"I have all of the following books already prepared, so educational publishing of music is what I'm into, which I hope will grow and when my touring days finish, which I hope is never, at least I'll have something to keep me going.

"So pursuit of knowledge and enjoyment of reading are my big pastimes. I was a librarian by profession before I became a performer, so I suppose if I wasn't performing, I would like something to do with

---

again met up with their original party. A snow storm blocked further progress and they were trapped, snow-bound in the Rockies, in Sierra Nevada, (around Lake Tahoe), which gets more snow than 99% of the world.

In Mid-December, fifteen set out on snowshoes for help but only seven survived the one hundred mile trek, resorting to cannibalism along the way. They reached safety on January 19th, 1847. Four rescue parties set out but by the time they got through, in March, the trapped group had also been forced to cannibalism. Of the eighty-seven original travelers, forty-one died, forty-six survived.

books, maybe writing children's books, which I am doing right now anyway, or compiling song books for children. I'm a great believer in the power and the knowledge of children.

"It may have been Wordsworth who made the point that sometimes the child is father to the man. I know what he meant and I believe that. Certain other singers and writers have talked about how we must listen to the knowledge of the child, the child has perfect knowledge. When the child is born, it is perfect. Each day it becomes tainted by the world, by you and me. The child has no agenda. They say what they think. They are honest and uncompromised by society's judgments and attempts to make them conform. So children are fantastic. I would probably end up working with them and for them, in books and so forth, if I wasn't a performer."

"So I am very pleased to have that done and I hope that that will instill in some of the young people, both in the States and Canada, wherever Irish kids are. Whether it is Irish America, Irish Canada, Irish Australia, where these kids might hear the songs, learn them, and that might set them off on a road to follow the great heritage of Irish music all through their lives. It becomes more beautiful as you get older.

"Singing and performing for children is one of the great joys in my life, and perhaps that, in and of itself, might speak volumes. That I could perform for a four year old child and then perform for the President of the free world, I hope that says something about me and that my friends would at the end of the day say that I was a decent person and always did my best, both for them and for myself. Robert Burns said that to see ourselves as other see us is very important. I don't have any illusions about stardom or things like that, doing what I do. I would like to think that [people] would see me as being a decent, honest, compassionate sort of person, a person whose feet never left the ground.

"I really can't say I have any regrets at all. I spent a lot of time at my grandmothers when I was young and learned a lot of her songs. I regret perhaps I didn't spend more time with her. She lived in Keady, in the County Armagh and I lived in Omagh, in County Tyrone. I would only see her during the summer holidays or an odd weekend when we'd call in to see her. I only regret that maybe that I didn't spend enough time with my grandmother."

Personal regrets don't fit into Tom's schedule. He's made his way, on his terms, and he has blazed a trail that has earned him great recognition, honor and respect. If he could, though, he would change one thing about the world, "I wish young people read more, read more of their own heritage, their own culture, because it gives you a sense of place. It grounds you, it grounds a young person to know they are part of something that goes back a long way, they are part of something bigger. They are not alone. Sometimes young people today, I feel, have a sense of alienation. Whereas if they were to learn their native music and their native culture, they would know that they are never alienated; but are a part of something. They are a part of, something that is much bigger than they are. That's very important for young people, I think.

"I would insist that every country; the U.S., Canada, European countries, Asian countries, every child should be made aware of their own culture, from a very early age. They should be proud of it. They should be made aware of their heritage and they should know it, the way they know to read or write. Their culture and their songs and their stories should be taught to them at that age, because I think today that the young kids are being bombarded by the media on every side by hip hop and rap and house music and garage music and all this stuff, which is fine, but it certainly won't last and it doesn't reflect the heritage and culture of any kind anywhere in the world. Have schools teach all of their children, everywhere, their own folk songs, their folk stories, their heritage, their legends and where they come from. That is the one big change I would make if I ruled the world."

The love of books and learning are obviously ingrained in Tom. From his earliest days with the Christian Brothers, to performing from the age of eight, to the influence of his Uncle Tommy and the ballad boom, and through his professional performing career, Tom Sweeney has lived and breathed a dedication to the acquisition, understanding and passing on

271

of the knowledge of our history to all who thirst for it, no matter their age. "I'm nearly blind reading. The older I get, the less I realize that I know." While Tom enjoys a bit of golf and walking, giving tours of his beloved Omagh to friends who come to visit is a particular pleasure to him.

But the highlight of Tom's professional career came in the U.S., at the White House; he still speaks of it with awe. "It is very hard to cap this, I was invited by the President of the United States of America to sing at the White House and I couldn't think of a bigger honor; an honor not just to me, but to my family; my mother, my father, my grandparents, and from all of the people that I had learned the songs. That was a great, great moment in my life, a defining moment for me.

[It was] "In March, St. Patrick's night, 1998, to perform my *Anthem for the Children*, which I had written, wishing all the children of Northern Ireland a much better future. I recorded it for Schanachie Records in New York and somehow or other Bill and Hilary Clinton heard the song and invited me to sing Anthem for the Children at the White House on St. Patrick's night, 1998.

"Myself and Frank McCourt were the entertainers that evening. I sang my song and Frank did a reading from Angela's Ashes. It was a most amazing night entirely. The song is still quite popular. And you must remember as well, that evening of March 17th, 1998, it was one month before they signed the Good Friday Agreement here in the North of Ireland and all the political leaders from all the parties had been invited to the White House for talks. So when I sang my peace song, all the movers and shakers from Northern Ireland, and the Republic of Ireland and America, they were all there, so who knows, maybe my little quiet song of peace influenced the group someway. At least that's what I'd like to think."

Anthem for the Children

by Tom Sweeney

Since you've asked me what I'd like to have for Ireland
I'll tell you just as simply as I can
An easy heart for every Irish mother
And a decent, honest job for every man
I'd like to see her free with peace and justice
And every child to learn of Liberty
I'd like to take my brothers and my sisters home again
And never have to work across the sea.

Chorus:
This is what I'd like to have for Ireland
The country that has made us what we are
To breathe the air of freedom in her mountains and her streets
And give our children peace instead of war.

Since you've asked me what I'd like to have for Ireland
What I have to say is simple, short and plain:
Irishmen to think and act like brothers
And love to take the place of hate and pain
I'd have the Belfast man walk down through Galway
And everyone he'd meet to take his hand
I'd have the Corkman wander up to Derry on the Foyle
And feel that he is in his native land.

Chorus

Since you've asked me what I'd like to have for Ireland
To tell the truth the thing I'd like the best
Is Irishmen all looking to the future
And bygones would be bygones laid to rest
Let tomorrow be the time for laughing children
May they grow in love and friendship day by day
And may their understanding of each other give us hope
That in Ireland we can find a better way!

Chorus

Tom's passion for his heritage, his family, and especially, for children, resounds in all that he does. The legacy of love for the song tradition, first advocated in his family by his grandmother, Sarah Makem, is shining brightly within Tom, and all of the generations here and to come, that his work is inspiring. For a Festival Legend, there is no better definition.

Tom Sweeney Discography:

Tom Sweeney (With Barley Bree):

- No Man's Land (re released in the States in 1986)   (1983)
- Castles in the Air
- Barley Bree Live, Here's to Song
- Speak Up For Old Ireland
- Anthem For the Children
- Best of Barley Bree   (compilation CD)
- Love is Teasing (self-released LP and cassette)   (1993)

Barley Bree Live Show:

- The Wind That Shakes The Barley, An Evocation of The Uprising of 1798 in Prose, Poetry and Song

Barley Bree Video:

- Tommy Makem & Friends (w/ Cherish the Ladies & BarleyBree)   (1992)
- Barley Bree, Let's Have an Irish Party (with Anna McGoldrick, Carmel Quinn and Paddy Noonan Band w/ Ritchie O'Shea)

Tom Sweeney Solo:

- The Bard of Ireland   (1990)
- Fair Hills of Ireland   (1992)
- Songs of Ireland   (1994)
- Live @ Fernagh Cottage   (1996)
- Little Isle of Green
- Daisy A Day   (1999)
- Favorite Irish Poems   (2001)

Tom Sweeney Videos:

- The Fair Hills of Ireland   (1995)

Tom Sweeney's Children's Albums:

- I'm In The Mood for Singing   (1997)
- Happy Songs For Children   (1999)
- Sleepytime   (2001)
- A Family Christmas   (2003)
- All Together Again

New Children's Series, with Book and accompanying CD, debuting 2005:

- Book 1:   Nine Penny Fiddle; Irish Songs for Children(2005)
- Book 2:   In The Mood For Singing
- Book 3:   Happy Songs For Children
- Book 4:   Sleepy Time
- Book 5:   A Family Christmas
- Book 6:   The Animal Fair
- Book 7:   Nursery Rhymes
- Book 8:   Songs For The Car
- Book 9:   Songs Of The Season
- Book 10:   Alphabet Soup

Own Compositions:

- Anthem For the Children   (1998)
- Milwaukee 25   (2005)

www.tomsweeneymusic.com

VIII.

𝔅𝔞𝔱𝔱 𝔅𝔲𝔯𝔫𝔰

𝔗𝔥𝔢 𝔖𝔱𝔬𝔯𝔶𝔱𝔢𝔩𝔩𝔢𝔯𝔰 𝔍𝔫𝔟𝔦𝔱𝔞𝔱𝔦𝔬𝔫

by Batt Burns

Pull up your sugan chairs, my friends
Close out the green half door
And gather around the peat turf fire
As we did in days of yore.

I am glad you rambled in tonight, For the house was quiet and still.
Herself was carding sheep wool, while I, my pipe did fill.
There wasn't a word between us, you'd swear a row was on.
But memories were with us, of our children now all gone.

To America and England, those lands across the foam
Will they ever laugh and joke again, in our cozy Irish home?
You've waked us from our reverie. Maybe it's just as well.
Before those memories saddened us, and a tear or two were shed.

Your happy faces cheer us up. You've surely brought some news.
And from my store of yarns, sure you all can pick and choose.
Look to the blazing flame there, do you see what I can see,
Dark heroes, fairy castles, warriors fighting to be free?

There's leprechauns and fairy folks, Oisin and Finn Mac Cool
I can see them all so plainly there, from my little fireplace stool.

Come back into the past with me as I speak of olden days
When life was much more simple and we all had purer ways.

Oh there were no lounge bars or discos. TV we did not know.
Yet we had fun and sport a plenty, in the Kerry of long ago.

"I come from a very little town called Sneem, in the hills of Kerry.
We have very narrow streets there. In fact, the streets are so narrow
that the dogs have to wag their tails up and down, instead of side to
side, where I come from." - Batt Burns

**

The tradition of the *seanachie* (pron. *Shaw Nah Key*), or storyteller,
is as old as Ireland itself. Before television, radio and ballad singers,
entertainment was provided in homes and pubs through ordinary
folks telling extraordinary stories. These stories were passed on from
generation to generation only through memory and retelling.

None were written down and the ability to electronically record
these dramatic, comedic or illuminating stories didn't exist at this
point.   Whether called bard, storyteller or seanachie, this traditional
form of entertainer thrived for thousands of years. Some of the old
stories evolved over time but the essence of the story remained the same,
others, maybe even most, of the stories, were lost or replaced by new
stories and storytellers.

The world over, there is no more accomplished storyteller or *seanachie*
than Batt Burns. He has the awards to prove it too. A funny, insightful
and thoroughly engaging performer, Batt has wowed audiences from
his native Sneem, in the southwest of Ireland, on the Ring of Kerry, to
the farthest reaches of where the Irish and storytelling fans gather. His
ability to take an everyday occurrence from the rural parts of Ireland,
make it entertaining, understandable, educational and memorable, sets
him apart.

Batt lures his listeners with haunting accounts of ghosts, witty jokes,
adventurous stories, evocative poetry and traditional folklore. His
material is laced with Irish wit and humor and he draws heavily on the

work of famous Irish writers like W.B.Yeats, Brendan Kenneally, Frank O'Connor and Bryan McMahon.

Beyond the stories of love, magic, courtship, sea battles and voyages, verse was very much featured in the seanachie's repertoire and poetry is an integral part of Batt's evocative performances today. These stories and verse are often steeped in nerve tingling tales of ghosts and great adventure, of heroes and evil men; both comical and fantastical, of history and those who made it, and humor laced recitations. Both Batt Burns and Tommy Makem often recite from the poem *Ode*, by 19th century Irish poet, Arthur O'Shaughnessy (1844 - 1881).

Excerpt from Ode

by: Arthur O'Shaughnessy

We are the music makers,
And we are the dreamers of dreams,
Wandering by lone sea-breakers;
And sitting by deathless streams;
World-losers and world-forsakers,
On whom the pale moon gleams:
Yet we are the movers and shakers
Of the world forever, it seems.

Steeped as he is in the twin traditions of storytelling and verse, and having served his apprenticeship to a master story teller, Batt is a world wide treasure and a truly authentic Irish seanachie. He captures the ancient tradition, bringing it to life right before your eyes, as those who came before him did. The tradition is alive again, in the words and stories of Batt Burns.

Born Bartholomew Aloysius Burns on June 26th, 1941, Batt grew up within the seanachie tradition, much the same as the generations before him did.   His family first came to Sneem in the 1700's. Batt's grandfather, Michael Clifford, was a good singer and a seanachie but he was only one of the many that Batt heard as a young man. There were other seanachies that lived and roved around his home. Batt's father, Paddy, also told stories, but not in the seanachie sense, more of short witty or humorous tales.

Paddy was the village butcher. A man who would often come to help him, O'Sullivan, would compose stories on his feet, in the moment, or in the evenings, over a few cups of Batt's mother's tea. Although O'Sullivan was not formally educated and could not read or write, these tales were not retellings of the old stories but new ones created right then and there.

Batt lived with his grandfather from the age of about four until he was eleven years old. Batt's mother was the school teacher in a one-room school in a town of 350 people. Sneem is about the same size today. Another unusual characteristic of the town is that there are two squares. One used to be the Catholic square. Take the one lane bridge, like the crossbar of the letter "H," to cross over a small stream and you are then in what used to be the Protestant square. Both squares are equally gorgeous and reflect the look of small town Irish squares, unchanged, unspoiled, a gorgeous time warp that lets visitors see yesterday; today.

"I come from a large family of nine, and I was the top of the list [the oldest]. ... At a very early age I was introduced to my grandfather, who was probably in his mid-seventies. ... At that stage in his life, he had reared twelve children, finished with his family and was now almost back where he had started! I was very much attracted to him and, in retrospect, I realize his storytelling was my attraction. I spent seven years with him, almost full time.

"... I was a very mature person before I truly realized what a special experience I had with my grandfather. He was a simple man, living on a simple farmstead who struggled with the land to make a living. He had no extra money at all and traveled no further than thirty miles from home ever in his life. In his farm was encapsulated the old Ireland with the old traditions and celebrations - all of which he kept, because he was untouched by outside influences. Over shadowing all was his marvelous ability as a storyteller.

"He didn't do any reading, but he had thousands of tales in his head that he told me over the period of seven years. If I could remember a quarter of them, I would have all the material I would ever need.

"There was no electricity; radio and television were unheard of. So, all of the entertainment was homemade. On a typical long winter's night in Ireland, I would have him mostly to myself as we sat by the open peat fire and he told me stories. That had to be one of the most important experiences of my lifetime."[1]

Batt's grandfather did not urge Batt to become a seanachie because storytelling wasn't a job or a career; it was part of the fabric of life, the same as going to church or getting up in the morning. It was not something "to be," but rather, something that is. As a child, Batt "enjoyed the stories and forgot a lot." But storytelling as a career never entered his head. He was going to be a teacher. It wasn't until Batt was in his early twenties that he made a conscious effort to recover the stories of his grandfather and others. Attending a cultural fair, he noticed that the "revival" of traditional Irish culture did not include storytelling. Batt became determined to recapture the stories of his grandfather and of his heritage.

He couldn't go to his grandfather, for Michael Clifford passed away in 1962, at the age of eighty-seven. So instead, Batt looked outside if his surroundings, and inside his mind. "I delved into my memory and, sometimes, full stories came back to me. At other times, fragmented pieces were recalled, but I took notes on them all. On a few occasions, I found some of my grandfather's stories, which I had totally forgotten, hidden away in anthologies of stories which I picked up in bookshops."

"My generation saw the most changes of any [in their way of life]. The American wakes with their songs, stories and dancing were big influences. In the 1920's, the seanachie tradition was very much alive, before television or ballad singers in the pubs. There was talking and storytelling; they were a big part of it, depending on who was in town."

"When I left my grandfather's home, my elementary schooling was finished. In Ireland in those days, a high school education was denied to ninety percent of the people because there was no free education. Luckily for me, my parents could afford to send me to high school, so I went to boarding school at the age of twelve, and I stayed five years. I then went on to college in Dublin and qualified as a teacher.

"My first teaching assignment was in the poorest part of the city of Dublin. I went from the heart of rural Ireland to the other side of the coin! I had fifty-seven pupils in second grade, which was enough to blow away all the fancy ideas I had learned in college. After six months of teaching, I received a letter from home telling me that the principalship of the boys school in the village was vacant. ... At that time, storytelling had no part in my life at all.

"In the following years of my teaching, I began to settle once again into rural life. Whenever I was asked to do a party piece, I would tell a story, since I am neither a dancer nor a musician. That was the very beginning of my storytelling."[1]

Over the next thirty years, Batt and his family hosted an American teacher from the U.S., every year for three months, showing them what the rural Irish educational system was like. Five years after the start of this program, Batt decided to flip the coin the other way and go to the U.S. himself. Because he was studying educational systems so heavily, Batt decided to teach a course on the Irish educational system.

"… I quickly learned that the students were more interested in the asides and the poetry that came along with whatever I was talking about than they were in my teaching topic. Overnight, the course became storytelling and poetry rather than what had been originally planned. Two years later, when I was invited back, the course was broadly called, 'Irish Studies.'

"In preparation for the course, I was forced to look into my own background, and I realized I had forgotten the rare experience of my childhood. I had even forgotten the stories. … Today, I recreate my grandfather through the use of his brogue, the old hat, the glasses, and his thoroughly Irish stories. The stories my grandfather told were long involved stories that might go on for an hour or even for two nights. My problem was trimming the stories for the stage while still retaining the flavor of the story and the authenticity of my grandfather.

"At the conclusion of the Irish studies course, I was asked to do a one-man storytelling show at the University of Wisconsin at Green Bay, and that was really the beginning of my storytelling performance. That was in 1977."[1]

After thirty-three years as an educator, Batt retired as an elementary school principal in 1994. But winning the *All-Ireland Teachers Talent Competition* in 1983 had put thoughts of a second career into Batt's dreams and retiring allowed him to pursue those dreams, and a second career as a seanachie. He became a full time performer in the U.S. within months of retiring from teaching in the Irish public schools, but the life-long commitment to the teaching of others, around the world, continues:

"Teaching was a big part of my life for thirty-three years. I wouldn't change much in my teaching life but I'm glad I quit when I did. I got the chance to develop this career where most people in life only get a shot at one career.   Coming to the U.S. full time in 1994 [was a personal defining moment]. To break from a regular job, to have the courage to go from my regular job. Maura [Batt's wife] came with me too. Her encouragement was most important, without it, I probably wouldn't have done it.

"Coming [to the U.S.] for six years full-time in 1994 opened a whole new world of audiences. I'll always remember the audience response when I came to the U.S. I remember St. Patrick's night in 2004, when I did the Kennedy Center, in Boston, where so many Irish came and are [Batt also played the Kennedy Center in 2000, 2001 and 2002]. The National Storytelling Festival in 1994, in Jonesborough, where I was a featured storyteller – reaction-wise it was a memorable performance. It was not to an Irish audience and yet the reaction was fantastic.

"I like to perform where I can reach the most people, or at a retirement complex, where people don't have much light [in their lives]. I told stories in a juvenile detention center in Kalamazoo and it was hard to get started but within fifteen minutes, the story captivated them. Everywhere there is the element of the ability to brighten somebody's life.

Batt regards storytelling as entertainment. "The whole business of storytelling being used as therapy would be new to an Irish storyteller. I have never even heard of that idea until recently. I need to do a lot more thinking on it, even though when I look back on Irish history, I realize that we have had a long and troubled history, and perhaps storytelling was the therapy that brought us through it all. So perhaps stories as healing agents is not a new idea, only an old idea in new clothing."[1]

"Performing is like a drug, in a sense, if you have tasted a great response. In a bad response, you wonder why. Once you get a warm reception, it is difficult to get away from it.

"I had the opportunity to travel to Antigua, in Guatemala for the big Easter Festival, Italy, New Zealand. I get to see new venues and went around the world in 2000. You meet new people, great people you meet en route, the friendships you form. I love coming to the festivals, my first one in Cleveland in 1984, it was a new voice, in a sense, because there are so many there from the West of Ireland. [It] brought so many back to what they left thirty and forty years ago."

"The storytelling tradition is dying in Ireland. Just like the music. What has to happen is that, just like the music and dance workshops, we need the same for storytelling and ballads. There is now some movement to do that [in storytelling] but we need to do so much more. The music, song and dance are so prevalent but we need to involve storytelling too. I have made an effort to preserve my own stories. Quite a number are recorded on CD's [you can get them at www.battburns.com] and I have contributed quite a number of them to books and such. When I was teaching I tried to get the kids telling stories as well."

"I think storytelling is the most neglected if our Irish traditions. Our music and dance are vibrant and alive, supported by workshops and classes attended by young and old. There are no storytelling workshops. No teaching of the skill of storytelling. Even our educational system supplies no training except in individual classrooms where the teacher is a natural storyteller and incorporates that art in the class. In our high schools, it is totally neglected, non-existent. So, in the land of storytelling, in the country that probably has the richest folklore of any country in the world, our tales are gathering dust in archives. It is long after the time to shake off the dust and get them alive."[1]

Others have noticed the dying seanachie tradition as well. Batt often incorporates modern Poet Brendan Kenneally's poetry and writing in his own shows, such as *The Story*, written by Kenneally around 1995. It is about the demise of the Seanachie. Kenneally is a Professor of Literature at University College in Dublin and the story speaks of the dying tradition that Batt is working so hard to preserve.

The life long love for teaching still continues for Batt today and he continues to teach children, and adults, both in the U.S. and in Ireland.

He and Maura present at assemblies in schools, trying to capture and engage kids of all ethnic backgrounds. Folk music and stories are just that, folk. Not Irish or Appalachian or any other. The similarities are easy to see.

Batt has presented programs at many universities in both Ireland and the U.S., such as Harvard, Notre Dame, Northwestern, Boston College, John Hopkins and Kent State University – where Batt was the Storyteller in Residence in 1995, and has been featured at festivals all over the Ireland, the U.S. and in New Zealand. He has also performed at Storytelling festivals all over the world, including; *The Corn Island Festival* (Kentucky), the *Timpanogos Festival* (Utah), the *Ann Arbor Folk Festival* (Michigan) and the *Masterton Storytelling Festival* (New Zealand). Batt is one of only two non-U.S. born storytellers to appear on the cover of *Storytelling Magazine* (Kerry Mallan, of Australia, is the other).

Batt has performed and taught at many other events throughout the world. He is the author of seven books on Irish history and culture and he has been honored as outstanding teacher and storyteller in the Republic of Ireland. He has also authored numerous books on geography and other topics for Irish elementary schools. He has appeared on *Good Morning America* and *The Late Late Show*, Ireland's most popular television program, on Channel 4, in England.

When performing, Batt is often accompanied by his wife, Maura O'Dwyer Burns, an accomplished concertina player from Ardgroom, in the Beara Peninsula area, in County Cork. Maura comes from along line of family members steeped in traditional music and song as well. Her late mother, Ella Mae O'Dwyer, was one of Ireland's best concertina players and a great exponent of the West Limerick style, which Maura has now inherited. Both Maura and Ella Mae were featured in a memorable concertina duet on an Irish National Television program, *The Pure Drop* some years ago.

The Burns have four sons; Bartley, Padraic, Liam and Killian. Killian is an accomplished accordion player and is following in his father's footsteps as a seanachie. Killian is also accomplished in Batt's favorite sport, Gaelic Football, and has won two All-Ireland medals with the Kerry Senior Football team.

Batt tours the world approximately five months of the year, three in the spring and two in the fall. For the rest of the year he conducts historical tours in Ireland. Since 1991, Batt and Maura have been hosting these unique tours, which endeavor to help travelers feel and sense the "Real" Ireland. Batt is uniquely competent to lead these tours, which immerse participants in the music, song, dance, storytelling, literature and rich history of The Emerald Isle.

In these tours, groups usually arrive at Shannon Airport and are transported to the scenic, beautiful, remote village of Sneem, Batt's home village, in the Kerry Hills. Sneem won the National Award for the best kept village in Ireland in 1987. Here participants become part of village life for a few days and mix with locals in the pubs, learn Gaelic song and hear traditional music from Maura. They also hear talks on history, folklore and storytelling from Batt, watch a farmer cut peat in the traditional style, walk exquisite mountain trails or take a boat trip in Kenmare Bay. On one of the nights, tour participants are guests in the Burns' home for an Irish "hooley" (old style Irish house party) at which talented entertainers perform. The tour then leaves Sneem and travels through the rest of Ireland, stopping at historical sites and meeting local people.

"I am far from being totally comfortable with storytelling. I have a thousand more things to learn yet. Every performance I give is different, evolving, like a pot in the hands of the potter. The thrill of storytelling for me is sharing something I really like, such as a poem, ballad or old folktale and finding out that someone else likes it just as much as I do. That is the great reward of my work!"[1]

"We have the best of both worlds [life in the U.S. and in Ireland]. I couldn't live in any other country [but Ireland]. I am too rooted in Ireland. You sacrifice the normality of life at home for a very irregular life on the road, but that is a choice. I have enjoyed it. When I stop enjoying it, it is time to get off the road. I wouldn't have it any other way."

Batt is the seanachie, the living, breathing story of Ireland, brought to life from the remotest parts of Ireland, his native Sneem, in Kerry. He often recites the Sigerson Clifford poem, *I am Kerry* in performances, for it rings of the ancient, the seanachie, and Batt Burns. But Batt is more, much more. He is not Kerry, he is Ireland, alive and well and continuing to spread throughout the world, the stories, verse, history and heritage of "home."

Batt Burns Discography:

- Stories & Poems of Ireland   cassette (1987) / CD (1994)
- More Stories of Ireland   cassette (1991) / CD (1994)
- Irish Tales for the Young & Old   CD (1994)

eStories:

- The Leprechaun's Trick
- The King with the Horses Ears

Books: A few of the many books Batt has written:

- Irish Offshore Islands   (1983)
- The Gaelthacht   (1985)
- The Focus Series (Series of four books for Irish School Social Studies classes)   (1979 - 1985)
- Multiple inclusions in various Anthologies

www.battburns.com

IX

Brendan Shine Band
Brendan Shine, Emily Shine,
Johnny Dawson

*"Having already played and recorded with my father, my
brother and my daughters, I would love to live long enough
to play with my grandchildren." - Brendan Shine.*

Brendan Shine has been involved in music since he was a young boy,
first watching his father play at the family owned *Kielty Dance Hall*,
then playing with his father in Kielty Dance Hall, and eventually,
heading out with boyhood pal, Johnny Dawson. Splitting time between
school, the farm and his intense inner need to play and sing, Brendan
eventually finished school, and concentrated on farming and music.
Performing became more and more a part of his life.

After five years with the *Ciaran Kelly Ceili Band*, from age fifteen
to twenty, Brendan and Johnny returned to their homes and while still
farming, started playing as *The Shine's Country Ceili Band*. In the early
performing days, the farm van became the tour bus, making the long
journey to Dublin markets every morning, after getting back from the
gigs all over the country the night before. But the twice-a-week gigs
grew to five or more nights as The Shine's Country Ceili Band were in
high demand and started playing all over Ireland. Brendan, singing and

playing the accordion, and Johnny, on drums, were joined by Brendan's younger brother, Owen, on keyboards.

Brendan and his brother, along with Little Johnny Dawson, toured and played wherever Irish music lovers gathered. The Brendan Shine Band burst onto the national music scene in Ireland with the debut of their first album, *The Best of Brendan Shine*. Brendan was already known across Ireland, England, Scotland and Wales at this time but the album solidified his place on the performing circuit. Soon that recognition extended to include New Zealand, Australia, Canada and the U.S.

Some of the signature Brendan Shine tunes that have reached the top of the Irish and English charts include Brendan's first hit; *O'Brien Has No Place to Go,* and *Where the Three Counties Meet,* followed by *Bunch of Violets Blue, Abbeyshrule, Far too Young, Sailor Boy, Dun Laoire, Where My Eileen is Waiting For Me, Turn Out the Lights, Down the Wrong Road Again, All My Roads Lead Back to You, Do You Want Your Old Lobby Washed Down Con Shine, Catch Me If You Can, The Rose of Castlerea, My Son, Shoe the Donkey* and *Celtic Tiger.*

Johnny, Brendan and Owen thought they would play forever. Unfortunately, life's random and sometimes cruel twists interjected. Owen passed away while on a tour of the UK, dying in a tragic accident in 1997. The passing of his youngest brother had a huge impact on Brendan and his whole family, leaving a hole that Brendan could not fill. He describes the first night performing after Owen passed away as the worst moment of his professional life. ""Owen was my bandleader from age fourteen to the time of his death at forty-four. I looked across the stage to my right to shout the next number to Owen, but he wasn't there – the loss and the emptiness was almost unbearable."

Eventually the grieving lessened and The Brendan Shine Band went on, with Brendan's daughter, Emily joining in, at first as a temporary replacement, but then, as the joy of performing overtook her, as a full member of the group.

Overall, Brendan has had twenty five chart hits in Ireland. He has earned four Silver, two Platinum and several Gold discs for record sales, along with scores of awards throughout his forty year career. He has also had over thirty-five singles hits in England and Ireland. *Do You Want Your Old Lobby Washed Down, Con Shine* remained in the Irish charts for seventeen weeks after debuting in 1979.

𝔅rendan 𝔖hine

"My fondest childhood memories are of working and living on the family farm, playing with my father in his band at all the local dances and helping to run the family dancehall, located beside our house. I have great memories of my school days – especially as I met my wife Kathleen (*nee* Kildea) while we were both in school in the local town of Athlone. My father awakened my interest and love for music"

Born June 2nd, 1947, in Portarlington, County Laois, where his father, Paddy, was the foreman manager of Bord na Mona.* Brendan Joseph Shine is the second youngest of six children. Brendan gave a strong hint of his traveling future by immediately moving to the family farm in Kielty (South Roscommon).]

Paddy Shine was a musician and owned a dance hall called Keilty Dance Hall, which is still standing beside the family farmhouse. Brendan played with his dad at Summerhill, a village just down the road from Kielty, twice a week at an open air dance called the Maypole. The ensemble was known as *Paddy Shine's Two Piece Orchestra*, with Brendan on the accordion and his father on Alto Saxophone.

Mary Frances Begley Shine, Brendan's mother, didn't play music, but her uncle, Charles Durney, was a renowned flute player. Brendan's grandfather, Patrick Shine was a talented musician and Brendan's uncle, Owen Shine, a National School Principal in Ballybay, Kiltoom, Athlone, was the first musician (an accordionist), to be broadcast on the first national radio station, 2RN. Another uncle, Peter Shine, was an All-Ireland Champion Irish Dancer.

---

* Bord na Mona-State run company which oversaw the production of turf and peat from the national bogs of Ireland. It was big industry and a large employer back in Paddy's time and seen as a very secure pensionable reliable job. The organization still exists today but its function is now centered around energy production as well as peat briquette production.

Brendan was a keen accordionist from an early age and won several competitions including being an All-Ireland runner up. "I was a pianist and singing in a ceili band. I got tired hanging around waiting to sing, so I took up the accordion to keep myself busy." Besides the accordion and piano, Brendan also plays the harmonium.

An accomplished pianist, Brendan was the organist and soloist in his parish church, at Drum, from his teenage years until well into the 1980's, when extensive touring made it impossible to continue. Brendan's brother Owen was an All-Ireland accordionist and pianist and his brother Colm plays the accordion as well.

Brendan grew up working on the farm and in the dance hall where he and his siblings helped "taking the door," serving the refreshments and spying on the adults from the balcony when long past bedtime. Brendan took a keen interest in the music and it was in the Kielty Dance Hall that Brendan first heard many of the reels, jigs and hornpipes he would later learn to play before performing in the Kielty Dance Hall himself. Brendan recounts that he often meets people all over the world who tell him with fondness how they met in Kielty Dance Hall!

But Brendan couldn't be held in the shadows, hiding but always watching, for long. The traveling bug bit again and Brendan hit the road, at the wise and experienced age of fifteen. "Johnny Dawson, who would be my drummer for forty years, and I ran away from school to join the *Ciaran Kelly Ceili Band*. We left for a six week tour from school and I sent a message home to my mother, saying: 'Gone on tour - see you in six weeks!'" Johnny and Brendan stayed with the Ciaran Kelly Ceili Band for five years.

"When I left the Ciaran Kelly Band, I formed my own band, *The Shine Country Ceili Band*. I have had my own outfit since and played a new style of music defined as *Country & Irish*," Shine explains. As 1980 approached, Country & Irish became huge in Ireland, and hastened the end of the pure country music dance bands that were featured in the dance halls all across Ireland.

"I wasn't the first but I probably dabbled in it. Country & Irish is strictly a breed of country music, it doesn't mean Country & Western music, it means Irish music, of a folk bend, with sentiments of American Country, but with Irish lyrics, performed by Irish artists and it's relating to Ireland. It got that name to define it from ceili music or traditional music or folk music."

The band performed nightly, but during the day, Brendan built a very successful market gardening business and earned a lot of respect as a carrot grower. He became recognized as an expert throughout the area. Brendan's land, in Moor lands, on the banks of the Shannon, was perfect for growing straight carrots in the soft soil. Most other market farmers upland struggled, because of the rocky ground, yielding bent and gnarled produce. "These carrots, in the real gentle Moor bogland, we were able to grow the carrots rather uniformly and lovely and straight. We became famous for that," Shine said.

"Seventy percent of my time is taken up with my career, with my music, and thirty percent with farming. But of course farming is ongoing, the farm still operates without me. Now I have a beef farm, with a pedigree herd. We're Pedigree Breeders of Irish Angus cattle. We breed Angus heifers on bulls, on pedigree cattle, and we also have a crossbreed herd of cows using Angus bulls. We're members of a Producers Group here in Ireland which promotes Certified Angus Beef. I could never imagine a time when I will not be performing, but if I wasn't, then I would concentrate on being a full time farmer."

"I started as a Balladeer. I learned a lot from listening to radio and listening to records. Television wasn't that prevalent in Ireland in the 60's. I knew that this is what I wanted to do for a living, when I first got paid for it, when I first did a nights work and I got paid for it. I realized this was a way I could make a living. I always had my mind set on being a musician and being a performer. There were several musicians and several performers in every household in our area, but none of them would have the ambition to go and make a living at it. I had, from the word go. It was a top priority with me and I said 'This is it. This is where I want to go.'

"You'd be sneered at and frowned upon when you'd be neglecting your school and your academic life to play music and you were, at times, being looked at as an outcast, amongst your family and teachers and people like that. They were said to always seek the limelight. It was considered a past time – a path that led to not a good lifestyle, lead them to things that might lead them astray. You weren't answerable to any institution or things like that."

But the love of music had a very firm grip on Brendan, and had gotten him into performing. That love is just as strong today, keeping him actively performing approximately one hundred and seventy gigs a year. His childhood home, Kielty, and now his family home in Taughmaconnell, [*pron.* Talk Mack Connell] near Athlone, County Roscommon (not Meath, Offaly or Westmeath, as reported so often), has had a huge influence on him and his music. His favorite song attests to that.

"*Moonlight on the Shannon River,* a beautiful melody and beautiful lyrics about a sight so familiar to us in South Roscommon -- the majestic River Shannon. When I sing this song it always reminds me of home as it is a song that can bring the sight of the rising moon on the Shannon to mind so easily. It is poetry in melody!"

Roscommon will always hold Brendan's heart but football is a close second: "[I love] Roscommon in the summer when the sun is shining and the air is heavy with the scent of the fresh mowed grass in the meadow, Croke Park when Roscommon are playing, Gaelic Football, Gerry O'Malley; Roscommon Football All Star, and Tony McManus; Roscommon Football All Star. I also remember Micko Dwyer, the legendary manager of the Kerry G.A.A. football team, stating on the show [Brendan's *Saturday Night Live* primetime RTE television show] that the one and only All-Ireland Final Kerry didn't deserve to win was the day they beat Roscommon in the early 80's. That was some admission for a proud Kerry man and testament to the great Roscommon team of the day."

"I have been very adventurous in my musical career, in actually attacking things, like I'd mix traditional music with Rock-n-Roll music. I'll use the accordion on a lot of music that normally wouldn't be used. It would all be within that vein of marrying music. I'd like to dabble in classical music. I'm a lover of classical music. I had an idea of the opera and the ceili. It is probably a product that I might mix some classic opera music and traditional Irish music. I have always pretty much followed my own path and created my own style of music. No regrets now or ever, Thank God," he says humbly.

Live appearances and radio are not Brendan's only platform to share his great love of Irish music and his homeland. Television first beckoned Brendan in 1982, and he appeared in *"Shine on the Shannon,"* a documentary on Athlone and its hinterland.

"This was a documentary about Athlone and surrounding areas. I, as a native of the area, was the narrator. We went to all the areas of interest and significance to me. In between the historic narration I sang relevant songs. *Moonlight on the Shannon River* was the highlight of the show and I sang it as we cruised along on a ship as the moon came up on the river. It was a great success and was rerun several times. The producer was Moya Doherty, of Riverdance fame."

Shine on Shannon was a huge TV hit, earning Brendan the highest honor to be given, when he was made a "free man" of the town of Athlone in a Civic Reception. A free man of a town is the highest honor a town can bestow on a citizen. In olden times when towns were walled, you had to have a key to get in, or a password. Being a free man literally means you get the keys to the town. The symbolism is that you had right of access to the town as an honored citizen. Brendan has shined so brightly as an ambassador for the town of Athlone.

Shine's own series, *Nice and Easy,* followed, with six shows in 1982 and another six the year after. Both shows were very successful, initially in Ireland and then later, in England as well. The final episode of Nice and Easy featured the first public appearance of his two children, Emily was five and Philippa was three. "We always intermingled and played music together, even when they were very young children," Brendan recalls. Bringing his two young daughters on the last episode is one of his fondest memories of the girl's early years and sharing music. Emily sat on Brendan's knee as they sang *God's Coloring Book.*

More recently, *LifeLines,* hosted by Karrie Crowley, did a series on performing families that were involved in Irish music and the Shines were featured. The clip of Brendan singing with Emily, from the RTE archives, was shown during the show and has been seen numerous times on television since.

Folks that Brendan admires include; Tenor John McCormack (also from Athlone), The Chieftains and The Sawdoctors in music, Actors Richard Harris, Ray McAnally and Brenda Fricker, and the person he admires beyond all others, Pope John Paul II.

"The Chieftains, as far as Irish music, bursting onto the worldwide stage, was big for me. I knew some of the Chieftains. I know Paddy Moloney; he played in a ceili band in Dublin, when I played in a ceili band. He same from the same background, the Irish cultural background of the traditional Irish music, that I came from.

"John McCormack singing at the Eucharistic Congress 1932 in the Phoenix Park was a defining moment in Irish music, as was when the Chieftains played in Japan. For me personally, when my song, *Do You Want Your Old Lobby Washed Down,* was sung to Pope John Paul II as he left Shannon airport after his visit to Ireland 1979, was a highlight"

When asked how his first gig went, Brendan had a laugh, and a story: "Our first gig didn't go too well! There was Owen, Johnny and I on the stage and two in the audience – a lad at the front and another at the back. The lad down the back was shouting 'turn it up!' and the lad up the front was shouting 'I don't mind swapping with you!'"

But his favorite place to play is in his own backyard: "Loughlynn Carnival, County Roscommon. It's a home gig and it reminds me of the good old days when all the community, young and old, came together to celebrate music, community and family values."

He also enjoys many sites in the U.S., such as; Nashville Tennessee; "A beautiful place, musically inspiring," Las Vegas; "The Buzz," Phoenix, Arizona; "A different world," and Boston; "Plenty of people from home."

Brendan is married to his life-long love and darling, Kathleen Kildea. "We married March 19th, 1972 in St. Ronan Church Taughmaconnell and this is still our home parish. It is the church in which my two grandchildren were christened. We had our wedding reception in Hayden's Hotel in Ballinasloe, County Galway, the nearest town, and then went to Moore Hall (a neighboring parish of my home, Drum, and Taughmaconnell). I still play in Hayden's Hotel and the Moore Hall Community hosts one dance a year, *The Harvest Ball* and I always play it. It always brings back memories of our wedding night.

"A great old tradition in Ireland is for neighbors to light bon fires along the route of the wedding party as they make their way to the reception. I can still see the bonfires all along the road the whole ten miles to the hotel and it was great to see all the well wishers on the way. We honeymooned in Paris.

"Our wedding day was very special. I can still recall vividly the little shop in Leeds where I bought Kathleen's wedding ring and remember with fondness the day we bought her beautiful headdress in Harrod's, London, while on a trip there. I still have my wedding cufflinks and I wore them to both my daughter's weddings. Kathleen was divine – she still is. It's amazing all the little things you remember."

Kathleen and Brendan's two children, Emily and Philippa, "both have sung with me since they were very young. They have sung with me every summer as part of the band while they were in school and college, touring all over Ireland and the UK."

Emily is a Psychologist and Teacher, as well as a professional musician and vocalist. She is married to native Athlone man John Halpin, who is a Consultant Engineer with Hewlett Packard. They have one daughter, Amelia. Philippa is a doctor and is married to John McDonnell, an Anesthetist. They have one son, William John and live in France.

Brendan has expressed the desire to play with his grandchildren some day. They will have plenty of resources to learn from. More than thirty-three albums, twenty-five number one hits, forty-five singles, four videos and now, four DVD's, show a prolific and highly successful career for the Roscommon man. He isn't done yet and hopes to play in Australia and New Zealand some day. The amazing similarities between New Zealand and Ireland have oft been stated, but Brendan would also love to study the successful farming that is prevalent there.

Emily Shine

Emily Mary Shine was born to Brendan and Kathleen Shine on December 17th, 1972 in the Coombe Hospital, Dublin. Emily went to school in St Peter's National School, Athlone and later attended secondary school in St. Joseph's College, Summerhill, Athlone and Our Lady's Bower, Athlone. She grew up in a household full of music and from the age of seven was able to sit at a piano and play anything she heard. She had a natural talent and while studying music in school was found to have the rarity, "perfect pitch." Emily's singing abilities were recognized at a young age and her amazing voice was widely acclaimed as she took leads in school musicals and led the church choir. She appeared on her father's TV programs with Philippa from the age of seven. It was obvious she had a great ability to entertain, as she oozed ease in front of audiences.

Kathleen ran the family village pub and Emily spent her childhood working there, spending time on the farm in Taughmaconnell and taking to the roads as a backing vocalist with her Dad for the summer holidays. Even while in College she returned every weekend to play and sing in the church choir in St Peter's Church, Athlone.

Music proves to not be Emily's only talent. She is a brilliant academic. While still in Secondary school, prior to University, Emily received a Teaching Diploma in English, Speech and Communications and graduated with an Honors Degree in Psychology from the world renowned *Trinity College Dublin*. An Honors Master's Degree in Psychology soon followed. She now teaches in various schools in the Midlands and West of Ireland as well as working in her Psychology post, sharing jokes and stories with Brendan, and touring extensively with the band.

Emily joined the band full time following the tragic death of her uncle, Owen Shine, in 1997. She was working for the Irish Society of

Autism at the time and would spend her days at work then drive to the gigs throughout the UK, and then return to her work the next morning. She initially joined the band short term, just to help her father out as he had no keyboard player to replace Owen, but the performing buzz and bug caught Emily and has been with the band ever since.

Now an integral part of *Brendan Shine*, the band, Emily plays the keyboards, and of course, sings beautifully. The voice, and her engaging, warm personality, has developed an extensive and ever growing number of fans wherever she appears. Emily helps arrange and produce all Brendan's studio recordings and together they have released two singles, *Under the Light of the Moon* and *The Tree in the Meadow*, one CD titled, *Like Father, Like Daughter,* and Emily features with the band on the new Brendan Shine CD, *Live as Ever*. Emily has been described as the "greatest voice in Ireland" by Tony Allen, of *Foster & Allen*.

Emily met John Halpin in 1991 and they married in 1999. They are now the very proud parents of a daughter, Amelia Joy Mary, born May 5th, 2005. They live in Liberty, Ballydangan, in South Roscommon, just five miles from her childhood home in Taughmaconnelll.

Music is Emily's language. She has traveled the world with the band and loves every minute of her musical life. She also loves reading and learning, and is presently taking some time out from the band to enjoy motherhood. She is looking forward to getting back on the stage soon. Emily has a truly rare talent, gifted, and is a born entertainer - Like father, like daughter!

Johnny Dawson

John "Little Johnny" Dawson was born in Athlone Town, in 1946. He attended the Local Tech School, where he met Brendan Shine and together they formed a school band. Johnny trained as a barber but was a natural drummer with amazing affinity for rhythm.

At age fifteen, he and Brendan left school in Athlone to go on tour with *The Ciaran Kelly Ceili Band*. Johnny and Brendan have been going on tour now for over forty years and Johnny has always been known as "Big Little Johnny on the drums." Despite his smaller stature, he is renowned all over the UK and Ireland as one of the best drummers in Irish history, with a special talent for Traditional Irish Ceili beat.

Johnny has overcome huge medical difficulties to date, including weeks of unconsciousness at the hands of a rare fatal strain of meningitis. He has had bilateral hip replacements but still drives the music of the band with his trademark sound. A real old time professional of the music business, Johnny is also an acclaimed singer, with a distinctive voice. He even had a song written especially for him by Shay Healy, called, *"I'm Little But There's Lots of Me to Love."* You won't hear a better version of *Galway Bay* or *I'll Take You Home Again, Kathleen,* than that sung by Little Johnny Dawson.

Johnny is married to Mary (nee Maloney)Dawson and they live in Ballymore, County Westmeath, where they breed Krufts award winning Cavalier King Charles dogs. Johnny is also featured on the new Brendan Shine CD, *Live as Ever*.

With a career spanning four decades with Brendan and the Brendan Shine Band, anyone who sees the band can instantly appreciate the unique relationship that exists on stage between these life long friends, forged over a lifetime of travel, challenge, laughter and one great success after another.

Just a few of the historic achievements and highlights of the Brendan Shine Band:

- Performing in Carnegie Hall, New York and Albert Hall, London.
- Introducing Cardinal Thomas O' Fiach on Brendan's Primetime TV show 'Saturday Night Live" for RTE.
- Having the Shine trademark song, *"Do You Want Your Old Lobby Washed Down, Con Shine"* played for Pope John Paul II as he left Shannon Airport following his visit to Ireland in 1979.
- Honored by President Mary McAleese in *Aras an Uachtarain,* for Shine's contribution to the Irish industry.
- Being made a *free man* of his hometown Athlone in a civic reception for promotion of the town and region through a documentary *Shine on the Shannon* for RTE National TV.
- Lifetime Achievement Award for Brendan Shine's contribution to the music industry presented in London by *Irish World Paper.*
- Receiving *Platinum* (100,000 units sold), *Gold* (50,000 units sold) and *Silver* (25,000 units sold) *discs* for record sales.
- Hosting two series of *Nice and Easy* for RTE and BBC, Shine's own show.
- In 1997, Brendan and his group won the Band of the Year award and the following year he received a Lifetime Achievement Award from The Galtymore Club, London.

𝔅rendan 𝔖hine 𝔇iscography:

Some of the more than thirty-three albums, forty-five singles, four videos and four DVD's that Brendan Shine has recorded:

𝔎ecords & 𝔆𝔇's:

- This is Brendan Shine (1970)
- Ceili House (1973)
- The Best of Brendan Shine (1974)
- Country & Irish (1975)
- Simple Love Songs (1976)
- New Roads (1978)
- Blue Misty Eyes (1982)
- My Old Country Home (1983)
- The Brendan Shine Collection (1984)
- The Irish Side of Brendan Shine   (1984)
  (a commercial collection, not an original)
- Memories (1985)
- With Love (1986)
- Moonshine (1987)
- Magic Moments (1989)
- I'll Settle for Ireland (1992)
- If You Ever Go Over to Ireland   (1993)
  (Reissue of album from the 1970's)
- Shine on 21 (1993)
- I Wanna Stay With You (1996)
- At Home in Ireland (1999)
- The Very Best of Brendan Shine (2001)
- Dear Hearts and Gentle People (????)
- Soft, Sweet & Warm   (2003) (reissue)
- Like Father, Like Daughter   (2004) (featuring Emily Shine)
- Live as Ever - Brendan Shine & Band   (2005)
  (recorded on location in Ireland, U.K., Cleveland's
  Irish Cultural Festival and the Caribbean Cruise).

Singles:

- Under the Light of the Moon   (2003)
  (Brendan and Emily Shine)
- Shine's Plan   (2005)   (Shine's Country Ceili Band)
- The Tree in the Meadow   (2005)
  (released just before *Live as Ever*)

Videos & DVD's:

- Live at Blazers   (1984)
- Live at the Circus Tavern   (1987)
- Shine On   (1993)
- At Home in Ireland   (1996)

X.

𝔇𝔢𝔫𝔫𝔦𝔰 𝔇𝔬𝔶𝔩𝔢

"I heard the phrase 'pog mo thoin (kiss my ass)'
and asked my mom what it meant.
She said it meant 'Peel the potatoes.'"

Dennis is an internationally renowned harpist, storyteller, historian and teacher and one of the foremost authorities on the harp and on Turlough O'Carolan, the greatest harpist in history.* His recorded tribute to O'Carolan is spell-binding and has moved many to tears. Dennis sings in English, Gaelic (Irish) and Latin and has played in front of international celebrities and national television and radio audiences

---

* *Turlough O'Carolan [Gaelic spelling Toirdhealbhach O'Cearbhallain], was a harpist, singer and storyteller born in West Meath around 1670. Smallpox, a usually fatal disease, robbed O'Carolan of his sight at the age of only eighteen. This was later found to be a blessing in disguise, as it found in him a gift for music. He was trained in the harp through the generosity of a sympathetic local woman named Mary Fitzgerald McDermott Rowe. O'Carolan's very first composition, "Si Beag, Si Mor," earned him great fame throughout Ireland and started his career. O'Carolan would often write songs in honor of his current host or the host's family. He called these tunes "planxties." O'Carolan left a legacy of harp music and songs unrivaled by anyone, before or since. O'Carolan died on March 25th, 1783 at the age of sixty-eight years, leaving one son and six daughters (his wife, Mary Maguire, passed away in 1733). O'Carolan was also known for his love of whiskey. "Est homo qui potest bibere" (He is a man who is able to drink), said Jonathan Swift. His dying words were said to be, "the drink and I have been friends for so long, it would be a pity for me to leave without one last kiss," and he died.]*

throughout the U.S., Canada and Ireland, and has a large following in Japan as well. He has been recognized and honored all over the world and has made guest appearances on many television shows, including *Murder, She Wrote*, starring Angela Landsbury, and has consulted, and performed, background music for many others.

This extraordinary harpist is a quiet man, introspective but with a surprising and engaging sense of humor. He is not afraid to poke fun, even at himself.

"I remember there was a time I was playing in New Jersey, in Holmdel, and members of Cherish the Ladies were there as well. We had to play on a promotional stage, really advertising some imported mead (honey wine), from Ireland. We were required to dress in costume. They just threw us together, without rehearsal. So it turned into a bit of a session. Well, between Joanie Madden in a toga and myself in tights with a wizards cape and Mary Coogan in some odd outfit, I remember swearing to myself that I'd never dress 'lep' (leprechaun) again, for ANY amount of money. But we could drink as much of the mead as we wanted."

Currently a college professor at Glendale College, California, where he has taught since 1979, Dennis teaches English and Reading and is Director of The College Learning Center, which deals with the use of technology and the Internet in education. He is also the Director of the Ireland Glendale Community College Study Abroad Program. He earned his masters degree in education in 1978 from California State University, Los Angeles. Dennis' father was a professor of Sociology at Glendale for thirty-three years. Dennis performs throughout the year and also conducts workshops on Turlough O'Carolan, as well as on the Gaelic language, the harp, Irish music and song and Irish history, just to name a few.

One of eight brothers, Dennis Mark Doyle, born July 29th, 1952, had to learn – and earn, his own way. Like Dennis, many of his family members were and are also musicians and/or teachers.

Dennis lives in Glendale, California but his people are from Newbridge (now Avoca), County Wicklow and then Shamokin, Pennsylvania, where his grandfather was a coal mining engineer and was taught to read and write by his wife, Agnes Louise Doorley, Dennis' grandmother. Like many other Festival Legends, Dennis has a family rich in music and respect for Irish history. Although his father, Mark Anthony Doyle, "couldn't play chopsticks," Dennis' great grandfather, Patrick Doyle, was a musician and band leader. His mother, Elizabeth (Betty) Louise Seigfried, played the organ. Dennis' wife of more than twenty-five years, Paula Anne Philo Doyle, is a singer and fiddle player as well and has sung with Dennis at Milwaukee Irish Fest.

Paula wrote a religious song called *Grace, Like Rain.* Dennis showed it to the folks at Milwaukee and they then surprised Paula by singing it on stage with a thirty plus member choir. Dennis and Paula have five children, ranging in age from twenty-one to seven; Evan, Michael – a drummer, Austin – a talented guitarist, Grace – an excellent singer, and Sarah.

Surrounded by nuns, priests and brothers with Irish accents, Dennis grew up in Catholic schools. These surroundings led to serious consideration of entering the priesthood and Dennis spent four years in the seminary. This led to his being part of the movement to a more folk music based liturgy. Many of Dennis's former classmates at the seminary have gone on to become very prominent liturgical composers.

Dennis decided on the teaching path instead and Irish music, and fans of the harp, have been richly blessed in being presented, in song and story; the history, folklore, influence and legacy of the harp, the Irish, and the often ancient traditions of the Irish heritage. These presentations are so enjoyable, and engaging, that it captures all those interested in the Irish culture, not just those interested in the harp. It quickly becomes obvious that you are in the hands of a true sage, a bard that is able to bring to life the harpist tradition.

"I fell in love with the music [of the harp] before I fell in love with the harp. I loved the music of the mandolin and organ while still in college and then heard *Give Me Your Hand.* I found the music for it but it doesn't sound right on piano, it is made for the harp.   I started to look at the harp but then, in 1982, my wife surprised me at Christmas by ordering one for me.   The box under the tree had a *How to Play the Harp* book and the instrument arrived soon after, in January.   When someone gets you a $1,000.00 instrument, you jump right in.   We were playing gigs about two months later, in March.

"A group of friends, around ten or twelve of us, got together for a session about every two weeks.   Then we got offered gigs.   I had always had a musical background and could play the chords even if not the melody.

"I would say that people who want to start the harp should start right, with a teacher who can show them the proper fingering and positions. Many start on the harp plucking in an intuitive way, which is likely all wrong, then, at some point they will need to relearn the whole process or they will never be fluent in the instrument. As the Irish say: *Tus Maith, leath no h'oibre* - a good start is half the job."

Dennis' first paid gig was playing Christmas songs in a store window, with speakers outside for passer bys – he was ten years old.   "When I was younger, my parents had bought an organ and you got free lessons with it. I took the lessons. Then, when I was a little older, as I was studying to be a priest, I didn't have access to an organ but played the piano. While in the seminary, I participated in the blossoming of the new liturgical music in the mass – folk music. One of my classmates was Bob Hurd, who wrote *In the Breaking of the Bread, Pan de Vida, The Mass of Glory,* and many other popular Catholic hymns.   [The movement] ... all started in church. In a lot of cases, we borrowed Irish tunes and put new words to them.   I did the cover photography for the first two albums [we put together], for a publisher called *FEL,* for Friends of the English Liturgy, and played the piano until I left the seminary. I then got married and grew interested in [playing] the mandolin. I loved the music and my wife gave me a mandolin. She plays the fiddle, which had belonged to her grandfather. We played gigs, weddings and such, and around St. Patrick's Day.

"In July and August of 1983, I made my first trip to Ireland, mostly playing Irish festivals and competitions. My first competition was at Granard. I stayed in Ireland long enough to see one of my favorite bands, *Clannad*, at Memorial Music Hall in Dublin.   I taped a lot of sessions while in Ireland and came back with a lot of new songs to add to my repertoire. I also bought books and music there that weren't available here.

"One of my major influences was Anne and Charley Hayman, who I met in L.A. Anne is an authority on the wire-strung harp, a traditional version of the Celtic Harp, played with the fingernails and wrote the preeminent book on how to play it.

"Starting in 1982, I studied with Sylvia Woods, at the Sylvia Woods Harp Center in Glendale, California, for five or six years. Sylvia was an All-Ireland Champion on the harp. In 1979 or 1980, she won the Fleadh Ceol (pron *Flah Kee ol,* which means *Feast of Music*).

National music competitions in Ireland were conducted first locally, at competitions called *Bun Fleadh,* winners then go on to county competitions and the top three finishers at the county level then advance to the Fleadh Ceol. Winners would also compete from Chicago, San Francisco, Los Angeles and New York.

Dennis's teacher, Sylvia, was a student of Alan Stivell, who played a lot of reed instruments such as bagpipes and the bombard, as well as the harp. Stivells' father revered the harp and was a woodworker. He built Alex a harp and Alex took the music, electrified it and raised the energy of the music, so that it had more appeal than as just dinner music. Alex is considered to be responsible for the revival of the instrument.

With the dawning of television, the harp disappeared with the bards and seanchies, who were no longer needed to provide entertainment. The days of fathers making harps for their daughters to play when guests came over were now ended. There was a shift in the way people received their entertainment and their news, from making their own, to relying on radio, and then television. "The old bards were the media of the time, conveying news, weather, sports, history, culture, family and regional event news," explains Dennis.   The bard tradition faded and has all but disappeared, except for cherished memory.

"Another influence for me was the group *Train to Sligo,* said Dennis. "Tom Moore, who wrote such songs as *Still Believin'* and *Cavan Town,* for Mary Black, was a part of the group, as well as Gerry O'Byrne, who later played with *Patrick Street.* They also had Paula Gershen, who had studied with Mary Bergin, on tin whistle. Fiddler Cait Reed and hammer dulcimer player Judy Gamerol were members too. Tom Moore had also taught some of the people in Clannad to play the mandolin. He eventually moved to Russia where he was taught Russian in Siberia. He married a Russian girl and is now back in Dublin."

"It has been six years since my last new recording, but right now, I am at the right level of fame and interest that is appropriate for me, given the kids and such. Once the kids are gone, I hope to do more shows, venues I haven't done before. It used to be five or six weeks gone at a time. …. It is very tough on the family when I am traveling. [For example], Milwaukee is ten days away from home, with the summer school. Paula is a really great performer but can't go with me, with the kids. So it is tough for her too, to not be able to perform. I occasionally do a study abroad program and I am bringing my family this year. Playing in a great hall or venue would be a dream.

"Some pieces I play regularly are original. I start nearly every set with *Austin's Planxty*, named after my third son. It is recorded on the album *Hibernia,* and was included in a Narada collection, *Faces of the Harp.* A tune called *Grace* is part of my repertoire now. Paula and I have written several religious songs, with Cathedral Press, published in a collection, called, *Songs of Celtic Christianity.* It is now out of print but it had a good run and I still get requests for some of the songs, including a piece called *Walk in the Light.*"

"In the 1980's when I was first starting my career, I was the opening act for Clannad at the Wiltern Theatre on Wilshire Blvd. in Los Angeles. They were looking for a local talent who fit the type of music Clannad played and since I sang in Irish, I fit their type of music. It was my biggest audience so far and the place was packed and I did very well. I couldn't see anything, the lights were so bright. Plus, I got the star treatment with a dressing room with a star on it!" Dennis relates with a bit of laughter. "It resulted in a lot of gigs, exposure on the local Irish program, and with local radio."

"[One of my favorite moments is] when I discovered that I was being treated respectfully and as a peer by some of my favorite musicians; like Tommy Makem, Danny Doyle and Mick Moloney. Over the years, I know that Irish harp music will not be as popular a music as most other kinds of Irish music, but I know that I have the respect of excellent musicians who are glad that I am doing something that touches our cultural roots. I don't think it will ever disappear; it's such a beautiful instrument and still a living sign of the Irish people. I meet Celtic harpists everywhere I play. There are actually little bands of them in cities all over."

"My first time at the Milwaukee Irish Fest and [I] was a performer in a smallish harp tent, it paid very little at the time. It started to rain, driving people into my tent. I got gigs all over the country after that because people running festivals all over the country got a chance to hear me."

Dennis has great admiration for many performers but specifically mentioned Mick Moloney, Tommy Makem, Cherish the Ladies and Joannie Madden, Eileen Ivers, Gerry O'Byrne, Sharon Shannon and Lilish O'Meara, who is a consultant to the Ceol Traditional Irish Music Museum, located on the West side of Dublin. He remembers when he first heard the Chieftains and the seminal *Bothy Band*, which included members Kevin Burke and Mihal O'Donnell, who Dennis recalls as producing the most gorgeous singing he has ever heard – it had a big influence on Dennis, making him determined to learn and include Gaelic language songs in his own shows.

"Makem and Clancy on Ed Sullivan, it introduced something completely new to American audiences. [The Irish] said, 'Hey, the Yanks like it, it must be good.' It influenced people like Bob Dylan, Rock-n-Roll and many other acts as well. Like the creation of the Ceoltiori Eireann, the predecessors to the Chieftains, by Sean O'Riada. Although he passed away young, the music went from a solo presentation to an ensemble. Riverdance was the same thing; people realized the whole Irish thing could be pretty cool."

If he weren't a performer, Dennis would be a performer, no argument. Dennis is a cantor and plays the piano at his parish church and is active in Boy Scouts as a Scout Leader, enjoys camping, being in the woods, photography and being a web master.

From County Wicklow to the coal mines of Pennsylvania to the sunny shores of Glendale, California, the Doyle families' journey has taken them far. Dennis' journey has continued as he spreads the music and the history of the harp to enthusiastic audiences all across America and Ireland. He is both a Festival Legend and a renowned harp master, whose teaching and songs have captured fans, and historians, the world over. Because of this remarkable man, the music and story of the harp lives on, expanding and captivating new audiences everywhere Dennis performs. He is truly a treasure and a living, talking, teaching history of both a time that was, and a music that still thrives and is relevant today.

Dennis Doyle Discography:

Recordings :

- *Be in My Heart, Celtic Hymns & Songs through the Day*, a collection of previously released tracks, but organized to provide a daily meditative experience, Ave Maria Press, 1998
- *Irish Meditations*, Incarnation Music,1997
- *Faces of the Harp*, a collection of harp pieces by various artists compiled by Narada Media,1997. Dennis' track is track one Austin's Planxty from his Hibernia recording.
- *The Minstrel Boy*, Incarnation Music,1995
- *Abbess: Hymns inspired by Saint Brigid,* Incarnation Music, 1994
- *Harp in Transit*, Woodenship Records, 1993currently out of print
- *St. Patrick: The Contemplative Celt*, Incarnation Music, 1991
- *Hibernia*, Woodenship Records, 1990
- *In the Mother Tongue*, Woodenship Records, 1988
- *The Harper's Return*, Woodenship Records, 1987
- *Far from the Shamrock Shore*, Innisfree Productions, 1985

Music by Carolan recorded by Dennis Doyle:
On Irish Meditations

- Princess Royal

On the Minstrel Boy:

- Fairy Queen
- Quarrel with the Landlady
- Miss Golding
- Planxty Safaigh
- Isabella Burke
- The Dark, Plaintive Youth

On Hibernia:

- Planxty Wilkinson
- Bishop John Hart
- Carolan's Welcome

On Mother Tongue:

- Bridget Cruise
- One Bottle More
- Mrs.Trench (Planxty Fanny Power)
- Lady Athenry
- Ode to Whiskey

On The Harper's Return:

- Captain Sudley
- Eleanor Plunket
- Colonel Irwin
- Carolan's Lament
- Fanny Power
- Blind Mary
- Si Beag, Si Mor
- Carolan's Farewell

Books and Publications by Dennis Doyle:

- *Irish Harp Music* by Dennis Doyle, Mel Bay Publications, Pacific, MO, 1998.
- *Songs of Celtic Christianity* by Dennis & Paula Doyle, Incarnation Music, 1995 with companion compact disk.
- *Teaching Irish to Americans in Milwaukee* by Dennis Doyle, essay in The Irish Language in the United States, Thomas Ihde, ed. Bergin & Garvey, Westport Connecticut, 1994.
- *Celtic Spirituality and Liturgy* by Dennis Doyle, an article in Parish Liturgy, March 1994, American Catholic Press, So. Holland, Il.

Other Accomplishments:

- Received a *Fainne* from the Curtin Branch of the *Conradh na Gaeilge* (Milwaukee, WI) for proficiency in the Irish language.
- Site Co-Chair of the Annual Conference of the <u>North American Association for Celtic Language Teachers (NAACLT)</u> in Glendale, California.
- Recognized as *"Irishman of the Year"* by the City of Los Angeles in recognition for work in promotion of Irish cultural activities.
- Received the Faculty Instructional Technology Award for "exceptional contributions integrating pedagogy and technology in student learning."

www.english.glendale.cc.ca.us/doyle.a.html

XI

The Makem & Spain Brothers (Shane, Conor & Rory Makem, Liam & Mickey Spain)

"... what the Makem Brothers have done is to restore the song tradition to its rightful place at the crossroads of history and music." - The Irish Connection[1]

As a family, the name Makem is synonymous with "legend" in the world of Celtic music. Shane, Conor and Rory are the third generation (so far) of Makems to perform on the world stage, and the inheritors of a grand musical estate.

The Makem brothers are a living, and performing (very successful in their own right), embodiment of all that their father, Tommy, stands for. Whether listening to Shane's quiet humor, Rory's Tommy-like tenor or Conor's great harmonies, Mick's deep gorgeous voice or Liam's wide variety of instruments, the Makem & Spain Brothers are insuring that the Irish Song Tradition - and the Makem family legacy - continues to shine brightly.

Besides the Makem Brothers and Tommy, the Makem family legacy, living the poetry of Irish music, is also well represented in this amazing family of Irish-born singers. Their grandmother, Sarah Makem, was a source singer and was visited by folk music collectors from all over the world, such as Pete Seeger, Diane Hamilton and Jean Ritchie, for her great store of old Irish songs. She was also the singing voice that welcomed millions weekly to one of the first international folk programs, the BBC World Service's *As I Roved Out*.

In the winter of 2003, The Makem Brothers joined forces with The Spain Brothers to form a quintet as unique as any in Irish music today. Mick's strong baritone and Liam's skills on the guitar, mandolin and harmonica are a perfect complement to the Makem Brothers' wit and harmonic brilliance. The result is a rare and electric onstage chemistry. The Makem & Spain Brothers are the only balladeers in their age group doing what they do. They should be recognized, and treasured, for carrying on when others take the easier path, or have not even ventured down the road less taken at all.

The Makem and Spain Brothers have played before millions on both sides of the Atlantic, including national slots on American public television and Irish talk shows, appearances at Symphony Space in New York City, the World Cup and the Guinness Fleadh. Their sound comes from powerfully backed, precise harmonies, varied instrumentation and a strong appreciation for the history and progression of folk music.

Each member of the band offers great contributions to the group, another case of the whole being much more than the sum of its parts. Rory is *The Musician,* guiding and driving the sound of the group. Conor is *The Songwriter,* bringing new songs and diversity. Mick is called *The Voice* by his band mates, one listen to the gorgeous deep sound clearly tells why. He also is a songwriter. Shane is *The Historian,* gathering material that tells the story of what they are singing and how it fits into the Irish scene at large, going back as far as it goes. Last, but certainly not least, Liam is *The Collector,* or as his bandmates also call him, *Mr. Moneybags,* for always buying new instruments. He is also a songwriter as well.

Signature songs, such as *Donegal Dance, Whiskey Row* and *Wild & Restless Foam,* all original compositions, as well as old favorites like *Road to Gundagia, Ha' Penny Bridge* and *Pretty Maggie O',* highlight the vocal and songwriting gifts of these tremendously talented performers and offers proof positive that the ballad tradition is alive and well, in the Makem & Spain Brothers capable hands.

Knowing Irish music almost inherently, both the Makem and Spain brothers grew up at sing-songs and sessions frequented by some of

Ireland's best known and most prolific singers and musicians, and that is not including their parents. As professional entertainers since 1989, they have had the unique opportunity to learn and be guided by many of these performers, successful in Irish and folk music, past and present. For both the Makem brothers and the Spain brothers, carrying on the legacy of love and honoring the ballad or song tradition has almost been preordained since birth, even if they didn't know it until much later. Only Liam Spain had the life long desire to be an Irish music performer from a young age. Conor, Shane, Rory and Mick all came to their careers by life's chance encounters and then were bitten by the performing bug, which fuels their active involvement and dedication to preserving and promoting the Irish heritage to this day.

Shane

"Having a favorite song for me is a little like having a favorite food, sometimes I'm in the mood for steak, or Mexican and other times it could be….." – never to be pinned down, that Shane.

Shane Patrick Makem entered the world on August 14th, 1967, born in the village of Drogheda, between Dromiskin and Dundalk, in County Louth. He is the "old man" of the group although the Makem brothers do have an older sister, Katie. Shane was named after his Uncle Jack Makem (Jack is John, which is Sean, which is Shane in Irish), who was often sought out to play as he was one of the few Uilleann pipers left in Ireland in the fifties. It is believed Uncle Jack was the first piper to use a synthetic bag. When his old one wore out and would no longer hold air, Uncle Jack simply made a new one out of the inner tube of a tractor tire – something that had never been done before.

When not on stage and in public, Shane, like his brothers, is more of an introverted guy. Not necessarily shy, just introverted, a little private. But when "off-stage," among other musicians, friends and/or those they know well, each of the brothers are outgoing, welcoming and funny.

Shane remembers his first gig as going pretty well; "Everyone seemed to be having a good time, there was a lot of drinking going on, so we probably sounded great." His family's long legacy is continued from his grandmother, the legendary Sarah Makem, through his father, Tommy, his cousins Jim and Tom Sweeney (of Barley Bree fame), his grandfather; a renowned fiddler and bagpipe player, often sought out, and his brothers, Conor and Rory. The family legacy and love of Irish music, history and dance has continued into the next generation as well, Shane's niece, Molly, is an Irish dancer and numerous cousins are involved in Irish music and the arts.

In their home area of Dover, New Hampshire, Shane, Rory and a few friends got together and formed the *Seacoast Irish Cultural Association,* to bring back the interest in the culture and so that, in part, kids could have an opportunity to learn something about Irish music, dance and the rich cultural heritage so prevalent in the Irish heritage.

Shane remembers the great parties held at the Makem house. Songs and stories, with amazing guests like the *Irish Rovers* and artsy folks were often there: "It's not that I remember individuals because I was probably too young. But I remember that there was music going on there were people actually playing and singing music in the house. There was always that going on.

"That's where folk music really comes from and that's why it's still around. People would get together and that is what they would do to entertain themselves. The television wasn't on. The people were just entertaining themselves, sort of a camaraderie. People enjoyed themselves sitting around the home and playing music. They were real people, not someone that you hear on the radio that you were never going to meet or talk to. They would be well known, but I probably didn't know that at the time. They were just my parent's friends."

Tommy Makem had relatives in the U.S., working in the mill industry and upon leaving Ireland, Dover, New Hampshire was his first stop. He then continued on to New York. He also spent some time in Chicago, where he met his future wife, Shane's mother, Mary. Tommy and Mary were wed in Chicago in 1963 but returned to New York, where their first child, Katie was born, in Queens. Soon after, they returned to Ireland (in the mid-1960's) until coming to Dover, New Hampshire for good around 1971, when Shane was four.

Going through Dover Catholic School and St. Thomas Aquinas High School prepared Shane for the next step, a B.A. in English from Stonehill College in Massachusetts. After graduation, a friend asked Shane to accompany him as he took a car down to Austin, Texas. Shane went and liked it so much; he decided to stay for a while. He returned to Dover when his brothers got out of college for summer break so they could play music together.

In 2001, Mary Makem passed away, at the age of fifty-eight. She was the backbone of the Makem family and had a deep sense of justness and fairness to everyone. She often got involved when others wouldn't and instilled that sense of fairness in all her children. She is sorely missed.

"A lot of people would think of folk music as just a person, because they are playing an acoustic guitar. I would say folk music tells a good story, especially Irish folk music. One of the great strengths is that there is a good narrative in it - that tells me it is good. There is always a good story to a good song. It may be about a specific event - even if you don't have any idea of the history of that event, you can get something out of it, something bigger than that one thing. It's about something bigger, of using a distinct event and presenting it," Shane said.

He continued, "The fact that we can get up on stage and can change, have a positive impact on people, whether to get them more into Irish music or to change that they think folk music is boring - we can change their perception of that."

An example of this is when the band received an unsolicited email from someone seeing them for the very first time: "We got an unexpected fan email. She was young; she said she thought that folk music was kind of this boring stuff that her mother listened to. But from the first song, she was just enthralled by what we were doing. We can change people's notion of what folk music is. I think people think of folk music as one person singing about their emotions and a lot of people might consider that boring but I think what we do is pretty interesting [the reality of what folk music is, in contrast to the perception of what folk music is] and to be able to make an impact on somebody like that [makes me proud].

"When I was a child, I knew what my father did but didn't see him doing it all that often. Now that I am in the same position, I have learned that you can't call in sick at this job. My father would be on stage no matter what. He performed with an ulcer, in great pain. I was in the emergency room one night and was on stage the next. I got off stage and people told me I was just green. You just have to go out there."

"Life is different than I imagined it would be. When I was young, I never even thought about playing music, until I was about eighteen and started playing in a rock band. Then I moved on to playing these songs that I sort of already knew, in my head, just from osmosis. I never really pictured myself as somebody who would be able to go and do a five day a week, nine-to-five job. Even when I was in college, I never expected to be going around the country playing music. I didn't really know [what I was going to do].

"[But] when I was in college I had a roommate who worked at a folk club. He had forgotten some work or something, and asked me to bring it in for him. After I left, the owner reprimanded him for having a non-employee in the kitchen. When he found out who my father was, he didn't seem to mind the kitchen infraction and asked if I wanted to play there. I called Rory to see if he was interested in playing it with me -- this was in November or December -- and we were scheduled to do a gig there in, I think February. Rory and I both got guitars for Christmas, learned forty or fifty songs over Christmas break, then played our first gig."

The Makem Brothers as a band came into being in 1989, after Rory graduated from high school, but the Makem Brothers were playing individually and together in local sessions and gatherings for a number of years before performing on stage. Shane and Rory made their professional debut in February of 1989 at the Blackthorn Tavern in North Easton, Massachusetts. Conor joined them in November, 1991 at the Tom Clancy Memorial Concert in Symphony Space, Manhattan, New York. Brain Sullivan, a base player, was added to the group when they had a gig on Boston Commons and needed a base player, they liked him so much he stayed for years.

The Makem Brothers and Brian Sullivan made their first festival appearance at Cleveland's Irish Cultural Festival in 1992, followed two months later by the Pittsburgh Irish Fest. The Makem Brothers have four albums, plus a demo tape, which sold from 1992 to 1995, but is no longer available; *Outstanding in a Field* (1992, Out of print), *On the Rocks* (1995), *Who Fears to Speak* (1997), *Stand Together* (2001). The Makem & Spain Brothers first post-merger recording was *As Others Did Before Us* (2004). It is plain to see that both families' legacies burn brighter than ever.

Shane loves living in Dover. A lot of family; Tommy, Katie and many relatives all make it home. He also loves Montana for no reason. Armagh, the whole west coast, "Derrynoose [the town where the Makem family came from] has great scenery. I know a lot of people and have a lot of relatives there. South Armagh gets a bad rap [for the troubles and history that has occurred there, among the British forts on the hills] but it has a lot of great things. My favorite places are usually where I am right now."

Although Shane loves the festival season for seeing old friends, fellow performers and other attractions, he loves returning home and the feeling of sitting on the couch and relaxing, maybe reading (when the infrequent opportunity arises), after leaving out on Thursdays and then returning on Mondays, while gigging. He recently finished *A Confederacy of Dunces* by John Kennedy O'Toole but his favorite author is Flann O'Brien. Some of his favorite memories revolve around the early years at Milwaukee Irish Fest. "The post parties [limited to only performers back then], were pretty amazing. Great sessions…never see some of these guys on stage together… those were pretty amazing."

One of Shane's personal defining moments came after he and Rory had played a few gigs together and developed a little confidence. He began to realize that he really could do it. The shy, introverted side could be left at the stage entrance. "The hardest part was talking in front of people, figuring out what to say, between songs, that's interesting."

"Most people don't realize that this is our job. Sometimes we have to treat it that way. There is actual work involved. People are sometimes fond of telling us the way we 'ought to do' things. They get upset when they ask for a favorite song that we do not know as a band and then ask us to play it anyway." Shane has no regrets: "Everything you do makes you who you are," he ended.

Shane would love to have seen Pete Seeger perform, Hank Williams too. But talking about March 13th, 1966, when Tommy Makem and the Clancy Brothers awoke the sleeping giant of Irish music in the U.S. by appearing on The Ed Sullivan Show for the fourth time, got Shane to really open up: "…they made it broadly socially acceptable to be Irish in this country. Like any other ethnicity, people wanted to blend in, wanted to be 'American.' When they heard Irish music on the most popular TV show in the world, it was ok to be Irish. That's pretty amazing. It had the same kind of impact on the Irish as Kennedy being elected President and as Riverdance."

One of the goals of the Makem's is to try to make the music readily available to anyone who wants it, not having to search high and low to find it. They hope to continue on their path of spreading the songs, stories and history of Ireland as their career of choice.

There are so many entertainment options today, from cable and movies, computers, DVD's, MP3's and a thousand and one restaurants and clubs. Like the balladeers, the live shows are dying. Live shows that used to draw five and six hundred people are now drawing one hundred. Irish facilities are not booking bands every weekend, shows and dances that I went to, on most weekends, as a child. The explosion of Irish festivals is the only thing that is keeping that tradition, and livelihood, thriving. Incredibly talented groups and performers are struggling to even make a living in this world. The Makem & Spain Brothers are one of the groups who are fortunate enough to be able to make performing their careers.

"I would like to be remembered as, hopefully, somebody who was able to take the music and pass it on to younger people, the way it has been done for hundreds of years," said Shane.

Conor

When asked what he wished people knew about him, Conor answered with a quip, then aimed at typical Irish stereotypes, "I've never taken part in an International Conspiracy. I guess I'd point out that just because I'm in an Irish band, doesn't mean my favorite food is corned beef and cabbage. While it's a once a year food for most people, we have the luck of sampling it all year. In truth, my favorite food is Tex-Mex."

Conor Brendan Makem, born September 29th, 1968 in Drogheda, County Louth, is the second of the three Makem brothers, third child after his sister, Katie.

"My grandparents grew up in a different era. After being in school in America for a few years, maybe third grade, the principal confiscated my snuff (tobacco that you snort to clear your nose). I was snorting some during recess to clear out my nose and she saw me from across the playground. She ran over and grabbed it from me, yelling:

"'What is that? Where did you get this?'

"I said 'It's snuff. It clears your nose out.'

"She yelled, 'Where did you get this?'

"I said, 'From my granny.'

"She just shook her head."

"That was the beginning of the cultural differences. A few months later I was sent to speech therapy. It was myself, some kids with lisps and two other Irish kids. It's not the fact that the teachers sent me there that beguiles me though, but that the speech therapist didn't recognize that the three of us had accents. I guess she must have thought there was some sort of epidemic making kids sound strange.

"After about a month, my mother found out I was in speech therapy and asked the principal about it.

"The principal asked, 'You never noticed anything wrong with the way he talks?'

"My mother told her I had an Irish accent, but that that was it.

"'Oh' said the principal.

"And the Dowleys and I were pulled out of speech therapy. But after a month of watching sock puppets tell me 'You must speak like this,' and my repeating 'I must speak like this,' and being told that that was good, I lost my Irish accent."

Being introduced to music from such an accomplished family history didn't guide Conor into the music field, initially. It was only after seeing Rory and Shane perform at the Blackthorn Tavern, near Stonehill College, that Conor remembers feeling an epiphany – "... realizing that this is what I would like to be doing."

Conor's first gig as part of the Makem Brothers went quite well – performing at a memorial benefit concert for Tom Clancy. There were many different acts performing and the Makem Brothers performed two numbers. Conor could be the first person in performing history whose very first time in front of a microphone was also his professional stage debut, at New York's Symphony Space. Prior to that, his brothers wouldn't give him a microphone to practice into.

Things have changed for the better and being on stage is when Conor is happiest. He and his brothers are fond of saying that their favorite place to play is where ever they are at the moment and they mean it when they say it. Years of practical experience had ingrained the ability to make each show energetic, engaging, educational and memorable, even when they have performed the songs hundreds of times before.

But it is the sessions in and around the Makem's home that spark so many of Conor's memories and stories. Although good sessions are hard to come by, they are cherished all the more because of it. It is obvious that those sessions had a big effect on each member of the Makem & Spain Brothers, whether from the incredibly accomplished company they played with and/or listened to, or the great legacy of the respect for the Irish heritage with the love passed on to them by their parents, friends, and frequent visitors.

"When Liam [Clancy] was living in Dover, when my father and Liam would get together to practice, sing a few songs, that's when I first began to notice that my father was singing Irish music, as opposed to just singing songs. The fact that it was 'Irish' first began to register and I first got an appreciation of what he did," said Conor.

"Our generation has lost the ability to communicate, to hold conversations," he continued. Televisions, music, the bars with their blasting noise, all make it even harder. In the old days, when none of this existed, people actually talked. We get our personalities from the things and people around us, through talking to others. Now people get it from movies and TV. The world has shrunk. You could fit it in your pocket. Yet people are so homogenized. From the mass media, their personalities are formed, not from each other. Old people weren't dealt that hand. They learned who they were and then went out into the world and found who they were all over again. That's why I love talking to older people; they have the great stories and experiences to share."

Conor also loves doing creative things and is happiest when eating. Pizza and Mexican food are favorites. Interests for a career would be beer manufacturing (he is just joking – sort of), video production or somewhere within his fascination with science, if he had started younger and got the necessary volumes of training required. "What could be more profound," is how he described the idea and excitement of making new discoveries in the universe.

When not performing, the middle Makem brother is a part time (three days a week) reporter for the *Rochester New Hampshire Times*. Initially working full time, Conor left the job when his show schedule did not allow for the full time required at the Times. The paper was then purchased by *Foster's Daily Democrat*. At the request of the editor, John Nolan, Conor returned to the paper in August of 2003, part time. This allowed him to still meet the band's tour schedule. His first story was on a cousin, Charlie Boyle, who had the "World's Best Tomato." Conor's predecessor had been trying to get Charlie to agree to an interview for quite a while. When Conor came on staff, the editor sent him out to get the interview, figuring if anyone could get it; it would be Charlie's cousin. Conor eventually got the story. "Old School," Charley was the last of a dying breed of hands on farmers. Charlie's favorite thing to do was to sit around the house after hours, drinking Budweiser and singing all night long. "Great sessiuns," Conor remembers.

Just like Shane and Rory, returning home from traveling is one of Conor's favorite things. When on stage, or even at a gig, festival or concert, performers are in a constant state of being always "on." Even when not "on" and walking around the grounds or sitting quietly relaxing, the Makem and Spain brothers are constantly approached, shook, slapped on the back, asked for autographs and hugged. They enjoy the interaction but it is often constant. The only respite is to leave the festival grounds, and miss all the great music and activities around them.

Most performers are very ready for being "on" to be "over" by the time the traveling ends for the week, month or tour. When returning from a gig on the road, like almost every other full-time performer, Conor loves to just chill out and watch TV, with *The Food Network*, *West Wing* and *Freaks and Geeks* being among his favorites.

Self-described (although his brothers also readily agree) as "having different thought patterns than other people," Conor's view of the top three defining moments in Irish music history is illuminating;

"Turlough O'Carolan, the world-renowned harpist, historian and song collector, his collecting of tunes preserved a lot of tunes that would be lost.

"The Clancy Brothers & Tommy Makem on the Ed Sullivan Show [four times from March 12, 1961 thru March 13th, 1966] – People were proud to be Irish again in the U.S. They traveled back to Ireland and brought that pride with them. The native-born Irish in Ireland became proud again too. Until then, they didn't consider themselves as worthy. They didn't have any pride in being Irish, from centuries of being downtrodden, centuries and centuries of being told that you're inferior. Even when they came over to America, there was a lot of sentiment against the Irish. The Irish-Americans, once they moved over here - [saw the] 'No Irish Need Apply.' The Irish were considered beneath slaves, a lot of times. Maybe it extends from a bit of that. They didn't feel worthy. It wasn't until my father and the Clancy's, I think, had a big part in people realizing that their culture really was something special.

"Riverdance – people started forgetting about the songs, unless doing *sean nós* [unaccompanied] singing. If you were singing with a guitar, you weren't Irish, it seemed. But Irish music is folk music; it changes. The banjo and the bouzouki were added to Irish music in the 20th century, yet most people consider them traditional. But the guitar was added then too and, for some reason, a lot of people wouldn't consider it traditional.

"Riverdance showed that traditions don't have to be stuck in the past. It was new and different but still a lot of tradition is showcased. Two things that compliment each other so well, tunes and songs – they belong together and are such a great focus of music. Riverdance brought that tradition back into focus, the tunes are now following."

"For me personally, seeing my brothers perform for the first time was an exciting moment.

"My mother dying [in February, 2001], so young, it was unexpected. When you are thirty, you don't expect your fifty-eight year old mother to be dying on you. Lung cancer, she smoked her whole life. I constantly told her to quit but she always replied with the fact that everyone in her family lived into their nineties. It was the most emotional time of my life. It is the cycle of life. It doesn't matter if you are young, energetic – [it] doesn't matter. When your time is up, times up. My sister moved in with my father. We were always close but not an emotional family. We are protective of our family [however], have pretty good pride in family."

Besides pride in family, each of the Makem brothers lives and breathes pride in their Irish heritage. The work that they do daily to preserve and promote it is action, not just words. They daily live up to their creed of walking the walk and spreading the beauty of the Irish traditions, folklore and song. As Conor explained, "I am pretty proud of the band right now. Because I feel like it is totally different than just about anything that is going on right now in Irish music and I feel that we are moving in a direction where I think Irish music has been lacking. I think it is moving the music forward, in a way that I would like to see the music move forward. For a long time, we were sort of stagnant.

"We have a style with the five of us, it is a whole different feel than any other band out there, I think. I also think there is a severe lack of people singing ballads in our age group. There are some, but there is [almost] nobody doing it nationally or internationally in our age group, doing the stuff that we do. We kind of see our band holding up the tradition in our generation, keeping the tradition not only alive, but living."

"I would never have foreseen this. There are some times you have to pinch yourself - in realizing you do such an enjoyable job. I was going to be a computer major in college. But I took a few classes, and I always got A's in computers, but I realized I didn't want to spend my life sitting in front of a computer. And then, of course, computers got really big and I realized I would have been really rich if I had just stuck with them. That's when Shane turned me on to English." Conor graduated from Stonehill College in 1992 with a degree in English Literature and a minor in philosophy.

Conor's has a few favorite locations to visit; "In the U. S.: New Orleans; a lot of fun, Portland, Oregon; I love the area, Butte, Montana; just great. We went to a real speakeasy there. We were walking around an empty building and a tow historian took us on a tour, where we got the first drinks served in the place since the 1940's. The scoreboard was still on the wall, all filled out with team names. There was stained glass in the ceiling, light came through the little squares - the place was under the sidewalk.

"I like Dallas, Houston, Pittsburgh, Cleveland, Butte; fun cities. Festivals too, we don't get to see much of the cities but get to see our friends. In Ireland, I like Derrynoose (Makemville) – a few miles outside of Keady – many, many relatives and friends live there. You feel like you know everyone. Dingle, it's a cool town. Galway, it's as big as you need."

"My favorite unknown performers would probably be John Nolan, poet and story-teller, also editor of Rochester Times, knows a lot of neat songs. I don't know if they [people of Rochester] realize what they have, The Spain Brothers, up until a couple of years ago, then they joined up with us. The Spain's fattened our sound. We can really get into harmonies; can belt it out without drowning each other out."

The Makem brothers had seen the Spains perform at a Dover pub called *Biddy Mulligan's*, the Makem's local hangout. They enjoyed them so much and saw that they were doing the same kind of music that they then made a point of going to see the Spains when they performed at Biddy Mulligan's on Friday nights after that. After a while, the five future partners had a session at Shane's apartment and realized they had something much better together than playing separately. As Shane mentions, when asked about Liam and Mick, "Those guys are like brothers to us - we know what each is thinking." *The Makem & Spain Brothers* were born and their engaging beats, wonderful vocals and retelling of the history of the songs they perform are gaining notice, and fans, everywhere they play.

"My favorite place to play would be Milwaukee Irish Fest – real fun one, huge crowd, stages are permanent, sound always good – the all-around experience. At most festivals there is no pressure to sell out the show, so you're not worried. Plus you get to see old friends. Liam Spain's or my house – session places, where everyone shows up, it ends up being a blast – whole lot of beer and a whole lot of singing. And Charlie Boyle's – great sessions too," Conor said.

A few other favorites in Conor's life; "Inside Newgrange is amazing – My father was there for Winter Solstice, which is booked out for twenty years with princes and scientists. You see the sunlight coming through the hole. He said it was the most amazing thing he had ever seen in his life. The Irish countryside, it brings calmness, whether viewing or walking. The first time you fly into Ireland, if daylight, you pass over the, as Johnny Cash said 'Forty Shades of Green.' Fields and square patches of green.

"When you look off stage and see thousands listening and enjoying [the show]. It's not just the view, very few can see that. Anyone can see the Grand Canyon, we are so blessed to be able to do that [to play in front of thousands]."

The Makem and Spain brothers also have a few favorite lessons they've learned over the years; "Most lessons are things you can't even say. The reason I get mad when I see people are not kind or polite is from my parents," said Conor. "They made me everything I am and value. We don't drink on stage. We used to, but our mother and father both told us; it just doesn't look good. If you want to be a professional, don't have a beer in your hand. Also, if we drink all day, we tend to not be able to stay up all night [to see old friends and play music].

Generation

by John O'Brien, Jr.

Tho' I walk thru the land, where ballads barely whisper
Still I hear their call and I come
They live within me; reverberate, sing out
I can't still their music, their breathing history in their hum

God, son of the father, chipping legacy into stone
Proudly stand the burden to pass on its honor
Generation to generation, fan the flames of the stories
To another generation, son of Makem, Conor

Rory

Rory Peter Makem, the young pup of the family, has a voice that rings of his father, when talking and especially when singing songs like *Jug of Punch* or *Holy Ground*. He was born October 26, 1969 in Drogheda, Louth, Ireland and plays 5-string banjo, mandolin, bouzouki, bodhran, guitar, harmonica, and his self-built base guitar.

Rory graduated from Bard College in New York in 1993 with a degree in Music Composition. Writing for orchestra instruments, the theory involved, technical aspects of music and instruments, and how to write for them comprised the main course of study. "And it hasn't hurt me, I've forgotten everything," Rory relates, almost seriously. He met his wife, Elaine, there and they married in May 2005.

"When I was a kid, I wanted to be a marine biologist but I didn't know what that was. [Later], I was told by a palm reader, *Leo the Psychic*, that I should be on stage.

"Through my adolescent and into my teenage years I listened to some of my father's music, as well as the ever present with my friends, rock-n-roll. I have a vivid memory of my father's and Clancy's reunion in 1983, when we went down to New York, at the age of fourteen. A light went on. I suddenly found folk music. I felt it just had more soul than I had noticed before. It is quite a vivid memory. [It was my] first time in New York, Concert Hall, all these people there to see my father. It was enlightening. It got me into listening to folk music, looking through my father's recordings after that.

"I immersed myself in my father's record collection. It was there I found *the Weavers*, *the Kingston Trio*, and *Woody Guthrie*. These led me to explore the early American music, the old blues players, and the old mountain players. I found Jean Richie and John and Alan Lomax. At any rate...I was hooked." Rory was the founder of a country band as well, while in college, called *Lisa, Lisa and the Country Jam*, "back in the early days," he says (1991).

"Although the folk song tradition is virtually inherent in my family, I came to be a professional almost by accident. My brother, Shane, had a college roommate that worked at a small Irish pub. The owner, knowing who Shane's father was, asked if he might be interested in playing a night at the pub. Shane called me.

"When I got the phone call from Shane though, I'd only piddled around on the banjo and guitar, I said why not? From there, we just fell into the 'Irish music profession.'

"What came about as a happenstance has become a crusade. Early on as a professional, I noticed there were no young people continuing the folk song tradition. Fred Hellerman once said of folk music, 'don't think you can improve on music without knowing where it came from' (or words to that effect.). The most important elements of the Irish song are melody and lyrics. The Irish are historically, among the most poetic cultures in the history of the world. The tradition of song was for hundreds of years, the backbone of the working class people. It told their story. It made them laugh. It made them cry. It helped them remember. It helped them not forget. The way the words are put together; the way the story is told; the way a melody complements the words; the way the rhythm compliments the melody; the way all these elements come together to create a mood, paint a picture, convey a feeling, and tell a story in a simple and elegant manner in the voice of the people. That is the folk song tradition."

"Out of the three brothers, Rory probably has the most passion for the music, for doing this." - Shane Makem

The first time Rory played professionally with his father was in 1993, in Tommy's hometown of Keady, at a memorial concert held in honor of the tenth anniversary of Sarah Makem's passing.

When playing with his father, Rory sings a song by Ewan MacColl, called *My Old Man*. It rings of old Irish, folk, Tommy Makem, and the ballad tradition exemplified in a song. Audiences often go silent when he is singing it. The passion in Rory's voice is unmistakable and gives chills as he sings.

An excerpt of Ewan MacColl's My Old Man

My old man was a good old man
Skilled in the moulding trade
In the stinking heat of the iron foundry
My old man was made
Down on his knees in the moulding sand
He wore his trade like a company brand
He was one of the cyclops' smoky band
Yes, that was my old man

My old man he is dead and gone
Now I am your old man
And my advice to you, my son
Is to fight back while you can
Watch out for the man with the silicon chip
Hold on to your job with a good firm grip
'Cause if you don't you'll have had your chips
The same as my old man

"I recall a story my father once told me," Rory said. "It was 1963. He and the Clancy's were playing a room in Vegas or Palm Springs. The night before, Buddy Hackett had played the room. He left a note in their dressing room. 'Knock 'em dead boys. Remember, someone saved up all month to come see you.'"

The story's message is something the Makem and Spain brothers exemplify each and every day, on stage or not. They remember the working man, share the same values and strive to provide a lifting, educational and memorable performance for everyone that comes to see them.

"(The Makem & Spain Brothers) show people of many different backgrounds that old songs don't have to die, if a small group of men or women love them and make sure to get together once in a while to sing them." - Pete Seeger[1]

"The first time I met Pete Seeger, I was eighteen and on my way to college. He told me you learn more out of college than in college. He was right," Rory softly recalls.

"The first time I saw him [performing] was at the Lowell Folk Festival. It was Pete and his banjo in front of four thousand people. He had them in the palm of his hand. He had them all singing four part harmony. He was incredible."

As the wisdom and work of generations, dedicated to preserving and promoting the heritage to all groups, is passed down to Rory, and from him onward, certain conflicting ideas seem to reoccur. "At various events in Irish America, I have noticed a tendency for the organizers to continually ask the question at their numerous committee meetings, 'and what are we going to do for the kids?' They answer that question with face painting, petting zoo's, carnival rides, bobbing for apples, three legged races, slides, big blow-up Barney things that can be jumped on.

"If these are indeed cultural events, the idea is to expose the culture to the patrons; this includes the children. How is a child to gain an appreciation, if not an interest, for something that adults tell them they wouldn't be interested in? 'You go pet the llama while we go see the guy playing the uileann pipes.' A llama can be [seen] at any 4H county fair. An average Irish-American kid is going to have precious few opportunities to hear the pipes played live. When that kid that wasn't given the chance to see the piper becomes a teenager, at the same event, they will gravitate to what is familiar to them, and I rarely, if ever see them in the audience."

"Generally, I am living my dream about performing. I have met and played with many of my heroes. I get paid to do something I feel is important and enjoy doing. There are people that appreciate what I do. If anything, I would like to bring folk music to a wider audience, and change the perception the media has created for folk music over the past forty years. What the pop culture media considers folk music is not folk music. I can understand why young people have an inherent dislike for what they think is folk music.

"Folk music has the perception of being someone wearing a black turtle neck, wearing a beret, singing 'I gave my love a cherry,' Peter, Paul & Mary [as in Animal House]. When I think of folk music, I think of a house party and everybody enjoying themselves and singing great songs and playing good music and dancing, sing-alongs and tunes and everybody pitches in and helps, has their own party piece; a little dance or something."

To bridge the gap between perception and reality, "We have to just keep doing what we are doing, keep doing it. In this time of a watered-down, meaningless, disposable, one-world culture, there are very few young people continuing that tradition. This is why I continue trudging upstream. I feel it is my birthright, my purpose."

Mick

"I believe that anytime we add an original song into the line-up, we are not only preserving our heritage but we are continuing to spread the word, so to speak. And I think that is very gratifying." - Mick Spain

"After more than 13 years, the Makem Brothers have spun into a musical cocoon and emerged as the powerhouse Irish vocal group of their generation. During the winter of 2003, the Makem Brothers joined forces with Irish music's <u>Spain Brothers</u> to form a quintet as strong and unique as anything offered in Irish music today. The result is a musical act far greater than the sum of its parts and an electric onstage chemistry that few acts ever achieve.

"The Makem Brothers and the Spain Brothers realized the magic that a combined live performance could possess after honing their craft at private sessions together over several years. Their subsequent polishing created a sound that is unmatched for Irish singing bands in their generation.

"Their sound comes from powerfully backed, precise three-part harmonies, varied instrumentation and a strong appreciation for the history and progression of folk music. They are also talented songwriters with an ear for 'timeless' songs.

"Mickey and Liam Spain are second-generation performers who learned songs at their father's knee in the mill town of Manchester, New Hampshire. Mick's strong baritone voice and Liam's endless skills on the guitar, mandolin and harmonica had always set the duo apart, but now have enabled a seamless transition to a five-man group."[1] - From www.Makem.com/bio

Michael (Mick) Harry Spain grew up with Irish music, walked away from it and has never left. Although it took an auto accident in 1991 that ruptured a disc in his lower back to bring Mick back, the songs he heard each day in his childhood had just been hiding below the surface. His father gave Mick a guitar and a song book for something to do while laid up. Mick learned three cords (Liam laughingly chimes in here; "And here he is," – implying that he is the same now as when he first learned the cords. Mick counters with "and I learned one more"). It didn't take Mick long to learn the songs because he found out he already knew the words. All those days of waking up in the morning and hearing his father singing and playing folk music in the kitchen finally paid off.

"To be honest with you, performing was the last thing I ever thought I would be doing. Growing up I was always fascinated with the law, but not as an attorney or a policeman but some other aspect. What aspect, I don't know. Later on, I had decided that I wanted to work with kids so I went to college and pursued a degree in elementary education; I was going to be a gym teacher.

"Growing up, I was never into playing music. I loved listening to it but didn't think I would ever be able to play an instrument. Some say I still can't! I was more involved in sports. I remember my father, who is very musically inclined, would try to get me to learn how to play something. I distinctly remember a day when he was teaching me how to play the trumpet, the neighborhood kids were out playing ball in the street and I'm inside developing calluses on my lips and I thought this is the last thing I want to be doing.

"So I put off learning how to play a musical instrument. Liam was the one who developed a taste for playing at a young age. He was very interested and very capable of playing an instrument. In my late teens and early twenties, watching him play, made me wish that I had learned how to play something. There was a time though, before I was in kindergarten, that I used to play the frying pan. Yep, a frying pan, right out of my mothers kitchen. I would hold it like a guitar, pretend to strum and would sing something. I was so good that I was encouraged to go to the corner store and play for the proprietor. He'd laugh and give me something....my first paying gig. That was the extent of my musical abilities until my mid twenties when, literally by accident, I came into what I now do for a living.

"In 1991, I was involved a car accident in which I ruptured a disc in my lower back. As a result, I was unable to perform my duties as a rental agent at an automobile rental facility in Boston. During my recovery my father gave me one of his guitars, a *Weavers* song book and a capo.

I learned three chords. Contrary to popular belief, I have learned at least two more since then, and taught myself to play.

"As this was going on, I hadn't realized how many songs I knew just from hearing them as a kid. After a while, even though I had only been playing for a bit, I knew my life would not be the same. For so long, playing music was not a part of my life. Hell, I didn't even know I could sing. Now, I can't imagine my life without it. As I was learning, I obviously couldn't afford to make a living at it, still can't, so I continued working.

"I eventually left the car rental industry, moved back to New Hampshire, and got a job working for the State of New Hampshire, where I was able to combine my interest in the law with my desire to work with kids. I was a counselor, working with juvenile delinquents. I enjoyed the work but it was very stressful and during the ten years in which I worked, my back got worse. I eventually needed surgery, which I had in June of 2004.

"I had my spine fused and it's now the best it has felt since the accident. The constant pain was too much and so affected my day to day life. I wasn't expecting a miracle from the operation just a little relief, what I got was far beyond what I was expecting. The recovery was three months in a back brace with the first month confined to the house. At my one month check up the doctor said I was ok to leave the house and ride in a car. Later that afternoon, we (the band) drove to Ohio - I laid down the entire trip.

"It was during this time that things with the band were picking up, and my desire to continue with the state was waning, so I decided to leave that position. Now, during the off time with the band, I substitute teach in the elementary schools.

"Music was never a part of my life growing up. I was into athletics. I played baseball, my dad tried to get me to play the trumpet…. I didn't think I could sing. Now I can't imagine my life without it. The day I picked up a guitar, I didn't know it then, but that changed my life. You think the way life is going to go, get married, have a family, you don't really see it coming. It was a whole different route. I'm glad it happened."

As Mick and Liam state in their recording of *Fields to the Stones*, an album of working man songs:

"…[This] is a diverse collection of songs honoring the workers, their lives and the plights … a fairly ironic concept for two people who have yet to find their 'niche' in the workforce. It's not for the lack of effort, mind you, for we have pursued success in a variety of careers. In fact, fate may have linked us to you long before this recording. For instance, one of us may have rented you a car, or sold you a used car or tried to sell you insurance for an existing car. We may have stocked the shelves at your local supermarket, mowed your lawn or tended your garden. We may have bottled the beer(s) you drank, picked up your weekly trash, delivered your newspaper or your furniture or, heaven forbid, dug your grave.

"Now we know this appears to be a 'colorful' work history and that some may view it as us being better at finding work than retaining it. We, however, would like to think of it as us being fortunate enough to realize, often in the early stages of employment, that happiness best be pursued on another path. By the time this recording was completed, we believed we had found that path." - From *The Spain Brothers, Fields to the Stones*, Red Biddy Records, 2002

"You get to play with people you grew up listening to," Mick said. "I still can't believe it sometimes. I got to play with two of my heroes [Tommy Makem and Liam Clancy]. Playing with Tommy, every time is exciting, but the first time, standing up on stage next to him, someone I had grown up listening to, was simply incredible, very difficult to put into words. I get the same feeling every time he sings *Four Green Fields*. I honestly can't believe I am up there next to him. I consider myself an extremely lucky individual and I love all of it. I don't consider it *work* because I enjoy it so much. Work always had a negative connotation. All the time we're getting to meet new people.

"Up to this point, I'd have to say the birth of each of my children, my marriage to Dawna, and playing on stage with Tommy Makem, are the top defining moments in my life. I first met Dawna in a bar that Liam and I used to play in, she was the bartender. In fact, I took up drinking alcohol just to get know to her. However, the more I got to know her, the more drunk I got, and then it was the more she didn't want to know me. Some how I won her over and I am a better man for it. She is a wonderful woman.

"We married on June 18, 2005. I had been married before, for ten years and separated for three, before getting divorced. I have four children, Elizabeth, who is twelve, Michael is eleven, Emily is nine, and Patrick is eight."

"I wish I had started playing music earlier, I wish I was a better musician. I would have liked to have taken lessons [Mick now also plays the banjo and bodhran as well]."

Mick is the fourth child of six born to Marie (nee St. Onge) and Michael (John) Spain, born on April 23rd, 1966 (after Catherine, Anne and Elizabeth and before younger brothers Padraic Martin and Liam Eoin (*pron. Owen*)). Marie's family is from Canada. The maternal side of Joe's family is from around the Mayo/Galway area, but the paternal side is a bit of a mystery. Michael's father passed when Michael was only eight years old and the family roots are unclear.

Michael played guitar and sang and you can hear his voice on the original Tommy Makem song and recording *Freedoms Sons*. He also wrote *Calling Me Home* (recorded by The Spain Brothers, *Fields to the Stones* album) and *Lightning on the Draw* (recorded by The Spain Brothers, *Heroes and Rogues* album).

"My father goes by Mike and he still plays music around the house. I remember when I was growing up he was playing in venues five or so nights a week and worked as a probation/parole officer during the day. My mom stayed home with us six kids. I don't know how they did it. They sacrificed a lot, but they did what they had to do.

Sometimes, my dad would have some of the guys from the various bands he played in over to sing songs, and of all the guys that came through door, there was one guy that my brothers and sisters were always glad to see. He wasn't a great singer, didn't play an instrument, but he worked in a neighborhood store. He always had a candy bar for us and that was far more important than any song, to us."

"I am eight years older than Liam, so when we were growing up, we were at two different periods in our life. I had my circle of friends and he had his. There were occasions where I would let him tag along with me, but that was strictly for our own entertainment purposes. Back then, Liam bore a striking resemblance to me and my friends would call him "Little Mick". My how the times have changed! Liam and I have another brother, Pat, who is two years younger than me and when I went away to college, Liam and Pat formed a bond mostly based on practical jokes. Pat was the mastermind, possessing a very devious and crafty imagination as well as a smooth, polished personality, which he was able to get Liam, with out much effort, to do all the dirty work. I, well I was the target. Liam and I really didn't get close until he was in college and we started performing together.

"Back when Liam and I were on our own, we used to perform in a pub in the town in which the Makem brothers grew up. Whenever we played, they would come to hear us. This evolved into a friendship which led to playing at sessions together which eventually led to the merging of our two bands. I say this because one of the first times I met Conor was in that pub. It was around Thanksgiving and I was on stage introducing a song. I had asked the handful of people listening what was the most popular Thanksgiving song. From the bar area I hear, *The Croppy Boy.* Now I have no idea today what the hell the song was that I was going to sing, but I am certain that that was not the one I had in mind. And I believe that was my first introduction to Conor Makem.

"Playing with the Makem boys, for me, was just like adding three more brothers to the family. It was always a natural feeling. No nervousness or uneasiness, it just seemed like a good fit. Maybe it was because we grew up listening to the same type of music (although I did grow up listening to their dad, they never had to listen to mine), but we all seem to have the same styles, likes and dislikes. I think that is what translates to an audience when we are on stage...the natural, easy going style.

"The Spain Brothers are playing a well chosen hand of cards, but their opening hand is a promising one, and they are an act to watch out for. They have strong full bodied harmonies and a hearty enthusiasm for their chosen material.

"Their singing is strongly reminiscent of Liam and the late Paddy Clancy.

The comparisons are obvious to the Clancy Brothers/Corries mix of multi instrumental versatility with an added touch of backwoods Americana." - Folk Roots, London, UK[1]

Liam

Liam Eoin (Owen) Spain, born June 20, 1974, started playing guitar at age thirteen, backing up his father in gigs at clubs and bars and such. He made his parents buy him a guitar after seeing John Fogarty play *The Old Man Down the Road,* but did not sing back then. Liam got into performing jokingly, explaining, "It got me into the bars and I wanted to be like my father, I admired him and that's how we kind of came about it. I still enjoy it as much as then and wouldn't think of doing anything else. Irish music has been very good to us and [with the merging with the Makem Brothers]; I wouldn't want to change anything.

"I remember, the first time playing with Tommy Makem in my hometown. My parents were in the audience, and when we were playing *Go Lassie Go*, I glanced over to my left to see my brother and Tommy singing together and I thought to myself, 'Holy !@#$, we grew up listening to him and now we are on stage together.'

"It was a huge moment in our professional careers, I mean we spent our whole lives listening to the Clancy's and Tommy, his music in our house, and for us to get a chance to share the stage with him, let alone in our hometown, was something beyond surreal. It was also very, I don't know if rewarding is the right term or not, but the audience had former teachers, friends, and neighbors in it, and it was just great for all of them to see my brother and myself up there doing that. I still remember getting a little chill when we were singing *Go Lassie Go* near the end of the show. I looked over and my brother was taking a verse, and Mr. Makem was playing whistle, there he was right next to my brother, I just thought 'yeah, this is cool.'"

"I continue to be a performer because I love the songs so much, and I feel honored to be trying to carry on the song tradition." I know it seems odd, and I am sure I was the only kid on my block who aspired to be this, but I wanted to be a folk singer for as long as I can recall, I guess my father had a huge influence on that.

"Pete Seegar, the Clancy Brothers, Tommy Makem, were also huge influences. They were able to blend class and integrity in their playing. I would love to play with Pete Seeger and Bruce Springsteen.

"....I know a lot of people might already know how good a guitar player he is, but I wish people knew how great a songwriter Norman Blake is. He writes some of the best traditional songs I've ever heard [*Whiskey Deaf, Ridge Road Gravel,* to name a few].

"One of my favorite moments was meeting Doc Watson on a street corner in Boston, a guy I admired all my life. We were going to see his show and he and Jack Lawrence, his guitar player, were walking down the street towards us. We got a picture with him."

In remembering their first gigs as The Spain Brother's, Liam recalls, "I was a sophomore at the University of Vermont, there was a bar I used to hang out in called *The Blarney Stone.* I got to know the owner a little and I asked him if he wanted any Irish music for St. Patrick's Day, I told him I played a little with my brother. He replied back, 'Irish music on St. Patrick's Day?' An Irish bar owner had never thought of having Irish music on St. Patrick's Day. Amazing.

"About a week after that, we were playing at a friends bar in Manchester, New Hampshire, and on all the promotional material they made (posters, flyers, etc.) We were listed as *The Spades,* not *The Spains.* Now that's respect!

"Although I love being on stage and performing, I really don't like being in the spotlight." Liam left college at age twenty to join with Mick and form *The Spain Brothers*, performing all of the East Coast and Midwest until joining with the Makem Brothers.

"We first met, oh I don't know, seven or eight years ago. Mick and I were playing in a bar in their hometown, Dover, that's about forty five minutes from where we live in Manchester, New Hampshire. They happened to show up one night, either to have a beer or check us out, or both, and I guess they kind of liked it. They started coming back whenever we were there and we started talking and such. They really enjoyed the songs we were doing and they said it was great to see people their age doing this kind of thing.

"Eventually we coaxed them up on stage with us for a song or two. From there, we started having song sessions at each others houses, and started hanging out a lot more. The first professional gig with them was in 2001, I think. Rory had a chance to go to Thailand to work for a PBS series, so Conor and Shane asked us if we would like to fill in.

That was a pretty easy decision. The show went great. And it just kind of snowballed even more from there. They would come and sit in at some of our shows, and we would do the same for them. And then in November of 2002, I got a call from Conor asking us if we would like to join the band on a permanent level, and here we are."

Mick talks about Liam, "I would have to classify Liam as a musician, as well as Rory. People have commented to me how much they love it when Liam and Rory switch instruments, referring to it as the 'show within the show.' Liam is quiet and reserved and very unassuming. He has a quick wit and an ability to fall asleep anywhere, anytime. In fact, on the recent tour to Ireland, Liam positioned himself on the floor of the coach, between the last two rows of seats, and fell fast asleep. Word spread through the bus and it wasn't long before people from the front made their way back to take pictures.

"If it wasn't for the fact that he rarely has money, you could call him 'Mr. Moneybags,' as he is always buying new instruments. I've lost count of how many guitars he has. You see the instrument line-up on stage; the bouzouki, mandolin, and one, sometimes two guitars, all belonging to Liam. He also has quite a collection of harmonica's hiding on a table behind him."

"We sort have taken this on with honor," Liam says, "trying to keep this tradition alive, we are the only ones of our age group doing this. We have no competition but at the same time, if there were a few more acts our age doing this, it would be a better thing for the song tradition itself. It is kind of an honor for us to be trying to keep this song tradition alive, and we intend to keep doing it and trying to bring it to a larger audience."

The future of Irish music, present in the Makem & Spain Brothers, has traveled through three generations (so far); from Sarah Makem, through Tommy and into the Makem and Spain Brothers. We are placed in time to see the legacy continue, grow and broaden. The past still shines as brightly as ever but the future has a new glow, a new energy, that extends the accomplishments of the past and writes its own success story - called the Makem & Spain Brothers.

Did you know…

- This has been the busiest year since the 1980's for Tommy Makem and the busiest year ever for the Makem & Spain Brothers!
- Conor sings and plays: guitar, base, flute, concertina and tenor banjo.
- Rory sings and plays: 5-string banjo, tenor banjo, mandolin, bouzouki, bodhran, guitar, harmonica, uileann pipes and his self-built base guitar.
- Shane sings and plays: guitar, bodhran, bagpipes and played with Rory in a rock-n-roll band.
- Mick sings and plays: guitar, banjo and bodhran.
- Liam sings and plays: guitar, mandolin, banjo, bouzouki and harmonica.
- All three Makem brothers are Black Belts in Tae Kwon Do. Conor was asked by the U.S. Olympic Team Coach to attend the pre-Olympic school. Conor went for a week to the school then decided to go on to college instead.
- Conor is a member of Mensa.

Signature Makem & Spain Brothers Songs: The Road to Gundagai

Traditional, Arrangement by Makem & Spain Brothers

Oh we started out from Roto, when the sheds had all cut out
We'd whips and whips of money as we meant to push about;
So we humped our blueys serenely and made for Sydney town,
With a three-spot check between us as wanted knocking down.

Chorus:
And we camped at Lazy Harry's on the road to Gundagai,
The road to Gundagai, five miles from Boonabri;
And we camped at Lazy Harry's on the road to Gundagai.

Well, we struck the Murumbidgee near the Yanco in a week,
And passed through old Narrandera, and crossed the Burnett Creek;
And we never stopped at Wagga, for we'd Sydney in our eye,
And we camped at Lazy Harry's on the road to Gundagai.

Well, I've seen a lot of girls, my lads, and drunk a lot of beer,
And I've met with some of both as has left me pretty queer.
But for beer to knock you sideways and for girls to make you cry,
You should camp at Lazy Harry's on the road to Gundagai.

Well, we chucked our flamin' wags off and we walked into the bar
And we called for rum and raspberry and a shilling each cigar;
But the girl that served the poison, she winked at Bill and I,
So we camped at Lazy Harry's on the road to Gundagai.

In a week the spree was over, and our check was all knocked down,
So we shouldered our Matildas and we turned our backs on town.
And the girls stood us a nobblers as we sadly said goodbye,
And we tramped from Lazy Harry's on the road to Gundagai.

Last Chorus:
Yes we tramped from Lazy Harry's on the road to Gundagai,
The road to Gundagai, five miles from Boonabri;
And we tramped from Lazy Harry's on the road to Gundagai.

Whiskey Row

Lyrics by Liam Spain,
Music by Mickey Spain

Well I came to Chicago in 1869
And I took me a place in Connelys patch
Started on the Railroad working the UP line
Walking those endless miles of track
Laying down those crossties and banging on the steel
In the cold, wind, and rain
From Palmer House, down to Marshall Field's
Every day was just the same

Chorus:
But at the end of the day
We'd all wait for the horns to blow
Then we'd make our way
Down to the bars on Whiskey Row

Now over at the stockyards the packers are winding down
They're all waiting for the closing sign
They'll rush the front gates, and storm the town
And take their seats upon the line
With their glasses on the counter, their feet upon the rail
A friendly smile and hello
All the laughing getting louder with every passing tale
Those golden days on Whiskey Row

Chorus

Now Palmer House has fallen
Pullman Cars are off the track
And there ain't no more Courthouse Square
And nothing is left standing, over at Connelys Patch
Since that mighty fire tore through there
But someday soon she'll reach up to the sky
Over the rivers flames and smoke
And she'll keep a lookout with a mother's eye
Over her boys on Whiskey Row

Chorus

When We Danced in Donegal

by Conor Makem

I remember the cattle were ill that year
For the winter was long and cold
And the old man was cursing near all the day
When he drove them to town to be sold
I told him that Jimmy had the lone of a car
And was driving to Donegal town
And I asked could he drive all the cattle
Just himself and the hound

Chorus:
Ah, but that was long ago
When the roads were driven slow
A man could whistle gaily
If he had a girl or no
When the piper played his tunes
And the fear a tighe would call
The night when first I met you
And we danced in Donegal

We took the road through Killybegs
And we drove by Inver Bay
Overtaking a tractor before Mount Charles
Who was towing a bushel of hay
The farmer he winked and his wee dog he barked
As he pulled to the side to give way
And as sure as the weather he went home
For a drop of the tay

The door to the barn was open
And the smoke was billowing out
And the fear a tighe was taking requests
And the dancers all started to shout
He called out the Siege of Ennis

And the crowd fairly gave out a cheer
And I knew fairly well that the night
Would be magic in here

Then Jimmy he tugged the arm of my shirt
And he pointed away to the wall
And I saw you and wondered why the prettiest girl
Wasn't dancing with no one at all
He told me a girl that was pretty as you
Wouldn't dance with a farmer as I
And I knew he was right, but I'd be damned
If I still wouldn't try

End Chorus:
And it wasn't so long ago
When the roads were driven slow
But a man can still whistle gaily
If he has a girl or no
And the pipers play their tunes
And the fear a tighe still calls
And I always will remember
When we danced in Donegal

Makem & Spain Brothers Discography:

Makem Brothers:

- Outstanding In A Field   (1994) with Brian Sullivan
- Outstanding In A Field (cassette)   (1994)
- On The Rocks   (1995)
- On The Rocks (cassette)   (1995)
- Who Fears To Speak (Songs of the Rebellion of 1798) (1997)
- Stand Together (CD)   (2001)

Makem & Spain Brothers:

- Like Others Did Before Us   (2004)

Spain Brothers:

- Heroes and Rogues   (1999) w/ Sarah Godcher
- Fields to the Stones   (2002)

Videos:
The Makem Brothers:

- Slainte, The Makem Brothers and Brian Sullivan   (1994)
- Live in Concert (w/ Soibhan Egan)   (1997)

A sneak peak at Book Two in the *Festival Legends* series, *Festival Legends, Trads & Ceili's*:

I.

Cherish the Ladies (Joanie Madden, Mary Coogan, Heidi Talbot, Mirella Murray, Roison Dillon)

"...[Cherish the Ladies] expands the annals of Irish music in America... the music is passionate, tender and rambunctious. In short, if you cherish traditional music, you'll Cherish the Ladies!" - Jon Pareles of The New York Times.1

The vision brought to life of folklorist/musician Mick Moloney, and sponsored by the Ethnic Folk Arts Center (on Spring Street in Lower Manhattan) and the National Endowment for the Arts, *Cherish the Ladies* began as a concert series featuring the brightest stars and new comers in Irish traditional music, designed to highlight the contributions of women to Irish music in America. *Cherish the Ladies* is the name of a traditional Irish double jig. It was recorded by The Chieftains on *The Chieftains No. 4.* (1973, track 9). Due to the brilliance and passion of these outstanding musicians, it is a name that is now synonymous with the very best that Irish music has to offer.

As Joanie Madden, leader and guiding force of Cherish the Ladies explains, "When we were starting out we had great help from banjo/ guitarist/ folklorist and scholar Mick Moloney, who critiqued us on our first early tours. It was his idea to get a bunch of women together celebrating the fact that the days of the male dominated scene were over. I always admired how he was so kind to all the young players coming up."

Joanie recalls the fateful call from Mick Moloney in 1983. Calling to congratulate her on winning three All-Ireland Gold Medals (in whistle, flute and a duet with fiddle player Kathy McGinty), Mick said he had an idea for a concert featuring the up-and-coming women of Irish music. He had run the idea by Martin Koening and Ethel Raim at the Ethnic Folk Arts Center in New York and they were interested.

Irish-American women had broken the barrier in the perception, completely true up to that point, that the best traditional musicians and performers were only those born in Ireland. But then U.S. born Kathleen Collins won the All-Ireland Senior Fiddle Championship in 1966. Future Cherish the Ladies members won in succeeding years, including Joanie, as well as Liz Carroll (fiddle) in 1974 and 1975, and Eileen Ivers (fiddle), nine times in the 1970's and 80's.

Joanie wasn't enamored with the idea initially, thinking that they would be typecast as a novelty group, based only on their sex. But eventually she agreed to the concert series. She recalls how Mick was searching for a name for this vision of a series of concerts and for the group of performers:

"'How about Cherish the Ladies?' Joanie suggested.

"'That's great, that's great! We'll call the series that,' Mick responded."

And a new legacy, unprecedented and still unmatched, had begun.

Twelve Irish-American ladies, all from New York, except for Philadelphian Soibhan Egan, took the stage in various high school auditoriums around New York. The series was originally only planned to last about ten days.

"It started small, a group of timid soloists playing in various high school auditoriums around New York. 'At our first couple of concerts,'

Madden recounts, '[Ethel Raim] came out and would announce what we were going to do, because none of us would talk on the microphone!' Despite their temerity, the musicians played brilliantly, and the concerts left audiences and critics roaring their approval. Cherish The Ladies' phenomenal popularity surprised everybody, including Moloney, who later commented, 'What started off as a very interesting and sort of fun idea became taken very seriously. The New York Times did a big story on it. Suddenly, they were sold-out concerts.'[2]

Those on stage during the first concert series included; Joanie Madden (whistle and flute), Mary Coogan (guitar, tenor banjo, mandolin), Liz Carroll (fiddle), Cathie Ryan (vocals), Eileen Ivers (fiddle), Rose Conway (fiddle), Maureen Doherty Mackin (button accordion, tin whistle, flute), Soibhan Egan (fiddle, flute, bodhran), Bridget Fitzgerald (*sean nós* singing), and three dancers; Eileen Golden, Maureen Kennelly and Mairead Powell.

"All good players, always good chemistry," says original founding member Liz Carroll. "That's Joanie knowing that this one will go along with that one and knowing the importance of that. We were all kind of shocked by how well we all got along. So, after we did the second tour and we realized that some pieces were going to be moving on, including me, we all started talking about who could be our replacements and that was number one, you just had to have good chemistry to go on the road and have the same experiences that we had.

"What I always find with Cherish is that you tap your feet to that music. There are a lot of groups that are impressive and you say, 'Whoa, they can really play." But you really do tap your feet to Cherish. They've got that great old swing to the music. So many of those same girls became part of the series, *Fathers & Daughters*. What a fun legacy that is."

Joannie continues: "In addition to helping us out, [Mick] helped Eileen Ivers and Seamus Egan equally get a footing in the business. He is a great role model to me…and I in turn try to help younger musicians starting out as much as I can. I don't teach because of the rigorous touring schedule but give as many master classes I can to the local kids and in other cities. You have to give back to the music that has given [me] so much."

"[Cherish the Ladies] ... have grown from a one-time concert concept to an Irish traditional music sensation, literally the most successful and sought-after Irish-American group in Celtic music history. [Al]though initially the group won recognition as the first and only all-women traditional Irish band, they soon established themselves as musicians and performers without peer and have won many thousands of listeners and fans of their music. With their unique spectacular blend of virtuosi instrumental talents, beautiful vocals, captivating arrangements and stunning step dancing, this powerhouse group combines all the facets of Irish traditional culture and puts it forth in an immensely humorous and entertaining package."[3] From www.cherishtheladies.com

Mick Moloney pursued a grant from The National Endowment for the Arts to fund the first album for Cherish the Ladies, in their initial concert format. *Cherish the Ladies - Irish Women Musicians in America* was selected by The Library of Congress as one of the best folk albums of 1985. The first tour following the hugely successful opening series of concerts took place less than two years later. Cherish received a grant to tour again in 1989 and then a smaller grant again in 1991.

Then Joanie took the initiative and called the girls together again, to gauge their interest in forming a band, rather than just gathering for a concert series. All members agreed that they were having a ball doing the concerts and wanted to take the next step. So Joanie (flute and whistle), Mary Coogan (guitar, mandolin & banjo), Maureen Daugherty (accordion, flute and whistle), Soibhan Egan (fiddle, whistle & bodhran), Cathie Ryan (vocals), Bridget Fitzgerald (*sean nós* singing), and three dancers; Eileen Golden, Maureen Kennelly and Mairead Powell, got together in late 1991 and *Cherish the Ladies*, the band, was formed. Liz Carroll had a three month old baby, and couldn't join the group. Cherish played a dozen dates in 1991 and more than twenty in 1992. Eileen Ivers soon returned to the group before forming *Eileen Ivers & Immigrant Soul.*

Schanachie Records wouldn't bite on Joanie and Eileen Ivers' presentation for a new record but Green Linnet did. The Ladies knocked down the front door on the Irish music scene and released *The Back Door* on Green Linnet Records (1992). Eleven more albums have been recorded since and The Ladies just keep on; entertaining, energizing, and captivating audiences, the world over.

"'When it comes to material, says Madden, 'it's very much a democratic band. We get together, sit down in a circle, come up with ideas. It's definitely everybody involved. When it comes to material, it's everybody's ideas. All the musical memories come into force to create the sets and the arrangements.'"[8]

Cherish the Ladies have traveled all over North and South America, the United Kingdom and Europe, performing at the White House, in concert halls, at festivals and before national and international celebrities, royalty and most often, everyday people.

They have been named *Entertainment Group of the Year* by the Irish Voice Newspaper, named *Best Musical Group of the Year* by the BBC, and received the *Glasgow Royal Concert Hall's International Group of the Year Award* at the Celtic Connections Festival in Scotland. The Irish Voice Newspaper named Cherish the Ladies *Entertainment Group of the Year* and they were voted the *Top North American Celtic Act* by NPR Radio's *Thistle and Shamrock*.

"Of all the groups, Cherish really started mixing with the singers, the ballad singers; The Clancys, that type. I didn't know any of those guys. I know the trad musicians, period. When you sat down in the evening, you sat down with other trad players, the accordion and the fiddle are all mixed in there. Cherish kind of reached out, they know all of the ballad singers and Danny Boy [*come-all-ya's*] singers and rebel singers and all of that. It was a connection I certainly hadn't made with them on my own. They certainly all mixed much better because of Cherish diving in and saying, 'Yeah, we'll back you up as you sing this old song, or that old song.' There is a respect that I am not sure there used to be, so much, between them [singers and the trads]. Cherish kind of bridged the gap between the two groups." - Liz Carroll, original founding member of Cherish the Ladies, Jr. All-Ireland Fiddle Champion, 1974, Sr. All-Ireland Fiddle Champion, 1975, Sr. All-Ireland Duet Champion (with Jimmy Keane,), 1975, member of Green Fields of America, and currently touring as a highly successful duo with guitarist John Doyle (of Solas).

Cherish the Ladies have shared the stage with such legendary entertainers as; Tommy Makem, The Clancy Brothers, The Chieftains, Emmy Lou Harris, James Taylor and Joan Baez, to name just a few, and have also performed with dozens of symphony orchestras.

Cherish the Ladies symphonic career began with a phone call from the Boston Pops, who were interested in arranging new charts for a single performance at Symphony Hall in Boston. But Cherish the Ladies made their symphony debut with the Cincinnati Pops under the tutelage of Keith Lockhart. After the overwhelming response from the audience, Keith then took Cherish the Ladies back to Boston where they performed another four shows, including the prestigious *Tanglewood Summer Series*.

"The gig with the Boston Pops (the first time) was mind blowing," recalls Joanie. "I had always dreamed of doing it. It's crazy that we're doing this show. I felt that we were doing something for Irish music in America, of when it was played and where it was going."

These successful collaborations led to their Grammy nominated album *The Celtic Album*, released in 1995. Cherish has performed with many of the top symphonies in the country and play with more than twenty symphonies each year.

Cherish the Ladies are recognized and admired throughout the world and were one of the first Irish traditional bands to perform in Argentina. An opportunity to realize another dream, playing in Australia, came along but the group had to delay taking advantage of going to the "Land Down Under:"

Rambles' writer Jamie O'Brien quoted Joanie in his profile of Joanie and *Cherish the Ladies*, "'We had to make a choice between the Guinness Tour of Australia and doing an album with the Boston Pops,' Madden recalls. The band chose to take part in the orchestra's The Celtic Album, a move which proved highly advantageous. "(Conductor) Keith Lockhart went to (RCA Victor) and said, 'They're the next Chieftains. You'd better hire them right now!' And that's what happened."[8]

But talent like this can not be held back and Cherish the Ladies eventually did tour Australia and New Zealand, in September, 2004.

"They've never made a big deal about their role in traditional Irish music, but it was a totally male scene when they started and just look at it now." – Mick Moloney[4]

Although Cherish the Ladies started as an all-female ensemble, Joanie deemphasizes the gender aspect in the makeup of the band. The focus for Joanie stays on the quality of those sharing the stage, whether musicians, singers or dancers. A few men have played with Cherish over the years, and although it is rare, the emphasis is always on the magnificent talent of those on stage, not on their sex.

Cherish the Ladies have recorded fourteen highly acclaimed albums and their album *On Christmas Night* was chosen as one of the top Christmas albums of the year by The New York Times, Washington Post, The Village Voice and many other nationally syndicated newspapers. If the newspaper recognition wasn't enough, Cherish has appeared on *CBS This Morning, Good Morning America, Evening at Pops, C-Span, PBS* and *National Public Radio* in the United States and on BBC and RTE radio and television overseas. They were also chosen to represent Irish music and culture at the Official Cultural Olympiad at the Summer Olympics in Atlanta. Their newest CD, *Woman of the House*, under Rounder Records, was released in September, 2005.

Joanie Madden

Joanie is the drive and the passion behind Cherish the Ladies. Her infectious enthusiasm infuses both the band and the audience, turning a "quiet trad session" into an energetic show that leaves the audience dancing, clapping - and roaring in approval. Joanie is a Grammy Winner (in 1999 for *Paul Winters*, Best Crossover Album, on Celtic Solstice) and four time All-Ireland World Champion. She won three All-Ireland championships in 1983, on tin whistle, flute and in a fiddle duet with Kathy McGinty, winning twenty-five years to the day that her father, Joe Madden won his All-Ireland Championship for accordion, in 1958.

Americans were well known for fiddle champions but Joanie is the first American to ever win the Senior All-Ireland Whistle Championship, in 1984. Future Cherish the Ladies member Eileen Ivers also won the Senior All-Ireland Championship, on fiddle, in 1984, the last of her nine All-Ireland Championships, following the historic wins of American Kathleen Collins in the 1966 and Liz Carroll in 1974 and 1975.

From an interview with Dirty Linen's Steve Winnick - "After honing her technique for a few years, Madden was ready to take on [highest levels of competition in the annual Irish Music Festival], the *Fleadh Cheoil na hEireann* [*Flah Kee ole na h'eron*], the music competition that awards the All-Ireland championships. Madden describes the experience of the fleadh: 'Pressure's really on. There's four provinces in Ireland... and they only get to send two people from [each] province. So you're dealing with the eight top musicians from Ireland. There are two from Chicago, two from New York. So that's another four. And then you have two from England, and sometimes from Scotland, and sometimes France. Usually you have about sixteen or eighteen competitors. It was the cream of the crop. Anybody there was a brilliant musician.'

"In 1984, Madden concluded her competitive career by winning the Senior All-Ireland Whistle Championship. Had it not been for Moloney's continued support, music would be just a hobby for her today. "Without Mick," she muses. "...I'd probably be an accountant somewhere."[2]

God Bless Mick Moloney!

Joanie is the youngest person ever elected to the *Irish-American Musicians Hall of Fame.* Just a few of the other awards that weigh down Joanie's mantle include; *Traditional Musician of the Year*, the *Wild Geese Award*, the *Peabody Award* (for the ESPN documentary, *The Complete Angler)* and being voted one of the *Top 100 Irish-Americans* in the country, all for her contributions to promoting and preserving Irish music, culture and tradition in America.

"I am very proud to be among the strong Irish-American bearers of the music. It is great to be a representative going around the country, around the world, to represent Irish music." - Joanie Madden , on the Library of Congress' *Cleveland's Irish Cultural Festival's Legacy Project,* 1999.

Born in the Bronx, New York on May 26th, 1965 to Helen (*nee* Meade) Madden, and Joe Madden, Joanie Marie Madden is the second oldest of seven, with five brothers and one sister. Her family has a long history of both involvement and accomplishment in the traditional Irish music scene. As mentioned, Joe is an all-Ireland Champion on the accordion (1958) and hails from Portumna, East Galway. Helen, from Miltown Malbay in County Clare, is an Irish dancer.

Joanie grew up immersed in Irish music and becoming a musician was almost pre-ordained, despite her parents wishes for a career in accounting. She spent many family gatherings, special events and momentous occasions listening to her father and his friends playing, in formal or informal sessions.

"My earliest memories involve house parties with music and Clare Sets being danced around the house. By the time my siblings and I were six we could all do a Clare Set [each county has a "set" or dance attributed to them. The sets are the basis for a lot of the Irish dances performed today]. My father is a well known musician here in the New York area. He's a fantastic accordion player, in fact he was All-Ireland champion in his day, so I was very lucky to have known and played with all his friends. I never really wanted to do anything else – much to my parent's dismay in the early years."

From an interview with *Dirty Linen's* Steve Winnick: "I started fiddle lessons when I was about nine, and I hated that, so I quit that.

Then I started piano lessons when I was about eleven, and I hated that and quit that." Finally, she encountered the instrument that she would make her own: the humble tin whistle. 'I heard that instrument and I said, this is for me.'...."

Festival Legends, Trads & Ceilis, due out in 2007, goes on to tell of how Joanie came to be such a powerful contributor to the Irish music legacy, the trials and successes of the band, and a look at the other members, past and present. It then highlights some of the other Legends that have contributed so significantly to the popularity of Irish music in America, in the Trad and Ceili areas, including; The Kilfenora Ceili Band, Abbey Ceili Band, Mick Moloney, Joe Burke and many more. Book Three, *Festival Legends, The Balladeers*, will highlight the Balladeers, including Foster & Allen, Paddy Reilly, Dermot Henry and much more.

Favorite Links:

www.songsandstories.net
www.clevelandirish.org
www.makem.com
www.dannydoyle.org
www.liamclancy.com
www.dublincityramblers.com
www.thenewbarleycorn.com
www.tomsweeneymusic.com
www.battburns.com
www.cherishtheladies.com
www.english.glendale.cc.ca.us/doyle.a.html
www.theballadeers.com
www.ramblinghouse.com
www.zozimus.com
www.fiddle.com
www.scathan.com
www.storytellingworld.com
www.vertlift.com

Endnotes:

All sources are used with the permission of those sited.

Chapter I: Tommy Makem

1   Rambling House, Godfathers of the Ballad Boom www.
   ramblinghouse.com
2   The Mountain of the Women, Memoirs of an Irish Troubadour, by
   Liam Clancy. 2002.
3   From The Clancy Brothers and Tommy Makem by Ronan Nolan.
   Copyright Ronan Nolan, 2002,.
4   Information gathered from Makem.com.
5   Spotlight Online, *Tommy Makem Finds Peace in the Power of His
   Music.* Ross Bachelder, Spotlight Correspondent.

Chapter II: Danny Doyle

1   From Liner Notes, *Sprit of the Gael* (2002). Used with permission
   of Danny Doyle.

Chapter III: Liam Clancy

1   From *The Mountain of the Women, Memoirs of an Irish Troubadour,*
   By Liam Clancy. Doubleday Books, 2002.
2   From Rambling House (formerly www.irishmusicweb.ie). *Godfathers
   of the Ballad Boom,* by Ronan Nolan, 2002.
3   From CBS News Sunday Morning. Liam Clancy, Irish Troubadour,
   March 17, 2002

4   From; *Liam Clancy at The Main Point* by John McLaughlin. The Folk Life Quarterly, Fall, 1979.

5   From *The Clancy Brothers and Tommy Makem* by Ronan Nolan. Copyright Ronan Nolan, 2002.

6   Sean McGuinness, Dublin City Ramblers, inside cover of Dublin City Rambler CD, "On Holy Ground, A Tribute to The Clancy Brothers and Tommy Makem.

7   Mick Moloney, November 1991, from liner notes *The Clancy Brothers with Tommy Makem, The Luck of the Irish.*

Chapter IV: Johnny McEvoy

1   From "A Reason to Smile," an interview with Joe Jackson 2003.

Chapter V: Dublin City Ramblers

1   From www.zozimus.com/host.htm.

Chapter VI: The New Barleycorn

1   From Irish Fiddler James Kelly: A Matter of Tradition, by Hollis Payer. www.fiddle.com

2   From August 1st, 2000 interview with Peanuts, Ohio Online Magazine.

Chapter VII: Tom Sweeney

1   From *Sweeney: Carrying on the traditions of Ireland* by Ed Paukstis. www.scathan.com, November 1995

Chapter VII: Batt Burns

1   From "Batt Burns," interview by Kathy Unvergazt. Storytelling World. Summer/Fall 1995. Used with permission of Dr. Flora Joy, Editor, Storytelling World. www.storytellingworld.com

Chapter XI: The Makem & Spain Brothers

1   From www.makem.com.

Chapter XII: Cherish The Ladies

1 John Pareles, The New York Times Critic, Friday, November 26, 2004

2 From "The Long Road: Joanie Madden and Cherish the Ladies" by Steve Winick. From Dirty Linen #59 August/September 1995.

3 From www.cherishtheladies.com.

4 From "Passing it Up", interview by Helene Norway. Rootsworld, 2001.

5 Rambles, *Cherish the Ladies*, An interview with Joanie Madden by Jamie O'Brien.

About the Author

The author has been Assistant Director of Cleveland's Irish Cultural Festival for twenty-three years. The festival was founded by his father and John continues this legacy of love of the Irish heritage, and vision for the festival, an annual civic event with over 35,000 attendees. The festival is culturally focused and recognized as one of the best in the United States.

Active in the Irish community and with the Festival Organizers Convention, where he was a featured speaker in 2005 and 2006, John has been interviewed on numerous radio, television programs and newspapers. He designed, wrote and produced "The Legacy Project," a video for the United States Library of Congress, highlighting Cleveland's Irish Cultural Festival as "an event of cultural significance."

Printed in the United States
49036LVS00006B/145-156